C000093331

Lou Macari was born in 1949 and gı Ayrshire. After being taken on as an he went on to win back-to-back Scottish League and Cup doubles with the Bhoys before moving to Manchester United in a shock transfer in 1973. Macari's goals helped United win promotion back into the First Division in 1975, and two years later he played a part in the winning goal as United beat Liverpool 2–1 to win the FA Cup.

Macari went on to score 97 goals in more than 400 appearances for the Red Devils and won 24 caps for Scotland, scoring five times and representing his country in the 1978 World Cup Finals in Argentina.

After leaving United in 1984, Macari moved into management with Swindon Town, and also managed West Ham United, Birmingham City, Stoke City, Celtic and Huddersfield Town, winning three promotions, two championships with record points tallies and two Cups. He now works as an expert analyst for Sky Sports and MUTV as well as being a familiar face at Manchester United on matchdays.

FOOTBALL
MY LIFE

Lou Macari

BANTAM PRESS

LONDON • TORONTO • SYDNEY • AUCKLAND • JOHANNESBURG

TRANSWORLD PUBLISHERS
61–63 Uxbridge Road, London W5 5SA
A Random House Group Company
www.rbooks.co.uk

First published in Great Britain
in 2008 by Bantam Press
an imprint of Transworld Publishers

A CIP catalogue record for this book
is available from the British Library.

ISBN 9780593061084 (cased)
9780593061091 (tpb)

Addresses for Random House Group Ltd companies outside the UK
can be found at: www.randomhouse.co.uk
The Random House Group Ltd Reg. No. 954009

The Random House Group Limited supports The Forest Stewardship
Council (FSC), the leading international forest-certification organization. All our
titles that are printed on Greenpeace-approved FSC-certified paper carry the FSC logo.
Our paper procurement policy can be found at
www.rbooks.co.uk/environment

Typeset in 11.5/16pt Plantin by
Falcon Oast Graphic Art Ltd.
Printed and bound in Great Britain by
CPI Mackays, Chatham, ME5 8TD

2 4 6 8 10 9 7 5 3 1

Mixed Sources
Product group from well-managed
forests and other controlled sources
www.fsc.org Cert no. TT-COC-2139
© 1996 Forest Stewardship Council
FSC

This book is dedicated
to my wife and family

ACKNOWLEDGEMENTS

I have been helped along the way by so many, far too many to mention here. No slight is intended therefore towards those whose names do not appear below. My thanks then to: Sean Fallon, Bob Rooney and Jimmy Steele, the men who guided me at Celtic and helped put me back together on the treatment table; to United secretaries Ken Merrit and Ken Ramsden; to Martin Edwards, who carried on the United dynasty begun by his father Louis; to Tommy Docherty, Pat Crerand, Tommy Cavanagh, Dave Sexton and Ron Atkinson for picking me, Laurie Brown for fixing me and Cath on the United reception for putting up with me; to Debbie Lofthouse, who keeps corporate United running smoothly; to Gordon Taylor for all his advice; to Statto aka Andrew Edwards; to Bernard Paignton, my chief scout at Stoke; to Dick Bradshaw for recognizing my son Jon's talent at Nottingham Forest; to Brian Hillier for giving me my start in management at Swindon, and to Samesh Kumar at Birmingham, Peter Coates at Stoke and the Cearns family at West Ham, for subsequently investing in me; to Jon Trollope and John Menham for their different kinds of support at Swindon; to my mates Jack Trickett, Vinnie Sciarvo and Stuart Codling for their support in life; to my great friend

Joseph di Stephano; to bookmaker Fred Done for taking all my money off me; to my solicitors Kingsley Napley, and to all players and staff I played with and managed. And finally, to my friend Edmond Wan, get better soon!

My thanks also to Peter Fitton and Bob Russell, who gave journalism a good name reporting every kick in the national papers during my years at Manchester United; to David Meek, who kept the people of Manchester informed through the pages of the *Manchester Evening News*; to Mark Pearson and Steve Bower at MUTV, John Duggan at Today FM in Ireland; Tim Tuomey and Pat Dolan at Setanta, and Julian Wilson at the BBC.

Finally, my thanks to my literary agent, David Luxton, to Giles Elliott at Transworld Publishers for making this book happen and to Kevin Garside for his help putting it together.

CONTENTS

FOREWORD BY DENIS LAW

I was instantly delighted and enthusiastic when Lou Macari approached me with the request to contribute the foreword for his autobiography. We Scots have to stick together!

I'm immensely proud to say that Scotland has produced some terrific players over the years and that Lou Macari can count himself among the very best to have represented our country.

The fact that he played at the very top with Celtic and Manchester United is sufficient to confirm that he was a performer of the highest ability. Celtic and United are two of the biggest clubs in football with towering standards and both are followed by huge numbers of knowledgeable and passionate supporters. There is no place to hide at Parkhead or Old Trafford, they know their football and expectations are always sky-high. Becoming a crowd hero at both clubs, as Lou did, further emphasizes the lofty status he attained during his career.

I was in the later years of my playing days when our paths crossed at Old Trafford and with the national team.

I was, in fact, in my last season with United when Lou moved south from Glasgow to Manchester. He was also wanted by Liverpool, managed at the time by the incomparable Bill Shankly – my boss when I was with Huddersfield Town – which must have made Lou's decision about his future even more difficult.

He eventually resolved that his best option was to ignore Liverpool's overtures and take up United's offer of employment. I think he made the right decision, but we must take into account that I'm totally biased.

Lou's arrival at Old Trafford pretty well signalled the end of my time with United. I was in the side the day he made his debut against West Ham United, but that was the only occasion we appeared alongside each other in the famous red shirt. I was handed a free transfer at the close of that 1972–73 season whilst Lou went on to become a great favourite amongst the United faithful.

Our international careers also overlapped, but only just, with the two of us playing together five times in the Scotland team.

Therefore we played in the same side barely half-a-dozen times, but I saw enough first-hand during those games to realize that Lou was a top-class operator. He proceeded to enjoy almost eleven years at Old Trafford, helping the club to work their way back to a position of strength following the ignominy of relegation to the Second Division in 1974.

He later played briefly for Swindon Town before going into management, firstly with the Wiltshire club and later with major clubs such as West Ham United and Celtic.

All in all it adds up to a fascinating and colourful career in football which is more than worthy of the autobiographical record contained in these pages.

Lou Macari thoroughly deserves his place high on the list of all-time great Scottish players and the famous names who have worn the distinctive hoops of Celtic and famous red of Manchester United.

Denis Law, July 2008

Huddersfield Town, Manchester City, AC Torino, Manchester United, Manchester City and Scotland

PREFACE

LIFE AS A FOOTBALLER IS WONDERFUL. MY LIFE IN THE GAME has been wonderful. But there have also been personal tragedies that only now am I coming to terms with. It was only after I stopped playing that I realized how the loss of someone close can affect your mind and your judgement. Losing my father to cancer was hard enough, but there was nothing I could do about that. I only wish the same could be said about the loss of my mother and my son. The consequences of both their deaths are tough to deal with even now. I certainly don't have the same attitude towards the beautiful game that took me to Celtic and Manchester United in the carefree days of my youth. That's inevitable I suppose. Too much water has flowed under the Macari bridge. Part of the reason for writing this book was the opportunity it offered to look back at my life and try to make sense of all that has happened, good and bad – and there has been plenty of both.

The first words were committed to paper as English football

was pulling its hair out over the failure to qualify for the 2008 European Championship. Fingers were being pointed in all directions. No one escaped blame. The coach, Steve McClaren, and the players, hitherto regarded as a golden generation, were lambasted for their tactical and technical shortcomings. A root and branch inquiry into the state of the game in England was promised by the FA. The nation wanted answers. Too right it did.

The response to England's tame defeat at the hands of Croatia made me laugh. If England had held on at 2–2, no one would have said a thing. They would have gone to the finals believing they were among the favourites to win. Perception and reality have never been further apart. I look around at what's happening at clubs today and despair. Football is about attitude as much as skill, application as much as talent. Without the right mentality you can forget it. People talk about players being world class. Do me a favour. There are fewer younger players coming through. Where is the next Scholes, the next Giggs, Beckham, Lampard, Ferdinand, Rooney? The latter apart, there isn't a centre-forward playing in the Premiership today who would have caused anybody to lose sleep a generation ago. I'm talking about British lads here. We are supposed to have world-class centre-halves, but where are the centre-forwards they are keeping out? Where are the Alan Shearers, Mark Hugheses, Gary Linekers, Ian Rushes and Andy Grays? The top strikers are all foreign: Adebayor, Torres, Drogba, Berbatov, Tevez and Ronaldo. I can sound like a broken record when I talk about how it used to be, but the truth is inescapable. When I started out, British football was awash with world-class players. England were the World Cup holders, and Celtic were poised to lift the European Cup, followed a year later by Manchester United. That was no accident. The game was different then. The world was different then. There was a hunger about young players, a desperate desire to do well, a willingness to learn. These days kids come into the first team believing they have made it already. And who can blame them?

Let me give you an example. A friend of mine asked for a favour. He was selling his apartment, a posh place in Altrincham. He knew that a player had been to look at another apartment in the same block. He wanted me to push his place. He said he would do the player a deal. So I gave the lad a ring. He was a fringe player, barely out of the youth set-up. He'd had only a handful of games in the first team. The place was on the market for £900,000. I was happy to help out a mate and get the kid a deal, but I could not help thinking that some-thing was not right here, something to do with the state of the game. If a kid can afford a £900,000 pad before he can use a razor blade properly, where is the incentive to improve, to fight for a regular first-team place, to go the extra mile, to make a difference? That is what is wrong with today's game, or a major part of it. The hunger has gone. Kids don't want to work. They don't have to.

I played more than four hundred games for United over the course of eleven years at Old Trafford and scored getting on for a hundred goals. I was an FA Cup winner and went to a World Cup with Scotland, and the most I ever earned was £420 a week. The first car I bought was a second-hand Audi for a couple of hundred quid. To me it was like having a Ferrari. Today, the top players have a different car for every day of the week and a 4x4 for the weekend. I still have to work for a living. Ronaldo and co. will die rich men if they quit the game tomorrow. I'm pleased for them – I don't begrudge them a penny – but the wealth on offer to players now has changed the game. I can't say if it has changed the players as men, but having nothing made me the kind of person I am. It kept me honest and gave me a work ethic that saw me through as a player. It keeps me at it today.

The build-up to that Croatia game illustrated another key difference between my day and now. Money not only takes away the hunger, it empowers. The players have the power today, not the managers. We had no power. The Sunday after the Croatia game a newspaper ran a big story about some of the England lads at a lap-dancing club. It was Shaun Wright-Phillips's birthday. John Terry was there. Joe Cole apparently left early. That would not have saved me. I'd have been sacked. No matter what Jock Stein thought of me or my ability, I would have been out the door at Celtic Park. Gone. And that would have applied to anybody. That was my upbringing in the game. I would not have dared to step out of line for fear of the consequences. Nowadays you can do what you like. There is no discipline. There is no respect.

Even when I signed my first proper contract as a first-team player, £50 a week, I had no power. Celtic had the power. But I was willing to go along with that. The closest I can ever remember coming to a lack of discipline was at an Italian restaurant in Glasgow. Going to a restaurant was the one perk we enjoyed after games, though there was no booze or anything like that. Booze was taboo. Not even half a lager. One Monday before training Jock called a meeting. He said, 'Right, who was at the Vesuveo Saturday night?' A dozen hands went up. 'Right, which smart arse had a cigar?' A cigar! Someone had had a cigar and put it on the bill. That was a crime at the time. No one got drunk. No one stepped out of line. A cigar was enough to cause a scene at Celtic. Would there be an England team meeting over a cigar today when it's any excuse for a piss-up?

Croatia passed to one another at pace, created angles and ran with the ball, but they weren't special. Thirty years ago you could not have lost to teams like Croatia. You can now. These lads from Eastern Europe still have the hunger and the desire. They have not been softened by too much of everything too soon. They are still working at their game when our lads are driving home in their flash cars. Ask any Premiership manager when was the last time a player came back in the afternoon to work on his deficiencies. The silence will deafen you. And don't try to tell me that there are players out there who do not have a deficiency. There are hundreds of them. What are they doing to improve? Nothing. And people wonder where it has all gone wrong for England.

The decline does not stop at the border. I'm talking about Scotland too. And Wales and Northern Ireland for that matter. When I played for Scotland the squad for World Cups would be whittled down from sixty players or more. Now, on any given Saturday, in the Scottish Premier League there probably aren't sixty Scottish players kicking a ball in total. What chance do British teams have of competing internationally if players can't get a game domestically? It's a joke.

Manchester United have obviously become a great club again under Sir Alex Ferguson, who as a Scot from an era similar to mine shares many of my principles and beliefs. But something has been lost from the football I was brought up to play, and which became my life. Money has upped the ante. No one smiles any more. The fun is disappearing from the top end of the game. The consequences of winning and losing are too great. To me, football is and has only ever been a game. I'm not sure the players can say that now. Of course we moaned about bonuses. They made a big difference. But even then we were only talking a couple of hundred quid. Now we have moved into the era of global ownership and marketing strategies. Fans are seen as clients. The dynamic between club owner, player and supporter has changed beyond recognition.

This process has been catastrophic for the grass roots of the game – something that is felt more keenly north of the border, where cheap foreign imports flood the market. It has also made it nigh on impossible for Celtic to compete on the European stage, to repeat the glory days of the sixties. Celtic and Rangers are being slowly cast adrift from their Premiership counterparts as the money and power concentrate on a handful of clubs in England. And they say progress is good.

1

COCKNEY REBEL

PEOPLE THINK I MUST HAVE ITALIAN ROOTS BECAUSE OF THE name. Way back I'm sure I do, but that side of my ancestry I know nothing about. I have seen it written that I have relatives in a part of Italy near Rome, throwing up glamorous associations with Sophia Loren and Gina Lollobrigida. If only. I'm Scottish, through and through, although it might not have sounded like it when I was a lad. I was born in Edinburgh in June 1949 to Scottish parents. I was an only child; it was just Mum (Margaret), Dad (Albert) and me. We lived just outside the city in a mining village called Newton Grange. I don't know the circumstances, but the family moved to London, to Leytonstone, when I was a year old, so I grew up, believe it or not, as a cockney. And yes, I had the full cockney accent.

We stayed in London until I was nine. I used to watch my dad play on a Sunday morning at Hackney Marshes. That was my introduction to football. We'd travel to games in a motorbike and sidecar contraption. You don't see them any more but they were popular at the time. I would stand behind the goals and wait for someone to blast the ball wide then run after it and bring it back, just like any other young lad. My dad was a decent player. He represented the British Army, in midfield. I don't remember any details, just that he was good in possession and had an eye for goal. I get my physique and my style from him.

After the Marshes, the action would move to the streets of Leytonstone. We would be out every night kicking something round against a wall. A tennis ball or a full-size ball, it didn't really matter. The point is we were out learning the mechanics of the game. The ball became something that was connected to your feet. Second nature. By the time I was invited to Celtic many years later to train for the first time, there was never an issue about ball control. That was a given. You had to have it or the invitation was never made.

We lived on Leytonstone High Street. A couple of years ago when I was in London I decided to go back to check out my roots. I'd had neither the time nor the inclination to do that when I was manager, all too briefly, at West Ham. I jumped on the Tube, but when I got there I couldn't recall anything. I recognized absolutely nothing. Everything had changed. Or maybe it was me that had changed. So many details, even of my playing career, have slipped from memory. As you get older you are left with just as many impressions as details. And over time impressions can change.

My father was in the catering industry. A job came up in Largs, a seaside town on the west coast of Scotland – a bit like Brighton – and we moved back to the place of my birth. As a Catholic boy I had to travel to a school about forty minutes away. It was worth it, though, because St Michael's Academy in Kilwinning had a school football team. Not only that, the team I was in was the best group of players the school had ever had. Until then I had never played a representative match for anybody. The school in Leytonstone had not run to a football team. It was all jumpers for posts on street corners there. Some things remained exactly the same, however. Every spare minute – playtime, lunchtime, every day – we would be out with the ball, picking teams and playing the game. Every night after school we'd all be outside until it got dark. We'd tell the time by the sun. When it went down, that's when I realized it must be time for bed. My parents never had to worry about where I was or what I might be doing. The ball acted as a paging device. If they could hear that banging against a wall they knew I was nearby.

Playing football just seemed so natural. We didn't want to do anything else. In fact there wasn't much else to do. No video games, no internet, no computers, just fresh air and a football. I don't remember the cockney accent being an issue. As a kid, you get stick for something. I'm sure I got plenty, but it didn't matter. I would have given it back anyway. As an only child I guess I must have been a bit spoiled, though it never seemed like that. Money was tight. There were few luxuries, but my parents always made sure there was food on the table – tatties and stew. They were blissful days for a football-mad lad.

I was the centre-forward at St Michael's. People say I must have been the smallest centre-forward in Scotland. The way I remember it, everybody in Scotland was small. Just after I started with Celtic I was picked for the Scotland Under-18 schoolboy side. We played against England at Southampton. The pitch was heavy, as it often was at The Dell. Compared to us, the England team were massive. I had played against Irish and Welsh schoolboy teams, and they were like us. But England were huge, and I mean massive. I never got a kick the whole game: (a) I could not drag my legs out of the mud, and (b) they were just too big for me. Brian Kidd was in the England side, Mick Mills too. Mick was only a few inches taller than me but was twice as wide. Three or four of them went on to be top players. It was a lesson for me: if I had any ambition to be a player there was still work to do.

I'd got the call from Celtic at sixteen. Obviously, for a football-mad Catholic boy, going to Celtic was a big thing. The club used to go down to the Ayrshire coast to train in pre-season; the Scotland squad often did the same before big matches. I have a cutting from the local paper in Largs with a picture of a young lad in a Celtic scarf watching the players train. The caption reads 'Young Celtic fan watches his idols'. I was that fan – my first appearance on the back pages.

I was spotted in the normal way, playing for school and for the county, Ayrshire. It was all very informal. My father was approached and asked if I'd mind going to train at Celtic Park for two nights a week. This was the team of Bobby Lennox, Billy McNeill and Jimmy Johnstone, of Bobby Murdoch and Bertie Auld, a group of players who two years later would be labelled the Lisbon Lions, having beaten Inter Milan to become the first British team to win the European Cup. There was little sign of that when I was a supporter. I'd been standing on the terraces for five years, dreaming of one day pulling on that green and white shirt, but never thinking Celtic would be kings of Europe playing a thrilling brand of attacking football that others would copy.

Jock Stein had just arrived on the scene after taking over

from Jimmy McGrory, who had been in charge at Celtic Park for twenty years. It had not been the most successful period in the club's history. As a fan I was not watching the team win every week. Six weeks after taking over in 1965, Jock had his hands on the Scottish Cup – the first time Celtic had won it in eleven years. A year later Jock drove his team to their first League title since 1954, the first of nine successive championships. The atmosphere was incredible, and I was part of it; only a small part, but a part nevertheless. As a taster for what was to come the following year, Celtic added the League Cup in 1966 and lost out in the semi-finals of the European Cup Winners' Cup, to Liverpool. In 1966–67 Celtic won every competition they entered, landing the quadruple of League, Scottish Cup, League Cup and European Cup. It was a magical season. No one could believe it. You look back on that achievement now and it beggars belief.

In my opinion, what Jock Stein did at Celtic, winning the European Cup with a bunch of players who came from nowhere, was the greatest achievement ever in football. In his thirteen years at Celtic Park, 1965 to 1978 (when Billy McNeill took over), Stein led the club to unprecedented success: the European Cup (winners once, runners-up once, semi-finalists five times), ten League titles, eight Scottish Cups and six League Cups. We will never see his like again. How Jock gathered that group together and managed to drill them into a European Cup-winning team is something else. Ronnie Simpson was at Newcastle. He was not recognized as an outstanding goalkeeper. He came to Celtic and was brilliant. Bertie Auld was brought back from Birmingham City. John Hughes on the left wing was a big six-foot-two-inch rampaging rhino. Jock brought them together at no cost and not only won the European Cup but three years later made it to another final. And it wasn't just the winning, it was the manner in which they won. Celtic had to come from behind to win in Lisbon in 1967. Tommy Gemmell equalized, then Stevie Chalmers poked home the most important goal in Scottish football history. What a night.

To get to Celtic Park from school in time for training at half past six was a bit of an ordeal, the more so because Jock Stein did not appreciate late arrivals. I had to get my foot down to make sure I caught the first train to Glasgow Central. From there it was two buses. Catching the second, the 263 to Auchenshuggle, was crucial. Big Jock was strict on time-keeping. Regardless of how many trains and buses you had to rely on to get you there, if you were late you were in trouble. If you were on that last bus and it was running late you were always in a bit of a sweat because Jock would be waiting at the front door pointing at his watch.

The training sessions were for boys aged sixteen and above. As far as Jock was concerned we were possible Celtic players of the future. No more than that. There was no academy, no centre of excellence, no fancy concepts to send young heads spinning. We never felt we were near to stardom. That's how he ran the ship. It was great management. With him waiting for us, it sent the right message. It made us aware in no uncertain terms of the importance of punctuality and discipline. You were not there to mess about. This wasn't a kickabout with your mates, this was serious. If you didn't take it seriously you were out.

I always managed to make it just before the deadline.

The training was about building your strength, getting fitness levels up. You basically went through the door, slipped your training shoes on, then ran out on to what was then the biggest track in Scotland. It seemed massive to the eyes of a sixteen-year-old. For two years, that was it: twice a week running around that track. If you did well you would be selected to play a five-a-side game behind the goals. That was the only time you touched the ball. You never went on to the pitch, so that was a perk, a reward for your hard work. It felt wonderful to be included in that game for twenty minutes, playing at Celtic Park. If the ground was unplayable we would go on the terracing and play on the concrete under the stand.

There were no promises that you would be taken on as a pro. I was still playing for the school, the county, and Scotland schoolboys, so the club got to know all they needed to know about you from watching you in those games and from monitoring you in the training sessions. That's the way it was in those days. That's the way it should be now. If you were not taken on at eighteen, it was not a major disappointment like it is for youngsters today, who are affiliated to clubs from as early as nine. To be told you are not going to progress at any time during the next nine years at a club must be heartbreaking, because after any length of time they must all think they are going to make it. We never really met or even saw first-team players at that stage, unless they were injured and coming in for treatment. Even though Sean Fallon, Jock's assistant, was technically in charge of the training session, the great man would always be there, standing behind the goals for the five-a-sides, adding his knowledge as and when, maybe pulling you aside to make a point. The method of acquiring young players was simple in those days. Talented teenagers are now routinely signed on contracts worth hundreds of thousands. Clubs didn't operate like that in the sixties. They did not want to show their hands. They wanted to keep boys hungry.

I used to get home about 10.30 at night. My father would pick me up from the station, and in the morning it was back to school. There were no thoughts about travel tiring you out, or too many games. That is a modern phenomenon. In those days talented young lads all over the country were travelling to clubs twice a week to train. I'd bump into other boys at the station doing the same thing as me. One of those lads was Gordon McQueen, who was training with St Mirren. He lived in a little town just up from me called Kilbirnie, where my mother was from. Gordon and I got to know each other well on that station platform.

One night we asked this kid to go get us fish and chips from the chip shop. We didn't want to risk it in case the train came in. We paid him for the fish and chips before he left, and of course neither of us saw him again. Gordon has never forgotten that. He wants his money back. Somewhere out there is a fella who ought to know that big Gordon McQueen is looking for him.

When D-Day approached, there was no fuss. 'Come and see us next week and we'll let you know what's happening.' In you went. It was a simple yes or no. No bullshit with it. If you were successful, there was no going out and buying your first Cortina or Ford Anglia, or whatever was in fashion at the time. Even if they thought you were a talent of the future you would never be aware of that. Kenny Dalglish came through the Celtic ranks at the same time as me, and Danny McGrain, and David Hay. They didn't walk about thinking they were great players (which they were of course), they just got their heads down and worked. The press labelled us the Quality Street Gang. Jock didn't.

I signed my first contract with Celtic in 1968, at the age of nineteen. My first wage was £15 a week. As part of the contract you signed to say that you had come from an amateur side. If things did not go well in your first six months, you would go straight to that amateur team as a fall-back. I signed from a club I had never played for called Ashfield Juniors. That was another indication to players that there were no guarantees. 'If this doesn't work out, pal, you are an Ashfield player.' That was an incentive to pull your finger out, to take nothing for granted, I can tell you.

2

A CUB AMONG LIONS

THE MAN IN CHARGE OF THE RESERVES WAS SEAN FALLON, A Republic of Ireland man. Great man, Sean. He was a former team-mate of Jock's in their playing days at Celtic and had been at the club since the early fifties. Basically, the club was: Jock Stein, Sean Fallon, physio Bob Rooney, trainer Neil Mochan, masseur Jimmy Steel, who became a great friend of mine, and the players. So there I was, a Celtic player. I'd gone from following the team on the terraces to cleaning the boots and putting the shirts out for the Lisbon Lions. It was a great honour after being around the place for two years, getting two buses and a train every Tuesday and Thursday night. I'd adjusted. That is how it felt at the time. I was now sharing the same turf as the players who made up one of the great teams in British football history. Jock threw us all in together. There was no partitioning of players. That made us grow up fast. Even Jock got stuck in during training. Everywhere you looked there was a lesson to be learned. I could not have had a better footballing education.

All great teams build from the back. Jim Craig and Tommy Gemmell were superb full-backs. Gemmell's goals from left-back were often vital. His equalizer against Inter in Lisbon was typical, hammered with ferocious power. Craig was more considered at right-back. Because he had none of Gemmell's attacking flair he often went through matches unnoticed. But he was a clever fella, a dentist who graduated from Glasgow University. Jim always seemed to be in the right place defensively and was brilliant in the tackle. Incredibly, he won only a single cap for Scotland. He was way better than that.

Defence is about partnerships, and at the heart of Celtic's in the late sixties were Billy McNeill and John Clark. Billy was a leader of men – hence his nickname, Caesar – a traditional centre-half, brave in the tackle and terrific in the air at set-pieces. You felt safe with Billy around. He gave everybody confidence. Clark was a sweeper before they had invented the term. He used to clean up around Billy, a neat and tidy player and a great student of the game.

Bobby Murdoch and Bertie Auld ran games from the centre of the park – as good a midfield pairing as any I have seen. If you think Steven Gerrard can play, you would have loved Murdoch – a wonderful combination of power and touch. He had superb command of the ball, he covered every blade of grass, he could split a field with a pass and blow holes in the goals with his shooting. Again, partnerships, whether in defence or midfield, are about blending complementary talents. Auld was a converted winger who used his skill and balance to kill teams. He was not as dramatic as Murdoch but just as effective in his own way, and tough as old boots. Willie

Wallace led the line brilliantly alongside Bobby Lennox and Stevie Chalmers. Celtic paid a club record £30,000 to bring him to Parkhead from Hearts in 1966. Wispy was brilliant in possession and sharp around the box.

On the right was the incomparable Jimmy Johnstone. Jinky was one of the great wide men of all time, unplayable on an off day, never mind a good one. He was most people's favourite Lion. That's fair enough. He could do things with a ball at his feet others couldn't. Off the pitch he was a bit special too, always getting into daft scrapes. During one international meet-up at Largs he decided to take a rowing boat out to sea. But the tide was too strong and he couldn't bring it back in. I think the coastguard rescued him in the end. But what a player. He would not just beat opponents, he would destroy them. Ask Terry Cooper, who left the Hampden pitch dizzy after the great European Cup semi-final clash against Leeds in 1970. Big players do it on big occasions. Johnstone was great that night. Cooper and Leeds came north with a great reputation. They went home a little bit diminished.

Up front, Bobby Lennox and Stevie Chalmers had pace to burn, and great engines. It was an unstoppable combination. Beyond Parkhead, Chalmers is not a name people remember too much when talking about that great Celtic team, but it was his goal that made history for the club, a typically brave lunge to get to the ball first and stab it over the line before a pack of Italian defenders could clear.

It was in this company that I learned my trade.

There was no glamour attached to being on the groundstaff in those days, just a lot of hard work. We all recognized that we had major deficiencies in our game at which we had to work hard, including Kenny Dalglish, who was taken on shortly after me. I was weak physically. I didn't really have any great running power. The manager worked me really hard on that. We used to run every day from Celtic Park to the training ground through the streets of Glasgow. You'd almost be knocking over old women with their shopping bags. 'Oh aye, lads,' they'd say, waving at us as we jogged by. Jock Stein was big into fitness. It was of primary importance, one of the main reasons behind the team's success in the European Cup. The players were to a man incredibly fit. The second individual weakness I had to work on was my heading ability. It is fair to say that by the time I moved to England, where you had to be pretty decent in the air, I had gone from a player who had been completely out of his depth against England schoolboys in terms of presence and stature to a player able to handle that side of the game. That was down to Jock.

Believe it or not, Dalglish's problem was goalscoring. Fine player though he was, he struggled in front of the posts. So he would stay back in the afternoon with a couple of bags of balls, smashing them into an empty net, picking them out and doing it again and again. That was the instruction he was given. He knew that if he wanted to improve his game he had to work at it. Every afternoon it was the same thing, Kenny at the training ground firing balls into the net until it got dark. Looking at how things turned out for him, you could say it was time well spent.

It makes me laugh when people regard great players like Dalglish as naturals. Yes, a lot of it is about the gifts you were born with, but Kenny did not fulfil his potential simply because he was naturally gifted, he did so as a result of hours and hours of hard graft. He developed his skills. People wonder today where all the great British players have gone, but how can they get to the top now when no one tells them they have shortcomings and instructs them to work on them? They must have them, probably more than Dalglish, but as a rule youngsters are not required to come back in the afternoons and work on their games. You hear Sir Alex Ferguson talking about Cristiano Ronaldo working on his free-kicks after training with Wayne Rooney, Ryan Giggs and Paul Scholes, but is the same thing happening at Southampton, Tranmere or Walsall?

Returning to the training ground is, in the modern era, taboo, not to be considered. It's just not part of today's culture. It was part of ours because we had a manager who left you in no doubt that your future would be in the balance if you did not improve. Nowadays such a pressure does not apply. Clubs are so desperate for young players that they rarely, if ever, threaten to show them the door. It was the fear of failure that drove me on. It drove Dalglish on too, Danny McGrain and David Hay. Ask anybody who played with David at Chelsea and they will tell you his fitness levels were unbelievable. He was a freak. That came about because of what Jock demanded of him when he first walked through the door at Celtic Park. By the time he went south to England that attitude had become habit. It was ingrained.

I look at young lads today and I don't see that same application. There is no discipline. In fact they get the very opposite treatment. Talented lads at big clubs today are mollycoddled by comparison. 'Rest' is the watchword now. My argument has always been that if you can get a team to win the European Cup and then get to another final using Jock Stein's methods, then those methods are the correct ones. I know Liverpool, Chelsea, Arsenal and Manchester United have all been to Champions League finals in recent years, and won them in the case of Liverpool and United, but they have all spent millions getting there, largely on overseas players. For those teams without the financial muscle to buy success, hard work is the minimum requirement. And by hard work I'm not just talking about fitness, I'm talking about technique, working on all aspects of the game. I don't see anywhere near enough of that in today's game.

We'd spend two hours a day shooting, passing and the like. If Jock thought we were crap, he'd blow his whistle early. 'Right, you lot, back in the afternoon. Everybody. Fucking rubbish.' Just behind the training ground at Barrowfield there was a hospital. If you kicked the ball over the crossbar or wide and it went over the fence into the hospital, Jock would order you to go and get it. If you did it again, you went back. I don't know what the patients made of it. Even if he didn't like the way just one or two people had performed in a training session, everybody was back in the afternoon. So you were always on your toes. That work ethic kept us going for fifteen, sixteen years. All those players I was with at Celtic enjoyed long careers, rarely missed games. And when training was over it was back into your trainers and back to Celtic Park on foot. Jock would drive slowly alongside in his car shouting out of the window, 'Get a fucking move on!'

I was terrified of Jock. The first-team players were terrified of him, so you can imagine how a young boy just taken on to the groundstaff felt. He left you in no doubt he was the manager. His methods were so simple and productive. Forget about all the crap that has come into the modern game. It's all baloney. Take, for example, preparation for big games like cup finals. We used to go to a place called Seamill Hydro Hotel in

West Kilbride, just south of Largs. It occupies a beautiful spot on the west coast of Scotland and is popular for weddings. We'd go on a Tuesday, and that was it, locked away until the game on the Saturday. There were no WAGs on the scene in those days. Without being told, you knew what was required, what the arrangements were. Before we even started kicking a ball about – five-a-sides based on quick movement: the training area at the hotel was a bit of grass no bigger than a basketball court – Jock would walk us along the beach. Two miles each way. We did the same at night before supper. At the end of every day we'd probably covered eight miles. There were no tests to determine fitness levels scientifically. If you were twenty yards behind somebody Jock would just scream at you to 'get a fucking move on'. As I said, simple, but productive.

I knuckled down and continued to work on my skills, eager for the day when I could pull on the green and white hoops, run out and represent my club at senior level.

3

BOY TO MAN

THE DAY CAME IN AUGUST 1970, AGAINST MORTON – MY League debut. Jock did that with all the kids, threw them in against a smaller team. I say kids, but I was twenty-one. I felt like a kid though. And compared to Billy McNeill, Jimmy Johnstone, Bobby Lennox and those other giants of the game, I was a kid. Today I'd be an old man making my first appearance at that age. Theo Walcott seems to have been around for ever. He has already been to one World Cup as a squad member. He's unhappy at not being a first-team regular at Arsenal. He turned nineteen in March 2008, the month in which the first draft of this book went to the publishers. I'm surprised he hasn't got a book out himself. What's he waiting for?

Don't ask me how I did in my first game. I can't really tell you because there weren't any pats on the back from Jock Stein. He would never allow you to have in your mind the idea that you might have done well. He didn't want you to get carried away with things in the early part of your career. He did not want you losing the plot. Regardless of how well you did, you would be completely in the dark as to what he thought of you. You'd be in the team, then out of the team. We beat Morton 2–0. I didn't know I was playing until an hour before kick-off. I did not turn up expecting to play. It was nerve-wracking. I had stood on those terraces, I had played reserve games against Rangers in front of 20,000 fans, but this was the real thing. The first thing you notice is the crowd, the roar from the Jungle. Playing in front of them, instead of clearing up after them with the rest of the groundstaff, is something you never forget.

My only experience with the first team before my debut came a few weeks earlier, during an end-of-season tour to North America. Big Jock had done the same with the Lisbon Lions in 1966. This was my first foreign tour as a footballer. We played Bari in Toronto. Before the game, their goalkeeper made a gesture to Bobby Lennox indicating he was going to slit his throat. It set the tone for the match. As the game progressed I was smacked in the face a couple of times. Proceedings were getting out of hand. At half-time Big Jock walked over to their dugout to try to sort things out and ended up in a fist fight with their boss. He had to leave at half-time to catch a flight back to Glasgow to see a specialist about an ankle that was troubling him, but not before letting the Bari manager have both barrels and a right hook. In the second half the match descended into a free-for-all and was eventually abandoned.

You couldn't call Jock a coach in the traditional sense. He'd have a meeting before a big game, say in Europe, and he would hardly talk about the opposition at all, would not even mention them, beyond something like, 'You are playing the Spaniards tonight. You know what they are like.' He would concentrate on his own players, maybe hark back to a previous game and say, 'I don't want to see you do that again because you're fucking crap at that.' Team talks were simple, about playing to your strengths. 'Set-pieces, look for Billy McNeill' – exceptionally good in the air – 'All free-kicks, Tommy Gemmell' – unbelievable power in his shot – 'Any time you don't know what to do with the ball, give it to little Jimmy. He'll hold on to it for ten minutes.' Because we are now caught up in the intrigue of what goes on to win a game – tactics, technique and all – which is all crap, people don't believe it was that straightforward with Jock Stein and his European Cup-winning team. But it was.

Bobby Lennox talked about 1967 in a documentary about the Lisbon Lions. After the game the Inter right-back, Giacinto Facchetti, came up to Bobby and told him how the Italians took great pride in their fitness and could not believe how the Celtic boys managed to be fitter than them. He said they had never played a team like Celtic. But it is not rocket science, not a tactical triumph. Jock understood what his players could do and did not over-complicate it with systems and formations.

And we all had our feet firmly on the ground. It wasn't hard to when you were going to work by train and bus. When I passed my driving test I would sometimes get to borrow my dad's car, a Ford Anglia. If there was a game, we'd all travel up for the match together, me and my mum and dad. They would drop me off around noon then go and get a cup of tea and something to eat and come back for the kick-off. Afterwards they would take me home.

I was in and out of the team a lot in that first full season as a professional player with Celtic, 1970–71. One day in particular from that time will burn in the memory of every Scot, player and fan: 2 January, 1971 – the Ibrox tragedy. I wasn't involved in the match but went along with the squad. We were sitting in the bus at the end of the game, anxious to get away, as players invariably are. We had not a clue about the tragic turn of events inside the ground until someone came on to the bus about an hour after the final whistle and told us that dozens of people had died in a massive crush. We had opened the scoring after eighty-nine minutes, and then, in the closing seconds of injury time, Colin Stein had equalized for Rangers. There was chaos on the terraces. As the fans flooded out, barriers collapsed in one stairway, causing sixty-six deaths, many of them children. Suddenly, what had happened in the game was all irrelevant. The players sat on the bus in a state of shock. We couldn't get off, and the bus couldn't leave. When we did finally depart, the journey back to Celtic Park was sombre. Hardly anybody spoke. For the fans, the rivalry between the clubs is the most intense in the world. All that was set aside. It remains the one Old Firm game where what took place on the pitch is hardly ever talked about.

Five months later I was involved in my first really important game: the 1971 Scottish Cup Final against Rangers at Hampden. We did the usual preparation at Seamill then went up to Hampden on the bus. Jock never announced the team until an hour before kick-off so we were sweating all the way up on that bus, wondering whether we were going to be involved or not. I thought I was there just to make up the numbers that day. We got to Hampden, and I was named sub. I was chuffed with myself. There was only one substitute allowed in those days. There were 128,000 in the ground. Bobby Lennox opened the scoring, but just three minutes from time the teenaged Derek Johnstone, who would be part of the Scotland squad with me at the World Cup in Argentina in 1978, equalized. There was no extra-time in those days, so there was massive disappointment in the changing room. It was back on the bus to Seamill to prepare for the replay.

Back we come to Hampden late on Wednesday afternoon. It's a quarter to seven. We are in the changing room. Jock puts the team sheet up. I'm in. Jock doesn't say a word. He hasn't said anything at training. He hasn't said a word about it in three days. All of a sudden, I'm in the team. I didn't even kick a ball on the Saturday, so I'm thinking, 'What the fuck am I doing in the team?' Again there are 128,000 in the ground. I score the first goal, a little flick at the near post. The place erupts. Jimmy Johnstone then goes over in the box for a penalty. You can see it on YouTube – another reminder of how things used to be. Jinky gets chopped down. The Rangers full-back picks him up and more or less shakes his hand. This is Rangers–Celtic, don't forget, and he's congratulating Jinky for his trickery. There's no arguing with the referee, no appealing. Harry Hood puts the ball on the spot – 2–0. The place goes mad. Rangers get one back late in the game, but we hang on. In the dressing room afterwards there are congratulations, obviously, but no crap from the manager, just a low-key 'Well done.' Half an hour later we are on our way back to Celtic Park on the bus, where Mum and Dad are waiting to take me home.

Playing for Celtic at that time, every match was an adventure for a young player like me. It was such an honour just to be involved. It was not all about winning, either. On

23 October, 1971 we played Partick Thistle at Hampden in the Scottish League Cup. On paper it was a mismatch. It was a mismatch on the pitch, too, but not in the way anyone imagined. After thirty-six minutes we were 4–0 down. The only excuse we could have had was Jimmy Johnstone going off injured in the first twenty minutes. The sub, Jim Craig, was a right-back, not quite the same. Frank Bough informed *Grandstand* viewers of the score, then advised that they were trying to establish the validity of it because no one could quite believe it. He confirmed the score at half-time. In the end we lost 4–1. For me, Dalglish, Hay and the rest of the young lads coming through it was a wake-up call, reminding us that not every day had a happy ending. Thankfully those days were rare.

Regular first-team football meant playing in Europe. At a club like Celtic that was extra special. It was an opportunity to write your name in history. In March 1972 we were drawn against Hungarian champions Ujpest Dozsa. The first leg was in Budapest. For some reason Richard Burton and Liz Taylor were in town that night, probably filming. When they heard we were playing they became instant Celtic fans. Apparently Celtic supporters had taken over their hotel. The golden couple probably had no choice but to join the party.

It was Hollywood on the pitch that night. The Hungarian international Horvath put through his own goal to gift us the lead. I was playing up front on my own. It was hard work. The quality was high from both teams. Horvath made amends with an equalizer, but late in the game I sniffed out a half chance, and lobbed the keeper for the winner. I was part of a fantastic away win in Europe, and I felt I had really arrived. Jock was gradually reshaping the team, building a new set of

Lisbon Lions, and I was staking my claim alongside the likes of Kenny Dalglish, David Hay and Danny McGrain. George Connolly was another rising star. George was a brilliant player, cool on the ball and a great passer; the Scottish equivalent of a Glenn Hoddle or a Ray Wilkins. It is a mystery to me how he drifted away from the game.

Ujpest were a top side. They scored early in the return leg in Glasgow then sat back, hoping to hit us on the break. It was one of those great nights at Celtic Park: all-out attack from us, clever defending from them. I nicked a goal in the second half to send us through on aggregate. My stock was rising. I was carving a reputation as a fox around the box, a taker of half chances. Playing in Europe was a great learning experience for me. Everything was done that bit quicker. As a result, I was getting better.

For several years now I'd stayed as far away from Jock Stein as I could, always made sure he had nothing to pick me up on, kept my nose clean. The only time I went in to see him was when my contract was up at the end of 1971–72. It was the first time I'd spoken to him one-to-one. I had broken into the first team, the team that was the Lisbon Lions. I had scored three goals in two cup finals, and ended on the winning side each time. We had also won the League Championship in successive seasons as Jock continued a run that has gone down in Scottish football history. Aberdeen finished second both years, but by 1972 they were ten points behind us (and there were only two points for a win, remember), with Rangers a further six points adrift in third. So I was going in to see Jock with a body of work behind me. Or so I thought. He told me how well I'd done for the club. I was on £50 a week, and he said he would push my wages up to £55.

Compared to what the man in the street was earning – my father would have been on about £20 a week – it was good money, but nothing like the amounts players earn today, or even at the time in England. I earned enough to buy a decent car, a second-hand Audi, but nothing more than that. We made our money up on bonuses. But Jock controlled all that. If you beat Rangers you could be looking at £500 – enough to make your little legs run faster. Today there is no bonus that can make your legs go quicker. The players already have it in advance. The Rangers lads would be on the same bonus, so what you had was a real ding-dong affair for ninety minutes.

Losing to Inter Milan in the 1972 European Cup semi-final on penalties had been a real sickener. Both legs finished 0–0. I couldn't believe how aggressive the Italians were in defence. You don't see it much these days, even from Italian teams. If you went here or there, they followed you. If you went to control the ball there would be a foot in behind you. In those days you would accept a tackle from any angle; there was none of this 'no tackling from behind' nonsense. If you weren't tackled from behind it would be a surprise. There was nothing between the teams, it just didn't go for us on the night. I didn't take a penalty. Dixie Deans was the player who missed. In the early hours of the following morning, Dixie was snapped on Argyle Street standing alone at a bus stop. The caption in the paper read 'Loneliest man in Glasgow'. But Dixie was not the only one to suffer. Being told by Jock that there would be no bonus was an extra kick in the teeth, for all of us. That's what he was like. We were expecting as much as £1,000 a man for a win. The place was packed. We gave it everything. We were unlucky to go out on penalties. We didn't get a penny. I know one thing. None of us got rich playing for Celtic.

Pay day was on a Tuesday. The players would queue up at a little hatch. The top players like Billy and Jinky would have been on about £90 a week tops, but you never knew what your wage was going to be. You knew your £50 or whatever would be there, plus a fiver appearance money, but if you won on the Saturday you didn't know if it was going to be an extra £50, £75 or £100. It was all down to how Jock saw the game. The first man in the wages queue would open his wage packet. The lads would gather round. 'Well,' we'd say, 'tell us.' Too often the reply would be, 'Oh fuckin' 'ell,' which meant he'd short-changed us again.

The lack of bonus or appearance money after the Inter Milan game was the moment when one or two of the players started to get a bit disgruntled with the old regime. I'd been around the international scene a bit by this stage, and when you're away you speak to other players. I was hearing stories of up to £200 a week in the south. We were learning that a team like Leeds United would be given a certain reward just for getting to the European Cup Final; it was all written down in black and white. Billy 'Caesar' McNeill was the players' representative when it came to dealing with the manager. We'd often send him in to try to get a bonus improved from £20 to £30, stuff like that. More often than not he'd come out shaking his head. No chance. Players north of the border were beginning to feel a bit like second-class citizens.

Three weeks after the Inter semi we were back at Hampden in the Scottish Cup Final against Hibs. It had become a big game after the disappointment of the European Cup. Hibs were a strong team, it was a hot afternoon, and no one was expecting a walkover. They equalized after Billy McNeill had given us the lead, but we had Dixie Deans, who was keen to make up for his missed penalty – not that he had anything to prove. He scored his first, a header, before half-time, then went to town in the second half. His second, a brilliant goal driven in from the left, finished off Hibs. I helped myself to a couple, and Dixie ended the game with a hat-trick for a final score of 6–1. Afterwards it was the same old story: no fuss, no banquets, just straight back to Celtic Park, then home with Mum and Dad in the Anglia.

There was an unscheduled celebration, however. The route back to Largs took us through Paisley, where we often stopped off at our favourite fish and chip shop. In I went, happy as Larry. A few moments later a bus full of Celtic fans pulled up outside. In those days there was no great division between the fans and the players, who shared backgrounds and habits. You were one of them, they were one of you. Money had not yet driven a wedge between the parties. Next thing I knew, they were all in the chip shop. This was not something you could handle like you would when recognized on the train. With so many of them there was no opportunity to engage in polite conversation. I had just got my fish and chips and was rapidly looking for a back door to escape through when I was hoisted shoulder high and marched through the shop, and then the eating area at the back.

It was all good-natured stuff. No one came to any harm. I lost a few chips though.

4

FAREWELL MY LOVELY

IN THOSE PRE-BOSMAN DAYS THE CLUBS HELD A PLAYER'S registration. You couldn't leave unless they decided to sell you. Celtic held all the cards. I told Jock I wasn't happy with the offer on the table, and added that if the chance came to leave I would take it. And that was that. I walked out of his office without signing a new deal and continued with my work on the old terms. A few things were happening in my life at the time. I'd got married. I'd just lost my father to cancer. I was growing up, I suppose, but that's not how it felt at the time. I just felt as though I had to make a stand.

Once again, in 1972–73 we were soon on our way to winning the League Championship, and I was still enjoying my football, scoring goals and getting the adulation of the fans. There was not a sniff in the press about the fact that I hadn't signed a contract. A few months of the new season passed and still nothing happened. Then one night in January 1973, when I was sitting at home, the phone rang. It was late, after 11 p.m.

It was Jock. He told me that a car would pick me up in the morning and take me to England. I asked where I was going, but that was a waste of time. 'Just get in the car and it will take you there.'

The car came on time. Sean Fallon was in it. We headed south. I didn't have a clue where I was going. I told the wife that I would ring her when I got there.

By four o'clock in the afternoon I was standing in the Prince of Wales Hotel in Southport. Still Sean didn't tell me anything. I knew that Liverpool was on the map near here, and Manchester, but back then I didn't have a clue exactly where Southport was, apart from by the sea. I rang the wife, still clueless. We had a cup of tea and a sandwich, then got back in the car. Around six o'clock we made our way through the gates at Anfield. When we entered the city of Liverpool I of course realized we were heading for either Liverpool or Everton, but I never asked. In those days it just never entered your head to question the way things were done. You just went along with it because that was how Jock wanted it.

Before long I found myself in front of Bill Shankly. He offered me terms on the spot. He explained that when he'd first seen me a couple of years ago he told Jock that he wanted me and if I ever became available he would take me.

Liverpool had a big game that night, in the League Cup against Burnley. I went up in the stand to take my seat after arranging to chat again when the match was over. Sitting next to me was Paddy Crerand, the assistant manager of Manchester United. For some reason he could not sit next to the United manager, Tommy Docherty, who was in the directors box. 'What you doing here?' he asked. I told him I was about to sign for Liverpool. 'We weren't made aware that you were available for transfer,' he said. Nobody had been. Paddy told me not to sign anything. He went to see Tommy Doc at half-time, came back and told me that United were going to sign me. 'We're going back to Glasgow tonight. We are at the Excelsior Hotel at the airport. Come and see us tomorrow and we'll sign you there and then.'

Without asking about wages or anything like that, I made my mind up it was Manchester United. As a Celtic lad my team in England, the one I followed, was United. This was the club of Law, Charlton and Best. Liverpool were a good side, a real team with the likes of Kevin Keegan, John Toshack, Ian Callaghan and Steve Heighway. They were on the verge of becoming a great side. But once United came in, that was it. Then I suddenly realized, 'Fuck me, I've got to go back and tell Shanks after the game.'

Shanks, who had offered me £180 a week plus a nine grand signing-on fee – 5 per cent of the deal – was sitting behind his desk when I walked into his office. It was as intimidating as meeting Jock for the first time. He greeted me with that trade-mark 'Aye, ye all right, son?' which right away frightened the life out of me. I took a deep breath, then told him I needed some time to think about the offer. He was OK about it. Why wouldn't he be? He had no idea about what had gone on. He called somebody in. I didn't know who it was, but it turned out to be Bob Paisley. 'Bob,' he said, 'take this young lad back to the hotel. Make sure he's OK.' Sean Fallon had long gone. As far as he was concerned I was signing for Liverpool. Mission accomplished.

So there I was, heading away from the ground with Bob Paisley. I was booked into the Adelphi Hotel. I thought

Bob was just a member of the groundstaff, or someone loosely connected with the club. I remember asking him what Shanks was really like. 'He seems a bit aggressive,' I said, 'a tough man.'

Bob smiled. 'Oh he's tough all right.'

'He can't be any tougher than my first manager, can he?' I said.

'I don't know about that, son. It's probably touch and go.'

'Fuck me,' I thought.

The next morning I took my life in my hands and rang Shanks from the hotel. I told him I was signing for United. He was as good as gold. Wished me all the best. What an operator – real class.

I jumped on a train back to Glasgow. Waiting for me at the station was a fella called Jim Roger. We used to call him Scoop Roger. He worked for the *Daily Record* in Scotland and had got wind of the deal from Doc. He'd rung me at the hotel before I left and told me he would meet me at Glasgow Central and take me to the Excelsior. I knew Jim well, obviously, as a Celtic reporter. He took me to the hotel and got his scoop. Doc offered me £200 a week plus the signing-on fee, £10,000. It seemed an absolute fortune at the time – £3,330 a year for three years, less tax. Although it didn't exactly make me a millionaire, it was the biggest move of my career. I was now a Manchester United player.

Three years earlier, following the failure of Wilf McGuinness to fill Sir Matt Busby's boots, Jock Stein had had the chance to manage Manchester United. The drama had dragged on for days. Time stood still at Celtic before Jock decided he would stay. We'll never know how he would have changed the United story. Jock had his reasons for staying, and now I had mine for going. Celtic picked up £200,000 – a record for a player moving from Scotland to England – and I was off to Manchester.

5

DOC'S TARTAN ARMY

BECAUSE OF MY TIME AND EXPERIENCES AT CELTIC, I WAS conditioned to start thinking straight away about my debut for United that Saturday against West Ham. Preparation, preparation, preparation.

'Right, when are we off?' I asked the Doc.

'Just relax,' he said. 'We'll get on our way when we feel like it.'

We checked into the hotel for another night.

'We'll give you a shout in the morning,' the Doc added.

All I could think about was training. I thought we'd be up by at least six to get to Manchester for Thursday training, but it was eleven o'clock when the call eventually came. I offered to do some training that afternoon. 'Och, ye don't need to bother,' my new manager replied. 'I've seen you play.'

On the way back, in Gretna Green, we had a bump in the car. It was comedy-hour stuff. Crunch, into the back of a lorry. I was in the back. You can imagine what I was thinking. I was wondering what the hell was going on. It was my first day as a

Manchester United player, and I'd missed training and been involved in a car crash.

We eventually arrived in Manchester, and I trained on the Friday. There was no big unveiling for the press. After training the press lads were waiting at Old Trafford. They took a few notes and that was it, the top and bottom of the transfer. None of this sitting around all morning with coffee and biscuits.

Come match day there was snow on the pitch. It was barely playable, but it passed the inspection. My memory of the occasion is sketchy, though I shall never forget being handed the number ten shirt worn famously by Denis Law. Of course that was an honour, but it was also an embarrassment to me since the great man was also in the team that day wearing the number four. I also remember scoring the equalizer. Bobby Charlton got our other goal in a 2–2 draw. There is a great photograph from the match of Bobby Moore lying on the floor watching the ball go in the back of the net. What a picture that was! Come five o'clock I don't think I had any thoughts other than it was another day's work, just for a different club, albeit a massive one. At that point I did not have any understanding of any great differences between Celtic and Manchester United. That would come, though. It takes a while for things to unravel.

What I did find out quickly was the difference between the two managers post-match. The Doc was full of praise, probably went over the top. That wouldn't have happened with Jock. I'm not saying one was right or wrong, it was just a different approach. Doc's method came out loud and clear in the Sunday papers. He went overboard, hyping things up, yet it was only my first game. It put a little bit of pressure on to deliver. Maybe that was the reason Jock never did it. Everything was very low key with Jock. And in the final analysis all we had managed in that first match was a draw with West Ham – nothing earth-shattering.

I'd been with the Doc in the national squad. He was one of the funniest managers I worked with. Still is. Witty and sharp. If you liked the banter, which I did, it was a great strength. He used to call the United chairman, Louis Edwards, Big Chop Suey, because it rhymed with Louis. And he would do this to his face. Centre-forward Ted MacDougall was Drop Down Dead, which was probably what the Doc was hoping for. Ted had scored a lot of goals for Bournemouth, so he knew where the net was, but if the Doc took a dislike to you, that was it. The problem was, he took a dislike to everybody at some time or another. Most of the time it would blow over in a day or two then you would be back on side. Other times it didn't. It was Jekyll and Hyde stuff. Confrontation was a technique he was fond of, particularly with the more established players. It happened with George Best, it happened with Denis Law and it happened with Bobby Charlton. All three, like Ted, were gone within a year of my arrival. No one escaped. Winger Willie Morgan was very close to the Doc. You would never have guessed that one day Willie and the Doc would end up taking each other on in court over a disagreement. Even Paddy Crerand, the Doc's assistant, got fed up and left the club.

Sometimes it came to blows. Alex Stepney was a legend at United. He stopped *that* shot from Eusebio to help United lift the European Cup in 1968, for goodness' sake. He was in goal throughout the promotion-winning season of 1974–75. At one stage the previous season he was the leading goalscorer, courtesy of penalty kicks. At the start of the 1975–76 season he was told by the Doc before a ball was kicked that he would be second choice to Paddy Roche. Steptoe (as we called him) couldn't understand that and wasn't too happy about it. He was a senior figure at the club. The decision hurt, but it was not his style to kick up a fuss.

On the Friday before the first game of the season, Alex was training at The Cliff. In those days the first-team players always trained at Old Trafford on the Friday before a match. If you weren't in the first-team set-up you were banished to train with the reserves at The Cliff. As a policy, this never made any sense to me. What was the point of making players like Stepney, European Cup winners at that, train with the reserves? It was a slap in the face. And stupid when you consider that at any moment you might need to call on a player's services, which is exactly what happened.

Unbeknown to us, Paddy's father had died the night before, and he had had to rush back to Dublin to sort a few things out. With Paddy away, Alex got a call to come up to Old Trafford to take part in the first-team training session. There was no gear laid out for him when he arrived. We were doing a few laps around the pitch with Tommy Cavanagh, who was very particular about appearance: everybody had to be turned out in the same training gear. Understandable. This was Manchester United. So it was a bit embarrassing for big Alex to arrive later than everybody else for the session and in cobbled-together kit. It wasn't his fault, of course, but this did not stop him getting a tongue-lashing from Tommy.

It took a lot to rattle Alex's cage, but the next thing, Tommy was picking himself up off the floor. Alex had whacked him. Cav had basically taken it on the chin for the Doc, whose treatment of Alex had ultimately fuelled the violent response. The players were shocked at the way Alex had been treated. It seemed to be part of a pattern with the older lads who were there long before the Doc arrived. Needless to say, the incident cast a shadow over the day. Cav got up, rubbing his chin. 'What did you do that for?' he asked. Alex muttered something, and we moved on.

I was not immune. I came in for training one day and the Doc told me that I would be playing that night at Mossley, a small town up in the hills east of Manchester.

'Who's playing?' I asked. 'The reserves?'

'No, the kids.'

'What am I playing there for?'

'Never mind, just be there,' he said.

So I left training, went home and spoke to the missus.

'I'm playing at Mossley tonight,' I told her.

'What for?' she asked. 'A testimonial?'

'No, a game with the kids.'

'Why are you playing?'

'I don't know.'

I decided I wasn't going. I rang the Doc and told him.

'You'll be in trouble if you don't,' he said.

'I don't care,' I said. 'I'm not going.'

A little while later I got a call from Cliff Lloyd at the PFA. He warned me that if I did not go I'd be opening myself up to all sorts of strife. There might be a fine or a suspension, head-lines in the papers. I could be on collision course with the Doc. There would be only one winner in that situation. Still I refused. A few phone calls were exchanged after that, and eventually I saw the point and off I went.

I arrived at this small-town club in the middle of nowhere and all the journalists were there. Bob Russell of the *Daily Mirror*, Peter Fitton of the *Sun*, one after the other they asked me what I was doing there.

'What do you mean?' I said.

'We were told you weren't coming and we had to get here to do a story around it.'

I walked into the dressing room and the Doc was there. He was the one who had tipped off the press lads.

'What you doing here?' he asked.

'You told me to come to Mossley. I'm here.'

'Yes, but you don't really want to be here, do you?'

'No, but I am.'

'But you don't want to be here, so you may as well go home.'

So I left Mossley and went home. That was how it could be with the Doc. I have no idea to this day why he turned on me. Maybe he thought the goals had dried up. But I hadn't asked to be built up into something I wasn't. In fact it was the opposite of what I wanted. Then again, two days later you were the best of pals again, arms around shoulders. It was all very different to Jock Stein, and all a bit confusing.

6

LAW, CHARLTON AND BEST

WHEN I JOINED UNITED MIDWAY THROUGH THAT 1972–73 season, they were coming to the end of their great period. That is why I was there. Since 1968 they had finished eleventh in the League followed by eighth for three straight seasons. They hadn't won a trophy in that time either. The Busby era had ended. Wilf McGuinness and Frank O'Farrell had come and gone. Looking back, they never stood a chance. Sir Matt had been in charge for almost a thousand League matches over a twenty-four-year period stretching back to the end of the Second World War. He had fashioned two magnificent teams, almost single-handedly creating the modern Manchester United, building the club into an institution known all over the world. First there was the great team led by Duncan Edwards that perished on the runway at Munich. Ten years later Busby came again, lifting the European Cup with Best, Law and Charlton. When McGuinness departed in 1970 after a season and a half in charge, his hair had turned white. He hasn't got any now. O'Farrell had been in charge for a total of sixty-four League matches, losing as many as he won. In between him and McGuinness Sir Matt had returned to try to steady the ship.

The Doc replaced O'Farrell in December 1972. I was one of the new breed shaping the future. Until I arrived at Old Trafford my impressions of Law, Charlton and Best had been formed by watching them on the television. It was obvious that they were top players, and I quickly learned that they were all top guys too. When you arrive at a new club, especially United at the time, you are a little bit wary about the reception you will get, about whether or not you'll be accepted. When it came to it in my case, there was no problem at all.

Over those first few weeks, Bobby Charlton proved to me that he was a freak, a footballing legend who was better than I had thought in terms of application, dedication and attitude on the pitch. He was as unbelievable as George. His ability to get about the pitch was incredible. He was running wild across The Cliff years before I got there. When I got there he was still doing it. He was just amazing, defying his age, defying everything – a remarkable fella. And what presence. They all had that.

I was only seven years old when Charlton made his League debut at United, in 1956. He scored twice that day against Charlton Athletic and hardly stopped thereafter. He had been top scorer as long ago as the 1958–59 season, with twenty-nine goals. He ended up with more than three hundred goals in all competitions, and would finish the 1972–73 season top scorer as well, but with just six League goals. I was just behind Bobby with five goals in sixteen League games. The old First Division had twenty-two teams. Two got relegated. We finished eighteenth that season, narrowly missing the drop.

In the sixties, either Best or Law would score at least twenty goals a season easily. That is how much things had changed by the early seventies; it was remarkable how much the club still relied on Charlton. I am proud to say I was on the pitch when Bobby played his 757th and last game for United in April 1973 at Stamford Bridge. I did not know the Doc was thinking about how to bring the curtain down on one of the world's great footballing careers. In the end, Charlton did it for him. It was Bobby who approached the Doc to tell him he was thinking of calling it a day.

Bobby was a family man, quite quiet and reserved. He didn't say much. He didn't get involved in the banter. He preferred to let his football do the talking. I saw enough of him to judge him as a player, but not really as a person. Those who did had not a bad word to say. It was the same with Denis Law, The King, who left Old Trafford a few weeks after Bobby in the summer of 1973, picked up on a free by Manchester City.

A long-term knee injury meant that by 1972–73 Denis was a shadow of the player he once was. He had scored in a 2–1 home defeat by Ipswich on the opening weekend and in a League Cup game at Oxford, but that was it for his final season. But Law was arguably the best striker ever to pull on a Scotland shirt. He was a legend at United. And I was one of those bought to fill his boots. That was some undertaking – not that I looked at it like that, necessarily.

Best survived, but not for long. To see George in training was more of an eye opener than playing with him. As a player you knew what he was all about; it was only when you got in the same dressing room as him and shared the same training pitch that you realized he was not just another player. He was special. I'd been around Jimmy Johnstone, another genius, but Best was different. Best had Jinky's trickery, he was a powerful runner, he was brave and good in the air, and he scored goals. No flaws on the pitch. You couldn't get near him. He was as close to the complete player as I have ever seen.

There were a lot of comings and goings at that time, and I was one of them. When I walked through the door at Old Trafford I would not have believed it possible that Denis, Bobby and George were about to head the other way. Maybe other managers would have handled things differently, got a bit more out of Denis and Bobby, and certainly more out of George. A lot of crazy things happen in football, but George Best departing at the age of twenty-seven to play for a bunch of American teams and the likes of Fulham, Nuneaton Borough, Stockport County, Bournemouth, Cork, Glentoran, Hibs and Motherwell beats all. How was that allowed to happen? How did George Best, arguably the greatest player these islands have produced, end up at these places? You might see it as an early warning for the stars of today about what can happen. In saying that, George wasn't someone who left Old Trafford and sat behind a bar all day. It was more about the nightlife and the nightclubs than the booze at that stage. But the lesson is there. If that can happen to him, it can happen to anyone.

Strict discipline was not something that was instilled at United. I would walk around Old Trafford thinking, 'Bloody hell, that would never have been allowed at Celtic.' When you have great players in the team it doesn't matter as much, but when I arrived it was obviously not working too well. The true greats were starting to disappear. It was a period of great uncertainty at the club. The Doc had to manage this.

You can't build a team overnight, and in those days no team had a divine right to win. When you look back at that period, teams like Derby County could win championships. They couldn't now. Conversely, Manchester United could go down. Can you imagine that happening now? There was never a huge gap in terms of finances between United and other clubs, therefore the players in teams that today would be considered lesser clubs were just as good. I can't honestly say that I played against a team you could write off as rubbish. Competition was fierce.

As the relationship between the Doc and George deteriorated a lot of adverse publicity surrounded the club. In the build-up to games, none of that helped. We were fighting a losing battle. The players would have accepted George on any terms. He could have turned up at five to three every week as far as we were concerned. He was immensely likeable. But for a manager he could be difficult at times.

I remember rooming with him once at the *Daily Express* five-a-side tournament in London. It was a big event then. We were staying at the Russell Hotel in Russell Square. We arrived in the early afternoon, put our bags in the room, then George explained that he was due to meet two Japanese blokes from a Far East clothing company in reception at five o'clock. He popped out for a while, then at about four o'clock he returned to the room and explained that he had to go out again and wouldn't be able to meet the fellas from Japan after all. He asked me to go down there and tell them that he wouldn't be back. I asked him what it was all about. He said it was a deal worth a hundred grand to him, but he couldn't be bothered. He had other things on. So I had to go down and tell them he wouldn't be joining them. I couldn't get my head around it, but that was George. No amount of money could persuade him to do something if he didn't fancy it. That was an indication to me that in terms of reliability George could not always be trusted. That had been an issue even for the great Sir Matt.

George finally walked out almost twelve months to the day after I arrived, and he was a huge loss. Every player felt that. Five months later we were relegated. It was a surreal experience in so many ways. That 1973–74 season started with a 3–0 defeat at Arsenal, then we bounced back with home wins against Stoke and Queens Park Rangers. We then lost three on the bounce, all to the odd goal. As I said, teams were much more closely matched then. Anybody could hurt you. A couple of goalless draws at Elland Road against arguably the best ever Leeds side and at home to a Liverpool team about to become great boosted our confidence. But what we needed was a win. What we got were three successive defeats, two of them at home by the same 1–0 scoreline, against Middlesbrough and Derby County. A 1–0 win over Birmingham in October was followed by a run of five defeats and four draws. Not good enough. By Christmas the writing was on the wall. The glamour club of England was in free fall separated from the bottom rung of the First Division ladder by three teams: Birmingham, Norwich City and West Ham.

When you are in that sort of position, some people start to look for omens. On 29 December it was possible to think our luck might be changing. We were locked at 0–0 at home to Ipswich when Sammy McIlroy broke the stalemate. I added a second to send the fans into New Year's Eve with a smile on their faces. And fate seemed to be on our side: Denis Law, now at Manchester City, grabbed a late equalizer to rob

Norwich of a much-needed home win, Birmingham drew, and West Ham lost. We had some breathing space at last.

If I'm honest, my first year at the club was not what it might have been. I found goals increasingly hard to come by. It's not surprising really. I had never played in a struggling team before, and almost every game I played for United during those first twelve months was a monumental struggle. Charlton and Law had gone, Best was a couple of weeks away from joining them, and on top of that Ian Storey-Moore lost his battle with injury. Ian had joined United the year before me but had played only forty-one games. He had been a goal-every-other-game man in his eleven years at Nottingham Forest. When Frank O'Farrell signed him he was billed as another Best. Sure enough, he scored on his United debut in a 2–0 win over Huddersfield Town (you can guess who got the other). Unfortunately, Ian never got close to fulfilling his potential at Old Trafford, an ankle injury forcing him out of top-flight football at the age of twenty-nine. With him and Best out of the equation, the pressure piled on me to score the goals. It was never going to happen in that environment.

You could tell how lacking in confidence we were when it took an hour to find a way past Plymouth Argyle in the FA Cup third round at Old Trafford. I scored to take the pressure off a bit, but only 31,000 people were there to watch us – another indication that the light was going out so far as United were concerned. We didn't manage another win until March, by a single goal at Sheffield United, again scored by me. With ten games to go, Manchester United were in twenty-first place. I scored again in a 2–0 win at Norwich in the first week of April to give us hope. But it was never convincing.

The game that sticks in everybody's mind from that season, players and supporters alike, is the home fixture with Manchester City. There were two games remaining. We had to beat City to have a chance of catching Birmingham. Norwich and Southampton were in the same boat. It was three of the four to go down. All I remember from that derby is Denis back-heeling the ball into the net. It was a strange afternoon. Denis Law's last kick in professional football gave City a 1–0 win and sent United down. And I was on the pitch.

There were eight minutes to go when Denis scored his goal. Pandemonium broke out, fans storming on to the pitch. Police on horseback raced on to the playing surface to restore order. It was one of the iconic moments of the seventies – the day Manchester United went down. For the fans it was the blackest moment since Munich. No lives were lost so it can't ever compare, but as a footballing experience it was a desperate episode in the lives of Manchester United supporters. And players. We waited in the dressing room for the police to restore order. Four minutes after Denis scored we were told the match had been abandoned. The score stood. We were down.

People think there was only one hand on the knife, Denis Law's, but there were in fact three: on the same day Bob Hatton and Kenny Burns scored to give Birmingham the win that took them to thirty-seven points and safety. For the record, we lost our last match of the season, at Stoke, to finish on thirty-two points. In forty-two games we scored only thirty-five League goals. My share was five.

At that point the decision to join United and not Liverpool, who had finished runners-up to champions Leeds, did not look great. It was a dark hour for sure. But United had been in dark places before. The club had come back from Munich, it could come back from this. You have to take the long view in this game.

I did not win the medals I might have won at United, but I feel blessed just to have shared a dressing room with Law, Charlton and Best.

7

THE REVOLVING DOOR

WHEN PEOPLE TALK TO ME NOW ABOUT THE PACE OF THE modern game, it makes me laugh. Players like Bobby Charlton and George Best, and others like Alan Ball and Billy Bremner, players I had played with and against, were non-stop, and at a level few have ever reached or could reach. So I don't want to hear about fitness levels today. I have picked out only four names; I could pick out a hundred more from that era. I don't want to knock those modern-day players who are considered great in this respect; all I would say is that they would have to go some to compete with Charlton, Best, Ball and Bremner.

Every game to Bobby Charlton was a must-win game. At the age of thirty-six it was no different. It was the same with the others. Their ability to do it over twenty years was un-believable. I wonder if today's culture will ever produce types like that again. They weren't superstars as much as freaks in terms of their ability to last games and not get injured. There was no rotation then, remember. Too many of today's footballers have not had the same disciplines instilled into them. Culturally, the twenty-first century is a very different place. It produces a different breed of player. During my time at Old Trafford I would go home after training on a Friday and have a couple of hours' sleep to prepare for the game the next day. I felt it would give me something extra. And something extra was needed in the early seventies when pitches, balls, boots and kit were heavier. The physical demands were greater. And the players were harder. Peter Storey was an awesome opponent, a real tough nut. Chelsea had one or two, like Ron Harris. There was Norman Hunter at Leeds. You could go on and on. At Liverpool, Graeme Souness and Jimmy Case were hard lads. Tommy Smith was ferocious. Once, when I tried to go past him during a game at Anfield, his right fist collided with my belly. He just floored me. It was acceptable violence then. There was no rolling around on the floor. You just got up and gave it back when the referee wasn't looking.

The relationship with the referee was totally different too, one of respect. Respect for referees has become a *cause célèbre* at the FA, because there isn't any. You didn't want to step out of line in my day. As long as the tone was right, you could say almost anything to the ref. Neil Midgley was a great referee. 'Neil, you're having a fucking nightmare,' you would say. He'd reply, 'Not as bad as the one you're having.' In Ron Atkinson's first game in charge of United, at home to Ipswich, Arthur Albiston conceded a late penalty for a little tug on the shirt of Eric Gates. Eric went down. It was a debatable one. Not one player surrounded the referee. They accepted the decision, good or bad.

The only time I really got into trouble with a referee, apart from a couple of pre-season friendlies, was during the

Manchester derby at Maine Road in March 1974, the season we went down. Mike Doyle chopped me down. I fell on the ball and threw it in his direction. Clive Thomas sent off the pair of us. We refused to go. I didn't think Mike deserved to go; I certainly didn't deserve to go. There was no arguing as such, we just stood our ground. Clive ordered both teams off the pitch and back into the dressing rooms. He then came into our dressing room with the chief of police, who ordered me not to go back out. The pair then marched into the City dressing room and said the same to Doyle. We stayed put. That wouldn't happen now.

Players and officials were no different in Division Two, but going down with United was still a weird experience. At Celtic, I had known only success. All of a sudden I was playing at places I'd never been to: Cardiff, Oldham, etc. As things turned out, the Doc was the perfect man to have in charge. He told everybody we would come back stronger. He would say that, of course. But we did.

To help that process along, it was out with the old and in with the new. And there were an awful lot of those. Young lads like big Jim Holden (six foot two and eyes of blue), Alex Forsyth (could he smack a ball), Gerry Daly, Steve Coppell, Gordon Hill and Stuart Pearson were all top-notch. Others fared less well. Jim McCalliog, Alan Foggon, Tommy Baldwin and Ron Davies were in then out of the revolving door. The Doc also added George Graham, who by December 1972 was coming to the end of his days as a player at Arsenal. The Doc made him club captain, but he never hit it off with the fans. He was known as the Stroller at his peak. George has said many times to me that things did not work out at Old Trafford as he would have liked. He made his debut three weeks before mine and played more than forty games for the club. His last was as a substitute against Bristol City in Division Two in November 1974.

By then we were playing adventurous football, and winning. Our first match in the lower tier saw us at Brisbane Road, home of the Orient. I was back where it had all started for me, back in the land of my footballing father, where I took my first steps in the game fetching the ball for Albert Macari and the lads on Hackney Marshes. It was a tough introduction, but we won with goals from Willie Morgan and Stewart Houston.

Our first home game was against Millwall. We drew a crowd of 42,000 – the second biggest of the day anywhere in the country. Only Anfield attracted more. I was learning about the attraction and power of Manchester United for the first time. More than 18,000 had packed into Brisbane Road. Old Trafford wasn't jammed to the rafters, but there were more in the ground for the Millwall game than had watched us on average during the slide out of the First Division. Stuart 'Pancho' Pearson, who had been bought from Hull for £200,000, scored three minutes into his home debut. I was pleased. It looked like we had a striker who could find the net.

Two more victories followed to give us the flying start we needed, but for me it wasn't the best of starts. I scored a couple in the League Cup against Charlton Athletic, but I had to wait until the home game with Bolton on 25 September to find the back of the net in the League. In the game after that, at Carrow Road, we tasted defeat for the first time. Despite that loss we were three points clear at the top of the table and, as a team, full of confidence. By Christmas only two other teams had beaten us, Hull and Bristol City. The goals were now coming a bit more freely for me, and Pancho was a great strike partner, quick and strong. He liked to lead the line, leaving me to work the spaces just behind. We complemented each other well. The fans sensed the potential: more than 60,000 turned up on the last day of November for the home game with Sunderland, who were on a tremendous run of just two defeats in sixteen months. We beat them 3–2, and next up was Sheffield Wednesday, which proved to be probably the best game of the season in terms of entertainment. We drew four apiece, and I scored twice. The result gave us thirty-two points – a five-point lead over Sunderland at the halfway stage.

We were on a rollercoaster. The crowds were up at home, and away grounds were filled to capacity. The misery of that April afternoon when Denis did the deed seemed a million miles away. Yet it wouldn't be football without its dramas. As the year turned and I approached my second anniversary at Old Trafford, we hit a sticky patch. It began on 28 December, seven miles up the road at Oldham, home of the one and only Paul Scholes.

Boundary Park sits in the foothills of the Pennines. It is one of the highest grounds in the country, cold at the best of times and always, it seems to me, windy. Scholesy, a big Oldham fan, took his first proper steps in the game for Boundary Park Juniors, a club that can also boast Nicky Butt, the Neville brothers and David Platt among its old boys. With City unavailable, Oldham was the local derby for United. For a lad from Largs it was hard to spot where Oldham started and Manchester ended. The two are connected by the A62, which funnily enough is called Oldham Road in Manchester and Manchester Road in Oldham. It was effectively a long line of red-bricked terraced houses from Ancoats Street all the way up to Oldham town centre. Though Oldham had their own support, a good number of United fans hailed from the town. In those days it was not uncommon for kids from the satellite towns around Manchester, like Oldham, Stockport, Rochdale, Bury and Ashton, to support either United or City. A bit like Scotland with Celtic and Rangers. For many kids, their hometown club is a secondary consideration. So that day there were as many fans from Oldham supporting United as the team in blue.

The game was typical of a derby. Oldham threw everything at us. The place was crackling with atmosphere. A Scottish lad called Alan Young and winger Alan Groves ran us ragged. Groves was one of those players you see now and again who appear to come from nowhere and play like Pelé (four years later he was dead, from a stroke, I think). We never got on top of him that day and lost to a penalty scored by Maurice Whittle. It could have been more.

We lost our next game, too, against Walsall in the FA Cup on 4 January. We fancied our chances in the Cup. A run would have been nice, a chance to take on the big boys and check progress. But we went out after a replay. Perhaps it was a blessing, because the whole of January was a struggle. After beating Sheffield Wednesday on the 11th we had to wait until the middle of February for our next win, 2–0 against Hull. We lost the game after that, at Villa Park, but then started to turn the corner with three wins and a draw in our next four matches.

The 1–0 win at Bolton on 8 March, thanks to a goal from Stuart Pearson, was crucial. There were now just nine matches to go and we were still five clear on forty-six points. The return against Oldham at the end of March was another thriller. I scored in a 3–2 win, but the match was closer than it should have been. We were edging towards the line. On 5 April we were away to Southampton. If results on the day went our way, with just a handful of matches remaining, we could all but secure promotion. The atmosphere at The Dell was incredible. Everywhere we went, teams bent double to try to claim the scalp of Manchester United. This game was no different, but I slotted the only goal to lift us to fifty-six points. Barring a freakish end to the season, United were back in Division One.

The last game of the 1974–75 season was at home against Blackpool. Thousands were locked outside. It was like a coronation. We had won the Second Division Championship. The 58,796 crowd took the total attendance for the season at Old Trafford past the one million mark at an average of more than 48,000 – a remarkable number of people to have paid to watch a Division Two club that season and proof to me of what United was all about. Any doubts I may have had about the decision I made to leave Celtic and come to United ebbed away that sunny afternoon against Blackpool when I scored in a 4–0 victory to take my tally for the season to eighteen, making me joint leading scorer with Pancho.

8

UNITED ARE BACK

THE DOC HAD GREAT CONFIDENCE THAT THE TOP FLIGHT would hold no fears for us. The players were not so sure, but again the Doc called it right. We had pace out wide, strikers who could find the net, and in Gerry Daly another freak whose batteries never ran out. And he smoked. I reckon he must have spent his early days in Dublin running away from people.

The 1975–76 season could not have started better for United, or for me: I scored both goals in a 2–0 win at Wolves. Three days later we won by the same score at Birmingham, Sammy McIlroy getting both goals. Old Trafford was packed for our first home game. Sheffield United were the visitors, a team boasting the likes of Tony Currie and Alan Woodward. They were swept aside 5–1, and United moved to the top of the league with maximum points from three games.

Our first defeat came on 13 September against Queens Park Rangers, who alongside us were the early pace-setters. We also lost to Derby, another team that started well. Then it was the

Manchester derby at Maine Road. Though we had beaten City in the League Cup in our year in Division Two, it didn't have the same intensity as the League encounters. My first visit to Maine Road had ended with a sending-off. This was much more satisfactory: we drew, and I scored. All the goals came in a fourteen-minute spell. It was like Dodge City, shots firing in from all angles. The fans loved it. We were setting the standard according to the template set by Sir Matt all those years ago.

In November the Doc freshened things up a bit with the signing of Gordon Hill from Millwall. Gordon was a terrific asset, complementing Steve Coppell, who had joined the club in March 1975, on the right. Gordon was one of the best strikers of a ball I have seen, especially on the volley. He used to practise in hotel rooms with toilet rolls. Steve was the opposite of Gordon. He relied less on touch and more on efficiency, powering down the right wing. There was a simple economy of style in Steve, a quality recognized by the international side at the time. He would hit the byline then get his cross in. Gordon had to beat a man before he was interested in crossing to anybody. And if there was a chance to score himself, he would take it. That made him the more spectacular of the two, if not the most effective.

Behind them, Jimmy Nicholl and Stewart Houston offered solid support at full-back. Neither was eye-catching in the way Tommy Gemmell was for Celtic or Patrice Evra is in the present-day United side. They simply did what all good defenders should do – defend properly. But when the chance arose they could both get forward and cross the ball. The Doc encouraged that. He liked his team to be comfortable with the ball at their feet. Both Martin Buchan and Brian Greenhoff, our central defenders, were ball players. Martin read the game well, had great timing and was turbocharged across the turf. Brian was a converted midfielder whose great strength was his distribution. Our ability to attack from the back surprised a few teams that year and was a factor in our assault on the championship.

We were in the race all the way. January was a brilliant month for us with four wins, starting with a successful third-round FA Cup victory at the expense of Oxford. A week later we came from a goal down to beat Queens Park Rangers and go top of the League with thirty-five points from twenty-five games. Dave Sexton, who would later manage United, said we were the best team Rangers had played. That meant a lot. Every time I see the QPR goalie Phil Parkes I rib him about the shot he saved from me. I still don't know how he did it. I don't think he does either. I never hit one better.

After the FA Cup quarter-final win against Wolves – I had to sit out the replay with a bruised foot – talk of the double was in the air. I always get a bit nervous when that kind of stuff starts. I don't like to tempt fate, and in 1976 Liverpool were grinding out results like the machine they were, QPR were finishing the season like a train, and we were drawn against Derby in the semis. But as it turned out this match summed up Manchester United under the Doc for me, great football played on the deck at good pace with a pair of wingers causing havoc. Gordon Hill never played a better game in a red shirt. He scored twice, the second a trademark volley that screamed into the net from twenty-five yards. Derby could not get near us.

In between the Cup games we put away Leeds, Newcastle and Boro, scoring ten goals in the process. It seemed we could do no wrong. We were also a young side. Maybe we were beginning to believe in our own publicity. Then, straight after the Derby semi-final, we went to Ipswich and got hammered 3–0. With three games left we were on fifty-four points; Liverpool had fifty-eight points with one to play, QPR fifty-seven with one to play. With two points awarded for a win, we needed to be victorious in all three of those games to take it to the wire. What happened? We lost the first at home to Stoke and the second away at Leicester.

Incredibly, after such an exhilarating season, we limped across the line. We took that miserable League form straight into the FA Cup Final against Southampton. It should have been straightforward. They were a Second Division side. The bookies made us the shortest-price favourites in years. Southampton were not given a prayer. But finals are funny things; they can go well or badly without warning. We started well enough and could have been two up in the opening fifteen minutes. Steve Coppell got away down the right, and his cross was fumbled by the Southampton goalkeeper Ian Turner. I thought it was going to drop to me, but the chance went begging. Gerry Daly could have scored a few minutes later but he fluffed his shot from eight yards.

After that Southampton grew in confidence. Mick Channon and Peter Osgood started to come into the game. David Peach and Peter Rodrigues began to press from full-back. At half-time, with the game still goalless, doubt started to enter the mind. The match was not a classic. The longer the game went without a goal the more it seemed there would never be one.

Our best chance in the second half fell to Sammy Mac. Steve Coppell floated a corner on to my head and I flicked it on to Sammy whose header struck the woodwork. Mentally, both teams were gearing up for extra-time. The risk of losing was choking the game. Then, with seven minutes to go, Jim McCalliog, a former United player, slipped Bobby Stokes through and he slotted the ball past Alex Stepney.

Time seemed to stand still. Bobby looked offside. We couldn't respond. Southampton closed the game down. It was all over. No League Championship, no FA Cup, after coming so close to both. Tommy Doc said we would be back to win it next year. Everybody agreed, but without really believing it.

There was just one engagement left that year, the Manchester derby at Old Trafford. We raised our game and won 2–0. It felt good to end on a high. And back in August 1975 we'd have more than settled for third place in our first season back in Division One.

9

EUROPE CALLING

OUR SECOND CAMPAIGN BACK IN THE TOP FLIGHT, 1976–77, saw the return of European competition to Old Trafford for the first time since the 1968–69 season. Europe is woven into the fabric of Manchester United. It is part of the club's identity. We were back in the UEFA Cup, which back then was a difficult competition to win.

We played Ajax of Amsterdam in the first round. We lost the first leg in Holland 1–0, which set up the return beautifully. There is nothing like a European night at Old Trafford under lights. There have been so many great nights, from the early pioneering days under Sir Matt to the Champions League extravaganzas of the modern era. The United team of 1976 felt very much connected to the tradition of the Busby Babes. We were young and attack-minded. We burst down the wings. Ajax had won the European Cup three times on the spin. We were just starting out again. The atmosphere was electric as we walked down the tunnel. This was what the club was all about, why I had signed. The fans wanted to see how we ranked against the flair sides from Europe.

I felt ten feet tall when I opened the scoring that night. Stuart Pearson was injured, so Sammy Mac played up front with me. The Doc then took off Gerry Daly and pushed Brian Greenhoff into midfield. It was Brian who combined with Steve Coppell to supply the cross for Sammy's winner. A 2–0 win over multiple European champions. We were up and running.

And then we bumped into Juventus in the next round. The Italians knew Manchester well after beating City in the first round. The first leg was at Old Trafford. It is fair to say I have never seen a more cynical display from any team. Claudio Gentile, Marco Tardelli and Antonello Cuccureddu were brutal. Gordon Hill was kicked from pillar to post. Juventus had done their homework, identified the threat. Cut out the supply and United can't meet the demand. Up front they had Roberto Bettega, the darling of Italy at the time. Despite all that was thrown at us we took a one-goal lead to Turin, but it was never going to be enough. Juventus had too much nous for us at home and won 3–0.

The European game has now changed completely. Then the UEFA Cup meant something. So did the European Cup Winners' Cup, Fergie's first overseas success at United, when they beat Barcelona in 1994. Now the latter has gone and the former is just a device to generate cash. The Champions League is the only competition that matters. You might argue that it is even more important than the World Cup in terms of the quality of the teams (and England's big four are certainly better than the national side) and the global audience that tunes in every two weeks.

The Doc responded to this reverse by dipping into the

transfer market again, bringing in Jimmy Greenhoff from Stoke. Jimmy was a great taker of the half chance. He saw things early and was as brave as a lion in front of goal.

Our fortunes weren't much better domestically. We suffered a touch of second season syndrome in 1976–77, a home draw against Birmingham on the opening day just about summing up the state of play. It wasn't that we were trying any less or that we had gone backwards. We hadn't. It's just that other teams were on to us. Coppell and Hill were squeezed by opposition defences. They worked out how to break up our play. Just before the Juve game we were hammered 4–0 by newly promoted West Brom, managed by Johnny Giles. We also lost home games to Ipswich and West Ham. It wasn't until Christmas that we hit any consistent form, winning ten out of the next twelve League games.

That run coincided with the start of the FA Cup. I scored in the 1–0 win over Queens Park Rangers in the fourth round. After that we got our revenge against Southampton, and all of a sudden people started to talk about the Cup again. Doc's words about returning to Wembley to win started to carry some weight. Once we got past Aston Villa in the quarter-finals to earn a semi-final draw against Leeds at Hillsborough, the Cup dominated all our thoughts. April saw our League form tail off, so by the time we met Leeds, it was the Cup or nothing for us.

You always felt with Don Revie, the Leeds manager, that an angle was being worked. We stood in the tunnel for a good four or five minutes waiting for Leeds to come out. The buzzer, the signal to leave the dressing room and line up, had long gone. Eventually we had to tell the referee to go and get them. It was probably a Revie tactic to keep us guessing, make us sweat a bit more, make us feel exposed and vulnerable. With players like me, Coppell, Hill and McIlroy, we were not a big side. Martin Buchan wasn't big for a centre-half. Eventually the door opened, and one by one the Leeds players came out of the dressing room. It was like the land of the giants. Paul Madeley, Joe Jordan, Gordon McQueen . . . they got bigger and bigger as they emerged. As they lined up along-side us, Gordon screamed at the top of his loud Scottish voice, 'Come on, lads, we've only got to beat a bunch of fucking midgets!' It was intimidating yet funny at the same time. We just thought, 'Right, we'll see about midgets.' I'm only five foot five inches tall but I take great pride in not being bullied or intimidated by anybody.

We went out and beat a good Leeds side 2–1 with goals from Steve Coppell and Jimmy Greenhoff. It was results like that that told the players they were good enough. Suddenly the words of Tommy Doc were coming true. We had come back stronger, and we were going back to Wembley. We had not done quite as well in the League, but that's because the opposition had raised their game against us. It was a compliment.

That year we were the underdogs, but just as Southampton had beaten us the previous year, we stopped one of the great Liverpool sides from winning the treble. As an indication of how far we had come, we beat them on the Saturday, and on the Wednesday they went off to Rome to lift the European Cup for the first time.

And it was a great Liverpool side. I was at Anfield recently on one of the many occasions when Rafa was under the cosh from the owners. I asked a couple of lads what they thought of the current team, how many of them would get in their all-time Liverpool side. They said none of them, not even Steven Gerrard. This is not to say that Gerrard isn't a good player. He is. It is simply a comment on the difference in standards. Would Gerrard have got in ahead of Graeme Souness, Jimmy Case, Terry McDermott or Ray Kennedy? It is a fascinating question. The Liverpool diehards I spoke to thought not. Clearly, then, I am not alone in believing that the game is not producing the same quality of player it did a generation ago. No blame attaches to Gerrard for that, of course. The same could be said of the current crop at Arsenal, about whom much has been said. Give me the 1971 team any day. The present bunch wouldn't make it to the end of the tunnel with the old double winners.

But I digress. The point is that the FA Cup victory over Liverpool in 1977 was the first proper indication that as a club Manchester United were truly up and running again. We were proving it on results rather than hype, not simply trading on a famous name.

The United team that took to the Wembley pitch that May day was Doc's final creation, and possibly his finest. Alex Stepney was in goal, with Jimmy Nicholl and Arthur Albiston either side of Brian Greenhoff and Martin Buchan in defence. I had dropped back to midfield by then alongside Sammy McIlroy, who also started his United career as a striker. Up front, Gordon Hill and Steve Coppell provided the bullets for Stuart Pearson and Jimmy Greenhoff.

All the goals in that 1977 FA Cup Final came in the space of five mad minutes at the start of the second half. Pancho rifled in the opener for us, a typical strike drilled across Ray Clemence. Liverpool went up the other end and equalized with an even better finish from Jimmy Case, volleyed past

Steptoe. Then, three minutes later, in the fifty-fifth minute, we scored the winner, the ball taking that famous deflection off Jimmy Greenhoff's chest. The ball was played up to the halfway line. I outjumped one of the Liverpool lads (Emlyn Hughes I think), flicked it on, turned and headed for the box. The ball broke to me again. Jimmy was almost in my way. He was trying to get out of it because he was in my line of vision. His movement distracted me a bit. I mishit the shot slightly and I later learned that it deflected off him into the net. Things happened that quickly I did not have a clue that the shot had taken a deflection. I knew it wasn't a brilliant shot, but I also knew it would end up in the back of the net. I wasn't all that bothered how it got there. I knew what it meant: we were going to go on and win the FA Cup.

The first indication I had that the goal was in dispute was when Jimmy walked into the dressing room carrying a golden boot – the prize at the time for scoring the winning goal in the FA Cup Final. I had been waiting for someone to come in and give it to me, but I wasn't that bothered when Jimmy kept it. I didn't argue long and hard about it. I was just delighted to have an FA Cup winners medal, and winning the competition meant a route into Europe again. Since then, the debate has raged about who scored the winning goal. Jimmy and I could not have cared less. We had beaten Liverpool. That was the main thing.

That walk up the famous Wembley steps was one of the great journeys in football – if you were on the winning side. The difference from the year before was like night and day. I practically floated down the stairs the other side to start the party rolling out on the pitch. You have to have your picture taken with the FA Cup on your head, don't you? I'd seen so many others wearing that 'crown'. Now I had it on my head. Brilliant! The memories of twelve months earlier were still strong. After the Southampton defeat the banquet at the Royal Lancaster Hotel in London just fell apart. I was in my bed by ten o'clock. Twelve months later I was still up at five in the morning, throwing the FA Cup about in Hyde Park with some of my pals who had come down from Manchester. They took over the Royal Lancaster that night. It was a free-for-all. And not a security man in sight. Can you imagine what would happen now if Rooney and Ronaldo were caught chucking the FA Cup about in Hyde Park in the early hours?

That victory meant so much. It was such a big deal to a footballer to win the FA Cup in those days. It was not just the day itself and the medal, but all that preceded that: going down to London on the Tuesday, the build-up, the match-day rituals, BBC and ITV interviews at the hotel, the banquet afterwards, the trip back to Manchester and the open-top bus ride through the city. It was a real career highlight.

10

AYE AYE CAPTAIN

UNDER THE DOC, MARTIN BUCHAN WAS MADE CLUB CAPTAIN; he was definitely the right man for the job and took the position very seriously. He was like the head prefect at school. He liked to take control. Most of it was for the sake of appearances, which were very important to Martin.

On a match day he'd come into the dressing room saying this and that. We'd sit there and listen, then disregard everything he said and carry on as before. He liked the idea of being a leader. One day he bowled in shouting the odds about tickets for the players' lounge. 'Right,' he said, 'as you know, I take charge of the players' lounge. Last week I handed out forty tickets and I counted sixty-three people in there. What's going on? Come on, come clean.' The players used to go in and out bringing people in all the time. No one admitted responsibility, so Martin attempted to read the riot act. 'Right,' he said, 'I'm going to put paid to this. Next game you'll all get two lounge tickets each. It's a twenty-man squad, so that's forty tickets, plus one each for the opposition squad, that's sixty people in all. And anybody who thinks he's smart, I'll be on the lounge door on Saturday to collect those sixty lounge tickets.'

The next game was QPR in the FA Cup. No one believed for one minute that Martin would stand at the lounge door collecting tickets. I turned to big Gordon McQueen (who had by this time joined us from Leeds) and said, 'Fucking hell, Gordon, we've got to stuff him. We've got to get as many people in that lounge as possible.'

Before the QPR game I went up to the secretary's office and got about two hundred lounge tickets. At about two o'clock Gordon and I stood outside the players' entrance as fans made their way up to the Stretford End and handed out these tickets to supporters, distributing them willy-nilly, thinking, 'This is going to be fun.'

We won the match, and as soon as the game ended Martin set off from the pitch, with his kit still on, straight to the players' lounge.

Cup day was always a massive event. If you won or drew you went straight into the dressing room to gather around the little tannoy we used to have in there to see who you'd got in the next round. No TV in those days. James Alexander Gordon would read the results, then they would go straight to the Cup draw. On this occasion, of course, we passed Martin on our way to the dressing room, standing at the lounge door, waiting to collect his sixty tickets. The draw was secondary to Martin that day. It was all about the lounge. Fifteen minutes later he walked into the dressing room carrying a bundle as big as a postman's sack, and threw the contents into the air.

'Any interest, Martin, in who we get in the Cup?' someone piped up.

'Fuck you,' he said.

The Buck was a class act. The Doc thought so, too. We were at Mottram Hall, the team hotel that United used when we were preparing for games. My contract at United was up for renewal for the first time. Martin's was up, too. The Doc took me to one side in a private room and told me that he was going to make me the highest-paid player at the club, on £350 a week. Great, I thought. He went out of the room for a couple of minutes, leaving behind a piece of paper on the table. On it was written Macari: £350 a week, Buchan: £380. It was classic Doc and very funny. I never said anything. I would have accepted the contract anyway.

Humour was never in short supply. Fun made the world go round at football clubs. It was part of a player's identity. Gordon Hill would always be doing his Norman Wisdom impression. Well, he thought it was funny. To be honest, the Mr Grimsdale routine wore thin pretty quickly. Most of the lads would chip in with something. I was a practical joker. When Ray Wilkins arrived at Old Trafford in the summer of 1979 he was a bit of a fashion guru, or thought he was. He turned up in all the gear from the King's Road. Some of the lads thought he should be taught a lesson so I was instructed to nail his £100 shoes to the dressing-room floor, which I did. After training he came out of the shower to find them stuck fast to the floor. He reminds me of that every time I see him. It was all taken in good heart though.

The newspapermen were targets too. The *Sun*'s Peter Fitton and the *Mirror*'s Bob Russell once came with us on a pre-season tour to Denmark. I stole all their clothes. They appeared the next day in the same clothes they'd had on the day before. The day after that was the same. The lads were laughing their socks off. That was how it was. Towards the end of my career I remember taking part in a match with the Manchester press lads. I cut the ends off all their socks and put them in the teapot. You should have seen the look on their faces when they tasted that tea. Once, before a European tie against Juventus, the press lads organized a match with their Italian counterparts at The Cliff. I nipped into the Italian changing room and cut their socks in half. They didn't see the funny side. That particular practical joke was lost in translation. I made sure I brought with me new socks for all of them for the away leg in Turin. Nowadays players and press rarely meet informally. The old bonds that united clubs are loosening, and the game is the worse for it.

The exposure today, the hype, the inflated wages and the cult of celebrity have changed the rules of the game. Premiership players would not recognize Saturdays as we experienced them. For a start, all matches kicked off at three o'clock. At two o'clock the manager or his assistant – in United's case, Tommy Cavanagh – would go to the referee's room to exchange team sheets. This ritual was always a point of tension. You'd be waiting anxiously to see who was in the opposition line-up. Teams in those days were full of players who could hurt you. You wanted to know what the starting eleven was going to be. On many occasions we'd be sat there waiting for Tommy Cav to come in with Martin. Then, as he prepared to read out the names, he'd screw the sheet up, throw it in the bin and say, 'Load of fucking rubbish.' The players would fall about. Very funny.

I used to take myself off to the players' lounge until 2.30, with my kit on, maybe watch a bit of telly. I never used to go out for the warm-up. Players did their own thing. There was none of the carry-on you see nowadays, no consuming liquids or doing exercise routines. It was more a case of have a cup of tea, on with the kit, then slug it out for ninety minutes. They try to tell me that players are a lot more professional these days. If that is the case, then it follows that the players were unprofessional in my day – unprofessional enough for Celtic, United, Liverpool, Nottingham Forest and Aston Villa to win European Cups. Oh, and Leeds were unprofessional enough to give Bayern Munich the fright of their lives in the 1975 European Cup Final. Leeds should have won that night. If the Doc had come into the dressing room before kick-off giving Agincourt speeches we'd have thought he'd lost the plot. He was more likely to crack a joke. The talking was done during the week. Players understood the importance of the occasion on match days. Very little was said after the game either, win, lose or draw.

There was always a great buzz around Old Trafford, even when we weren't winning. That did not change throughout my eleven years at the club. It is difficult to define it. There is just something special about playing for Manchester United. It comes from every aspect of the club, from the manager to the fans. The supporters were brilliant. There was never any problem if you met them in the street. We would often go into town after training, get something to eat. These days players would not think about mixing with the fans the way we used to. That is one of the more disappointing developments in the game for me, the gulf that has opened up between the players and the supporters. The relationship between the players and the press has followed suit. After matches we would go to a pub in Sale and sit there with all the press lads. They had already had one go at getting the quotes for their Old Trafford stories; this was like a second round for them so they could get their stories for Monday's paper. We were genuinely friendly with reporters in those days. Supporters would be in there as well. That's all disappeared now. I can't understand why.

Under the Doc we were never big on tactics. We'd just go out and play. We were a rampaging, instinctive side. We were organized in the sense that every player understood the responsibilities of his position, but beyond that we didn't plan much. The one time it really backfired on us was the 1979 FA Cup Final against Arsenal. Though the Doc had gone by then, replaced by Dave Sexton, the template remained. At 2–0 down with eighty-five minutes on the clock you can say good-bye to the Cup. But that was never United's style. At 2–2 you should calm down a bit, shut up shop, accept that you have the momentum going for you, play for extra-time, take time to regroup. Given the chance again I'd make damn sure we kept the ball and closed the game down. Back then, in a daft Manchester United way, we believed we could go on and win the FA Cup in the final minute and a half of normal time. Madness. Arsenal went straight down the other end to complete one of the great finals of modern times. But that is what the FA Cup and Manchester United are about. On that occasion the club lost out, but as we have seen since, the approach has paid off spectacularly.

The timing of the Doc's departure could not have been worse for him or for us. A month after beating Liverpool in the 1977 FA Cup Final, he was out of the door. The last thing on the minds of the players when they discovered that the manager was having an affair with the physio's wife was the possibility that the club might sack him. I suppose it was just too awkward a situation for United. You can't have a high-profile employee playing around with another man's wife. It was impossible for the Doc to stay. You could not have sacked Laurie Brown instead.

Everybody had their ups and downs with the Doc, but you could not dislike him, and we were stunned by his departure. One day he was wisecracking around Old Trafford, the next it was all over for him.

11

THE QUIET MAN

DAVE SEXTON WAS THE DOC'S POLAR OPPOSITE. HE WAS ALSO AN excellent manager, one of my favourites. He was quiet, a straight talker, and tough with it. I would not have liked to get on the wrong side of him. He loved his boxing, and you got the impression he might knock your head off. Like me, he has also had to deal with tragedy in his family when his son drove his car off a cliff on the south coast.

Dave was a big thinker about the game. He knew everything about the opposition. His reliance on analysis was very un-Manchester United. We were all about playing off the cuff. The club was geared up for personalities. Sir Matt started that and the Doc carried it on. Then along came Dave with his tactical nous and professionalism that had worked brilliantly for him at Chelsea and Queens Park Rangers. His approach was more in keeping with what I had known at Celtic. In the short term, Dave was just what United, a club built on flamboyance, needed after the Doc; but in the long term his methods ran counter to the United culture. Ultimately that would cost him. He was hopeless for the press, guarded and private. He hated fuss and attention. He wanted to get on with things quietly. That was never going to work with the journalists after the Doc and Busby. But the players loved him.

Before every game Sexton would walk around the dressing room speaking to each of us players individually, trying to build you up, improve your performance. When he stood in front of you face to face, Dave was very convincing. There was a steely aggression about him. He was a hard man. Sometimes he could get his message across with a look. That never came across to the public. They heard this softly spoken figure and assumed he was weak. The public also mis-understood his methods. They saw him as overly regimented, defensive. He wasn't. Training was based around attacking strategies. It was all about going forward. If there were com-plaints from the players they came from defenders who moaned that there was not enough time spent on the defensive side of the game.

Dave had a generous nature. He treated the players well. He gave us all a gold watch as a sign of his appreciation for what we had done. When we got to the FA Cup Final in 1979 after beating Liverpool in the semi-final, he gave each of the players a painting by Harold Riley, which he paid for himself, and a gold sovereign. Riley had done sixteen special paintings of Old Trafford with a player standing on the pitch. I know of one lad, who had no appreciation of art, who threw his in the bin. I won't name him. All I can tell you is that he regrets it now.

We finished tenth in 1978, Dave's first season, and ninth in

1979. That was tough. On a personal note, my time under him could not have got off to a better start. I scored a hat-trick against Birmingham City at St Andrew's on the opening day of the 1977–78 season, Dave's first match in charge. Only three other players in United history have done that: Jack Rowley in 1951, Liam (Billy) Whelan in 1957, and Bobby Charlton in 1958. None has managed it since me.

In the early part of 1978 Dave moved into the transfer market to put his imprint on the team. In January, Joe Jordan arrived from Leeds for £350,000, followed a month later by my old fish and chips partner and Joe's Leeds team-mate Gordon McQueen for £495,000. Dave was building a new backbone at the club. For me it was the start of a long working relationship with Joe, who would join me in the dugout later in my football life as a manager. He was a fearless striker with a decent goal record. Gordon was considered the best centre-half in Europe and offered a tremendous goal threat from set-pieces. He was also very funny, which helped in the dressing room.

Gordon set the tone immediately. His move to United from Leeds was hugely unpopular on the other side of the Pennines because of the rivalry between the two clubs. Leeds had risen to become a major force under Don Revie. Their fans did not take kindly to United picking the cream of their crop. But Gordon summed up the situation thus: 'Ninety-nine per cent of players want to play for Manchester United and the rest are liars.' That cheesed off the Leeds fans even more. The rivalry with Leeds at that time was greater than that with Liverpool now, if you can imagine it. The fans used to walk around with 'I hate Leeds' badges pinned to their lapels. United also took Arthur Graham from Leeds much later. Since then, both Eric Cantona (perhaps Fergie's best-ever signing) and Rio Ferdinand have made the same trip across the Pennines.

But it took time for Dave to impose himself on the United regime. The League was a struggle in 1977–78. At times like that a cup run can help, but Dave was out of luck there too: we went out of the League Cup in the first round to Arsenal and the FA Cup in the fourth round to West Brom. The European Cup Winners' Cup did not last long either. We shipped four in the second round at Porto. Again, it was more about inexperience away from home than anything. We were nowhere near tight enough in possession or clever enough at closing down. In the return leg we won 5–2 – a typical Old Trafford night in Europe, but not enough. I felt for Dave Sexton.

We had a shocking run-up to Christmas, culminating in a 4–0 home defeat to Nottingham Forest. They had come from Division Two after us and under Brian Clough were about to take the First Division by storm. That was the team of Tony Woodcock, Martin O'Neill, Ian Bowyer, John Robertson, John McGovern and Larry Lloyd – a cracking outfit of unsung heroes. Straight after that, on Boxing Day, we went to Everton, a place where we rarely did well, and won 6–2. I contributed one for Christmas. But that was a rare feat that season. We couldn't beat the top sides and drew with too many of the mid-table teams. Largely a campaign to forget.

By the early summer of 1979, after another mid-table finish, Dave's honeymoon period was coming to an end. Getting to the 1979 FA Cup Final, our third in four years, was a much-needed boost, particularly as it included a victory, after a replay, over Liverpool in the semis. They were colossal matches for both teams. We drew the first 2–2 at Maine Road. After leading we were disappointed not to go on and win it – not that we deserved it necessarily. Kenny Dalglish gave Liverpool the lead, beating Gary Bailey, who had taken over in goal from Paddy Roche. Joe Jordan headed home the equalizer, and after Terry McDermott had missed a penalty for Liverpool, Brian Greenhoff put us back in front, only for Alan Hansen to score Liverpool's second eight minutes from time.

There was a fair bit of needle in the match. In the tunnel afterwards, Emlyn Hughes learned an important lesson: never take the piss with Gordon McQueen in earshot. Emlyn was shouting his mouth off, boasting about how Liverpool were going to turn us over at Goodison Park in the replay. 'Oh yeah?' says Gordon, and bangs him one. The tunnel was often the place for retribution; there was too much respect for the ref to step out of line on the pitch. Words were exchanged along the lines of 'see you on Wednesday'. On the day we followed up Gordon's punch with a win, Jimmy Greenhoff scoring the only goal of the game. That was a big win for Dave. The critics thought we'd blown it in the first match. So did the directors, probably.

Before the final against Arsenal, Dave came into the dressing room and sat a magnum of whisky on the floor in front of everybody. 'That's what we all need today,' he said, 'bottle.' He got what he wanted, to a degree, when we fought back from 2–0 down in the last five minutes. He must have thought we'd drunk it the way we responded after Sammy Mac scored that brilliant equalizer in the 88th minute. Something had gone straight to our heads.

Just like 1977, it was a beautiful sunny day. The Arsenal

end was a sea of yellow, reflecting the changed strip. The United end was traditional red and white – always gets the heart pumping, seeing that wall of support. Arsenal had started the game well and by half-time the trophy was practically theirs after goals from Brian Talbot and Frank Stapleton, who would later join United. Then, with the clock ticking over into the eighty-sixth minute, enter big Gordon and Sammy with two goals in two minutes. Suddenly the game had a completely different complexion. The momentum was ours.

The funny thing was, there did not seem to be any danger. Liam Brady picked the ball up and set off on a run. I tracked him, with our Welsh forward Mickey Thomas. We were inviting him to lump a long ball into the box because they did not have anyone forward. He didn't do that. Instead he just kept going, almost to the corner flag.

That'll do. Keep him there and he'll have to lay it back. Which, of course, he does, to Graham Rix. Mickey and I start charging towards Rix. He's right on the touchline. In the box defending we have Arthur Albiston, with Gary Bailey in goal. Rix has only Alan Sunderland to aim at. Gary comes to get it. If for some strange reason he misses it little Arthur is on hand to hook it away.

We knew this was going to be the last attack of the game. We'd nail them in extra-time.

Rix bangs the ball into the box. Gary misjudges it. Unfortunately, the ball drops invitingly for Sunderland. Arthur has no chance of clearing it. All of a sudden the Cup has gone again.

That was probably the most disappointing moment in my United career. People say it was the greatest final ever. It was

Left: In the back garden at Largs.

Below: Nice legs, shame about the tie.

Above and below: That'll be me one day. Watching my Celtic heroes train at the Inverclyde training centre.

Above: With my parents in 1963.

Below: Keepy-uppy king, *c*. 1961.

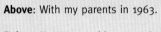

Above: The obligatory school portrait.

St Michael's College, Kilwinning, through the ages: **Top left** and **above** is 1963 (that's me with hand on ball in the right-hand one). **Left** is May 1966 (next to teacher). And me, **below**, aged fifteen in 1964 (*second from the right, front row*).

Left: In Scotland shirt, April 1967.

Below: In Celtic kit (I'm the one not signing the autograph).

Above: At home wearing my Celtic blazer, which I still have, May 1968.

Below: In the young Scotland team (*second from right, front row*).

Above: The Scottish mafia masquerading as young international footballers. Martin Buchan (*left*) looks just the same now.

Left: The Quality Street Gang relaxing in Bermuda.

Right: Celtic reserves with the Reserve League Cup after winning it at Parkhead.

Above: Celebrating the Reserve League Championship with Kenny Dalglish (No. 4) just behind me. Danny McGrain is kneeling on the left directly in front of John Gorman.

Right: On tour in Malta.

Bad hair days:
In training, **left**.
In Celtic kit (No. 10),
below.

Left: Alex McDonald
blows me a kiss in
the League Cup Final
against Rangers,
October 1970. Nice
fella, Alex, but not
my type.

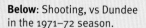
Below: Shooting, vs Dundee in the 1971–72 season.

Above: Running out of the tunnel followed by Paul Wilson and Bobby Lennox, Celtic vs Dundee in the league, September 1970.

Above: Accepting the congratulations of Dixie Deans after scoring fifth goal against Hibernian in the 1972 Scottish Cup Final and, **below**, posing with the trophy.

Above: Bottoms up! Celebrating in the bath after the club's fifth consecutive League Championship. (*Clockwise from bottom*) Bobby Murdoch, Bobby Lennox, Willie Wallace, Evan Williams, David Hay, Harry Hood, George Connelly, Tommy Callaghan, Tommy Gemmell and Jim Brogan, and me in the bottom right-hand corner.

if you played for or supported Arsenal, not if you wore a red shirt that day. There was despair in the dressing room. Dave was crushed. If the result hurt us, which it did, you can bet it hurt him more. He was football through and through. He had no other interests.

Here's an indication of his passion for the game. At the end of one summer tour we ended up with seven days in Hawaii. After a long, hard season and an end-of-season tour in America, it was brilliant. Waikiki Beach, Honolulu, Pearl Harbor – we did it all. Well, most of us did. All, in fact, except Dave. Five days in and we were all getting a bit concerned. We had hardly seen him. Around day six he appeared for breakfast. 'Where have you been, boss? What have you been up to?' He'd been in his room on a diet of American TV sport, absorbing everything. They play this stuff on a loop. He must have seen clips five, six, seven times – basketball, baseball, American football, anything. The idea that Steve McClaren is responsible for introducing American techniques into English football is a joke. Dave was at it twenty years earlier. He was engrossed in every aspect of every sport. And when he eventually showed up he wanted to organize a football quiz to fill the time. When you are on Waikiki Beach there are a lot of competing claims for your attention. Dave's football quiz was not one of them.

All that analysis made for a shrewd football brain, and Sexton never demonstrated that more than when he brought Ray Wilkins to Old Trafford in the summer of 1979 – a brilliant buy for United. Ray had his detractors, but for me there was none better at dropping the ball on a sixpence from anywhere on the pitch, with either foot. It marked a shift in emphasis from the all-out attack of Tommy Doc's team to a more considered continental approach. Liverpool had developed a passing game, and the feeling was we had to do the same. Sexton had known Ray as a kid at Chelsea. He was at the heart of the manager's thinking.

He made a difference too. Suddenly, games we had been drawing were turning into wins, and they were coming consistently: four wins in five in September 1979, the same in December, and in April 1980 we creamed six on the spin, starting at home to Liverpool. That run put us right in the championship picture. What we needed was for Liverpool to drop more points than us in the run-in. It didn't happen. Our fate was sealed with a 2–0 defeat at Leeds on the final day. It was a shame. We deserved something, having won twenty-four times and drawn ten with only eight defeats. We finished in second place, two points off Liverpool and five ahead of Ipswich in third – good enough to finish top in another year. That turned out to be the closest I came to winning the title with United.

Dave needed a signature purchase to lift the club one final rung, a striker he could rely on to get him goals, and in October 1980 Garry Birtles arrived for £1.2 million from Forest. Gary was the flavour of the month. He was twenty-four, had helped Forest to back-to-back European Cups, and had just broken into the England team. He'd scored thirty-two times in eighty-seven League matches for Forest and was getting better. He made his debut for United at Stoke. I was lucky enough to score on my debut. The monkey is off your back straight away. What Garry and Dave would have done for a debut goal. We won the match 2–1, but Garry didn't get his name on the scoresheet. Who did? Joe Jordan and me, and both of us would return to the Victoria Ground as managers. It took Birtles thirty games and almost a year to find the back of the net for United, when he scored against Swansea in September 1981.

Garry's goal drought was a mystery, a Saturday mystery. On Monday, Tuesday, Wednesday, Thursday and Friday, Birtles had no trouble scoring goals. In training he was a clinical finisher, neat and tidy around the box. We were all scratching our heads on Saturdays. He was not the first or the last to find Old Trafford a daunting place to work. Ted MacDougall struggled before him, Peter Davenport and Alan Brazil after him. Bizarrely, for an institution famed for its commitment to flair and attack, Old Trafford has proved to be a graveyard for a few unfortunate strikers. Birtles was one of the unlucky ones. Within two years of signing he was back at Forest, sold for £275,000, a fraction of what Dave had paid for him.

Mickey Thomas was another who openly admits he was overwhelmed by the Old Trafford experience. We'd turn up for training at The Cliff and Mickey would be nowhere to be seen, despite the fact that his car was always one of the first there. He lived in Rhyl and would drive over every day, making sure he arrived before everyone else. But we could never find him. When the whistle went to start training, Mickey would suddenly appear. More often than not he'd been in the dressing room with the reserve team players, where he felt more comfortable. You would never have guessed that he couldn't handle being a Manchester United player looking at his performances on the pitch, but behind the scenes it was all too much for him most of the time. The first-team dressing room was just too big a place.

The failure of Garry Birtles to catch fire more or less sealed the fate of my favourite manager. It's strange that you so rarely get the chance to say goodbye properly. The Doc went during the summer when the players had gone their separate ways. So too did Dave. At moments like that you understand where the ultimate power lies at football clubs – in the boardroom. We finished eighth in 1981, but with nine matches to go we were well off the pace. We had drawn too many games – eighteen in total. We were seen as safe under Sexton, and for Manchester United, safe is never enough. If you drew two and won seven of your last nine games, more modest clubs would throw a civic reception for you. Sacking a manager in those circumstances would be unheard of. But this was Manchester United.

The club had not won the League title since 1967, a period of fourteen years. In that time Liverpool had become the dominant force in English football, winning European Cups. United were no longer unique in that respect. And when Liverpool went slightly off the boil it was Nottingham Forest and Aston Villa that built great teams to reach the top, both of them adding the European Cup to their victories along the way. Old Trafford was becoming increasingly impatient. The club had led the way in Europe. This was Manchester United, the club of the Busby Babes, of Edwards, Colman, Taylor. This was Manchester United, the club of Law, Charlton and Best. Sexton had to go. But ask every player and to a man they will tell you how sad they were to see that happen. We really weren't far away.

The competition in that period was fierce, and the fans got impatient. They never really loved Dave like the players did. They saw him as dull. There was no razzmatazz surrounding him. Behind the scenes he was a gem. Had he been able to communicate that side of his personality to the fans the outcome might have been different. He might have been the one to create a great dynasty, like Sir Alex Ferguson did a decade later. Sexton was given four years.

12

LAST LEGS

AFTER DAVE GOT THE BULLET WE HAD A CARETAKER MANAGER, Jack Crompton, to oversee an end-of-season trip to the Far East. Jimmy Nicholl did a runner at Manchester airport before we caught a flight down to Heathrow. He decided he did not fancy it. When we got to Heathrow Gordon McQueen, Joe Jordan and I were talking with Mickey Thomas. He was saying he did not fancy it either. 'You're joking,' we said. He wasn't. He bet the three of us £20 apiece he would not get on the plane. We took him on, at which point he disappeared. He was not the last to get itchy feet. Sammy McIlroy actually boarded the plane for Kuala Lumpur then decided he did not want to go either. Poor Jack. We were still on British soil and he was three players down already. Jack was a lovely fella, but he had no control over the players. We knew a new man would be coming in, so we took advantage. Not in a malicious way, though. It was just fun, and nothing ever came of it.

We were moving into the era of Big Ron Atkinson, whose appointment, like Sexton's, reflected the need for a change in direction. The supporters wanted to see flair back on the agenda, which I believe Sexton would have given them had he been given the board's backing. Ron was seen as a larger-than-life figure. His West Brom team played with great panache. He brought the 'Three Degrees' – Laurie Cunningham, Cyrille Regis and Brendan Batson – to Old Trafford in 1979 and beat us 5–3 in a real barnstormer of a game. They also had a young lad called Bryan Robson who would follow Atkinson to Old Trafford in a record-breaking deal in October 1981.

Leaving Law, Charlton and Best to one side, Robson was probably the best I played with at United, an unbelievably powerful player. Interestingly, when he arrived at United he was a bit of an unknown. He wasn't someone who jumped out at you at West Brom at the time, probably because he was playing behind Regis and Cunningham. Len Cantello, an excellent player, was the man who often caught the eye in the middle of the park. Ron obviously knew better. After a couple of weeks chasing shadows at The Cliff it was crystal clear to everybody at United what a top-class performer the club had bought. Robson was never going to be a Bobby Charlton, whizzing the ball from one side of the pitch to the other; it was he who would be doing the whizzing, and effortlessly as well. He was a completely different type to any other player in the squad, not the sort of cultured, clever midfield player you might think would command the record fee United paid. He was not an Arnold Muhren nor a Ray Wilkins, who was a fantastic footballer. Wilkins came for big money too, £850,000, but did not get the credit he deserved at United. There was a lot of rubbish talked about him always passing the ball sideways, all this crab crap. You could be anywhere on the pitch and Ray could find you, drop the ball right on your toes. Ray was up there with Robbo, just in a different way. Robson was more eye-catching, more dynamic, and crucially for a United superstar, he attacked the box with venom, scoring lots of important goals.

Apart from the suntan, Ron was nothing like the Big Time Charlie figure he was portrayed as. There was no champagne. All that was a load of crap. He'd draw up a chair with a pot of tea and sit with the lads. He was very knowledgeable about the game. Dave would have liked him in his quiz team. Even though my time came to an end under him, I was impressed with Ron. He brought in Frank Stapleton in the August, just before Robson. Two great signings. Frank was top scorer for the club for the next three seasons – never prolific, but a one-in-three man, brilliant in the air and at leading the line.

Funnily enough, with all this talent in our ranks we had to wait five games for our first win of the 1981–82 season. Irony of ironies, it was Garry Birtles' first League goal for United that secured it. That sparked a run of nine wins in eleven League matches to put us in the mix. We kept it going all the way to March, but then a run of four games without a win, including a crucial home defeat to Liverpool, cost us badly. Despite five wins in our last six games of the campaign we could only finish third.

I had just turned thirty-two when Ron arrived at Old Trafford. At that stage in your playing career the emphasis shifts and you set different targets. You realize that staying in the team is going to be an achievement, and therefore staying at the club is going to be an achievement too. I stayed for a further two years. I was not daft enough to think there was going to be a regular place in the team for me. In my last couple of seasons I was sub in thirty-odd games, and there was only one sub allowed then, so I must have been of some use to the manager. In fact I was a dream sub for Ron. He could see I was no problem to him, that I always wanted to be involved. He knew that I wanted to play. I understood that I would not be starting; it was enough just to be in the mix on match day. I did not want to be sitting at home on a Saturday listening to the radio to see how the team was getting on. I still wanted in. But it is not about what you or the manager wants at that stage of a career, it's what your legs will allow.

In the League Cup Final against Liverpool in 1983 I came on for Kevin Moran and played at right-back. We ended the game with me and Frank Stapleton as central defenders. On this occasion Liverpool came out on top, though not before another young United prodigy, Norman Whiteside, gave us the lead with a thrilling strike. Alan Kennedy equalized, then, when our legs had gone and Frank and I were in defence, Ronnie Whelan fired an extra-time winner. I didn't make the team for the 1983 FA Cup Final against Brighton a couple of months later, which ended 2–2 on the day and gave us the immortal line 'And Smith must score'. Poor old Gordon. He was a fine player, and a Scot. We won the replay the following week at a canter, 4–0, with Robbo driving the team forward in characteristic style. He was the future. I was the past.

That League Cup experience was the first real indication to me that my playing days were numbered. Wembley was always a demanding surface, but clearly the old legs were not as quick as they used to be. Yes, it's your legs that tell you the end is near, and if you don't listen to them, you do pay attention when the letter telling you that your contract has been renewed fails to appear. There were no agents in those days. The club held your registration. When the term of your contract was up, they wrote to offer you a new one, with a bit more money, though not much. My last contract at United was for £420 a week. Considering I started on £200, that was not a massive improvement over eleven years. Players made their money in bonuses, from something in the order of £100 per League win to £3,000 for winning the FA Cup. But you had to be in the side to collect, and that's how it should be. There was a financial incentive for doing well. That's how you proved your value. These days they put the horse before the cart, pay you the money up front then expect you to perform. Where is the incentive there? There is no need to win, no need to strive.

The question I'm most often asked is this: do you regret not joining Liverpool in 1973? Had I done so I would have gone into a side on the up, one that was about to begin a phase of domination the like of which English football had never seen. Instead I joined United and left with a solitary FA Cup winners medal to my name. But my answer is an emphatic no. I played for Manchester United. In that final season, 1983–84, I passed four hundred appearances for the club and ended on ninety-seven goals in a United shirt. That'll do for me. Yes, the League title proved elusive. We had four top-three finishes after winning promotion at the first attempt in 1975, including a second to Liverpool in 1980. Liverpool were a great side, a great club, but my eleven years at Old Trafford could not have been bettered at Anfield, despite the success I might have shared in. I loved every minute of my time at Old Trafford. I was on the pitch when Bobby Charlton played his last game, against Chelsea in April 1973. I wore the number ten shirt when George Best kicked his last ball for United, against QPR on New Year's Day 1974. I played a part in the history of an iconic footballing institution. I have to be happy with that. The only downside was jumping in the car after the last game of the season knowing I wouldn't be back for pre-season training.

My last game in a red shirt was my testimonial on 13 May 1984 against Celtic. It was an emotional Sunday afternoon, saying goodbye to 44,000 people at Old Trafford. Celtic and United – I really could not have asked for more. People travelled in large numbers from Scotland. Tears were shed. Then it was over. I didn't have a thought in my head about what I was going to do next when I drove away from Old Trafford that night. It did not cross my mind that someone might employ me as a manager.

The thought took shape quickly enough, however. On an end-of-season tour in 1984 I learned I had the chance of a player-manager job at Derby. I cut the tour short to go for an interview. I was told I would get the job, but at the last minute I lost out to Arthur Cox. Player-managers were the in-thing at the time, and I knew I had to do something. A couple of months later Swindon answered the call.

13

CRY FOR ME ARGENTINA

BEFORE I STEP INTO THE WORLD OF MANAGEMENT, LET ME take you back to 1978 and the footballing adventure of a life-time – my only World Cup engagement.

I missed out in 1974. Four years later I'd made my mind up not to go to any World Cup. Bollocks to that. My mother had just died. The tournament was only three months away. In the immediate aftermath of her death the thought of going to a World Cup was a million miles away. Then the weeks started to pass. People came up to me saying things like 'It's your duty', 'You won't get another chance'. They were right about that. It turned out to be the only opportunity I had to share a stage with the world's greatest footballers.

In truth, my international career is not something I look back on with great fondness. I made my debut against Wales in 1972 when I was still a Celtic player and had twenty-two caps going into the 1978 World Cup, with five goals. I guess I was a little unlucky. Maybe there was some resentment in

Scotland towards players leaving for England. Maybe it was just that manager Willie Ormond did not fancy me. I wasn't helped by the fact that I joined a struggling side at Manchester United. I made my reputation in Scotland as a goalscorer; there weren't many goals flying in off my boot in the lead-up to the 1974 World Cup. Let's just say I didn't catch the eye at that point in my career.

The squad for the 1974 tournament in West Germany was arguably the finest Scotland had ever assembled. As I mentioned, United had, by 1978, a fair contingent of Scots; Buchan, McQueen and Jordan were all veterans of the 1974 World Cup, as was Kenny Dalglish from my Celtic days. Kenny followed me south of the border from Celtic in the summer of 1977, taking over Kevin Keegan's number seven shirt at Liverpool and playing against me in the Charity Shield match at the start of Dave Sexton's first season (a 0–0 draw meant that we shared the trophy). Kenny was by that stage the finished article, a world-class player whose status had been confirmed with the goal against Bruges at Wembley that secured for Liverpool their second European Cup win. All those failings of his youth, when he couldn't hit a barn door with a banjo, had been overcome. Kenny had a radar like few others. There was no great pace, but an uncanny sense of space and time always seemed to gain him an extra yard. I think 'mercurial' is the word often associated with Dalglish at his best. He used to slide into gaps, pulling the strings for his grateful strike partners when he wasn't hitting the net himself. He was helped by having his Liverpool team-mate Graeme Souness behind him – a Scottish version of Tommy Smith.

Had the 1978 competition taken place in Europe, I would have backed us to advance from our group, because Scotland had an embarrassment of riches. (It is worth remembering that after going to Mexico in 1970 as defending champions, England didn't qualify for the World Cup for the rest of the decade. The number of players playing in England out-numbered the Scots by ten to one, but it was Scotland pro-ducing all the quality.) Looking back, it was an achievement just to be involved; I never thought I would be at the outset, even though things at United were going all right for me. I would try to work out the make-up of the squad. Will they take six defenders, eight midfielders, five forwards, three goal-keepers? I'd go through the midfield candidates: Graeme Souness, Don Masson, Bruce Rioch, Archie Gemmill, Asa Hartford, Willie Johnstone . . . where was I going to fit in?

A total of eighty players were named in the initial squad. Can you imagine being able to name eighty players today in Scotland? That was then whittled down to forty, and at that point I was convinced I wasn't going. I just couldn't see how I would survive the cut to make the final twenty-two. I made it, and I was elated, but in the end I could not get away quickly enough from Argentina. In truth, I was still grieving for my mother; but even had I been in a better frame of mind there would have been precious little to smile about. And don't for-get, we were going to win the thing. We had the big send-off beforehand at Hampden Park in an open-top bus, Rod Stewart telling everybody in a song that 'Ole Ola, we're going to bring the World Cup back to Scot-o-land'. At one point our manager Ally McLeod was asked what he would do next after bringing the World Cup back to Scotland. 'Retain it,' he said. Most teams wait until they have won something before they set off on an open-top bus parade. Not Scotland. We did it first.

We got off to a bad start. Ally scrapped a planned press

conference when we touched down in Buenos Aires. It sent the wrong message, and it pissed off the press lads – not what you need when things go wrong. And they started going wrong very quickly. On the way to the hotel from the airport in Cordoba the team bus broke down. When we eventually arrived at the hotel, the place was terrible. To call it a hotel was a bit ambitious on the part of the hosts. They were still building it. When we walked through the door they were still nailing carpets to the floor. Fair enough, it had a swimming pool, which is useful in the sweltering Argentine summer. Shame it didn't have any water in it.

I was rooming with Martin Buchan, my team-mate at United. As I've already indicated, Martin, or 'the Buck' as we used to call him, was a unique bloke. I was one of only a couple of people who understood him, let's put it like that. Great player though he was, it would be fair to say that Martin Buchan had a lot in common with Peter Perfect. If there was a team meeting at five o'clock, Martin would turn up with two seconds to go. He was always on the dot. You could set your watch by him. Mr Perfect. To be fair, he was Mr Perfect on the pitch too. His performances were always polished and unflustered.

We changed rooms three times because they did not meet Martin's requirements. I can't be 100 per cent certain about the reasons. Let's say that in the first room there weren't enough coat-hangers, in the second room there was a bit of damp in the wall, in the third room . . . by which time I was saying, 'Martin, for fuck's sake!' I don't know how many hours it had taken to get to Argentina. Too many. Then we had another marathon to get to Cordoba and on to a half-built hotel on a bus that broke down. By the time we got to the third room I'd have happily slept in the toilet. As soon as we walked in the door of the hotel I knew Martin wasn't going to be happy. Eventually Ally McLeod offered us his room. It was no different to the others, but the fact that it was the manager's and he was prepared to give it up persuaded Martin to say yes. Eureka, he was content at last.

The food was no better. Soup was on the menu every day. It had a different name each time but it looked and tasted exactly the same as the day before. It became such a joke that one of the players suggested to a waiter, 'Why don't you fill up the swimming pool with that fucking soup?'

At our first training session we pulled up outside a big gated complex with a high wall around it. Ally stood up and addressed his troops, laughing. 'Right, lads, when you look at the training ground from the bus it might not look up to standard, but when you get on it you'll find it is definitely not up to standard.' Great. And he was right. The playing surface was terrible. We weren't used to the lush pitches the players enjoy today, but even so, this was ridiculous. Facilities at a World Cup should not be like that. The Scottish FA had been out, too, looked at the accommodation and everything and come back saying they were adequate. They weren't. That sort of thing has a terrible effect on players. Had it not been for Ally we would have lost the plot. He messed up with the press conference, but after that he was blameless. Every disaster that came along he would laugh and joke about, even about the record he made. The chances of that taking off were nil as the results went against us. Andy Cameron, a Scottish comedian, did get to number six in the charts before we left, but that was based around the fact that England 'didnae qualify'.

Of course our participation in the competition was hopelessly over-hyped and we completely misjudged the ability of the opposition, especially Peru, playing in their own environment in conditions that suited them – lively, bumpy pitches, oppressive heat and humidity. If Scotland went to a World Cup now in South America and faced Peru, everybody would be a bit concerned about that fixture. The Peruvian who did for us, Teofilo Cubillas, didn't even get a mention beforehand. When we played them a Scottish victory was a foregone conclusion. It was just a case of turn up, beat them and march on.

People had short memories. They forgot that we only scraped into the finals in the first place, by beating Wales controversially in our last qualifying match on 12 October 1977. Lose and it would have been all over for us, as Wales still had one more match to play, in Czechoslovakia, where we lost. Even a draw would have kept them alive. We had a bit of good fortune in that game. The first bit was Wales deciding to play the match at Anfield. They would have been better off playing in Cardiff or Swansea, a compact ground where the Welsh crowd would have taken most of the tickets, limiting the number of Scots in the stadium. The Welsh FA claimed it was for security reasons. If so, why they didn't do a deal with the rugby people I don't know. It cost them. We came out of the tunnel at Anfield to a massive roar from the Scottish supporters. You looked around the stadium and it seemed like a home match instead of the away game it was meant to be. That gave us such a lift. Wales had a good team, but we got the breaks. With twelve minutes to go, Joe Jordan and David Jones went up for a header. The ball hit a hand. Everybody in Wales swears it was Joe's. I didn't get a clear view (despite being only yards away) but I suspect they might be right.

Robert Wurz pointed to the spot and Don Masson tucked the penalty away. Joe kissed his hand. Dalglish made it 2–0, scoring on his fiftieth appearance for his country.

But to go back to the World Cup, I suspect that in a cool northern European climate we might have done better, but it was a different kettle of fish in the Argentine summer. The conditions were horrendous. There was no chance to acclimatize. The heat was too extreme. You would come back from training feeling like you had done three sessions, absolutely drained. There was not much in the way of nutritional advice, no specially prepared drinks packed with electrolytes to aid the absorption of fluids. It was a bottle of water and the soup for us.

Joe gave us the lead in the fourteenth minute against Peru. They equalized just before half-time, then Don Masson had a penalty saved. Cubillas killed us late in the game with two brilliant goals. He was one of the top players in the world, up there with other great South Americans like Ossie Ardiles and Mario Kempes. We were exhausted after an hour while they were running around as if it were the first minute. I came on as a sub, but to no great effect. We could not compete. The game just ran away from us. We wilted. And this was a team that had players of the calibre of Jordan, Dalglish, Gemmill, Masson, Rioch and Buchan – all superb players.

We might not have known how tough it was going to be before, but we did after that Peru game. And the nightmare was just starting. Willie Johnston tested positive for a banned stimulant. Before we left Scotland the players were given a list of substances with big fancy names. They sailed completely over everybody's head. We were asked if we had taken any of them in the last few months. Everybody said no. How would we know? After the games two players were tested from each team. Kenny Dalglish's came back clear; Willie's came back positive.

As soon as the words 'drugs' and 'positive' came back in the same sentence the place went mad. It was one of the biggest stories of any World Cup. Scottish player on drugs shock! The drug turned out to be a treatment Willie was taking for an injury which contained one of the substances on the list. He didn't know that and never could have, but he was sent home in disgrace anyway. It was ridiculous. The upshot was that Scotland became the big story of the World Cup for the British press pack. Don't forget, England weren't in Argentina, so Scotland were the focus for the Scottish and English reporters out there filing stories for their newspapers. And after Willie, it was open season. Reporters were looking for the next shock, the next disgrace. There were stories about players out on a piss-up in a bar. Complete garbage. The players were allowed out by the manager anyway, and no one was pissed. Next up, the players were being shot at as they climbed a wall to get into a casino. Yes, there were armed guards around the hotel, but that was routine at the time. The political situation in Argentina was unstable. No one was shot at. The casino was attached to the hotel. Going there now and again helped to pass the time. All of these crazy stories just further sapped the enthusiasm of the team.

Then we drew with Iran. Most of our supporters would have been hard pushed to find Iran on a map. Like Peru, this was another match we were going to win easily. The day of the match was my twenty-ninth birthday. Archie Gemmill and I were subs in the previous game but we started this one, along with Kenny, Joe, Man City's Asa Hartford and the Forest pair of John Robertson and Kenny Burns; Alan Rough, Sandy Jardine, Willie Donachie and Martin Buchan completed the team. You'd settle for that lot today. We took the lead just before half-time with an own goal, then tired again. The conditions were not a problem for the Iranian lads. They equalized in the second half and could have, perhaps should have, gone on to win the game. We hung on, and the mood was grim afterwards. The tournament was spiralling out of control. Ally was pictured with his head in his hands in the dugout when they scored. It summed up the way the squad was feeling. We were fed up.

We went into the last game at Mendoza needing to beat Holland by three clear goals. They got a penalty, and that should have been that. But in typical Scottish fashion we got closer than we had any right to do, given what had gone before. Morale was on the deck, we had not performed at all, we were a goal down, then we started to play. Kenny equalized just before half-time. That gave us a lift. At half-time our only thoughts were to go out there and give it a crack. Archie put us in front from the spot. He then went on to score one of the great World Cup goals, chipping the ball over the Dutch keeper after an incredibly mazy run. Archie's master strike is listed at seven in the FIFA list of all-time great World Cup goals.

There were twenty minutes left. We were one goal away from going through to the knockout stages, and here were two teams from the same part of the world. The Dutch were struggling as much as we were in the conditions. No one had expected us to be in this position. The pressure was off and we were starting to enjoy it. If we had scored the next goal who knows what might have happened.

There was no Cruyff in the Dutch side – he had boycotted the tournament for political reasons – but they had a player called Johnny Rep. Three minutes after Archie had the whole of Scotland dreaming, Rep pricked the bubble with a thunderbolt. Alan Rough never saw it. We went out of the competition, and Holland went on to meet Argentina in the final. Still, the victory was proof that Scotland did have the players to do well. But not in Argentina. And not from that hotel.

I left immediately. My wife was in New York visiting her parents in White Plains. She had watched the games at a cinema in Manhattan. I rang Alex Montgomery, my ghost-writer at the *Sun*, which was running my World Cup column, and told him I was going. He asked when. 'Tomorrow morning,' I said. After the game I had travelled back to Cordoba from Mendoza to get a flight to Buenos Aires. Alex was detailed to stick with me to get my World Cup story. That meant coming to New York with me, but he was still in Mendoza and could not get a flight from there to Buenos Aires. So he hired a taxi. It is more than six hundred miles to Buenos Aires from Mendoza across terrible terrain and mountains. The journey takes seventeen hours, and that's only if you make it in one piece. There were all sorts of stories about bandits and gunmen hiding out in the hills.

'I'll see you at the airport,' Alex said.

The next day I was there at the airport in plenty of time to get on the plane. There was no sign of Alex, and to be honest, I couldn't have cared less. An hour before the flight I saw a bloke in the distance who looked a lot like Alex. Sure enough, in he came, looking dishevelled, in need of a bath and a change of clothes. He'd been on edge the whole journey. He'd even had to threaten the taxi driver to get him to the airport on time when the man had wanted to stop in the mountains to have a fag break to recover.

We did the piece on the plane. I said a few things that I maybe shouldn't have done. The *Sun* must have been delighted. The article was so controversial it earned me a ban from the Scottish FA. I did two articles a week in Argentina. As you might expect, the last one was a summary of all that had happened, which, apart from Archie's goal, was not overly positive for anyone. I told a few home truths. Nowadays you would not get any international players putting up with what we had to in Argentina: the hotel fiasco, the food, the training facilities. All of these things were compounded by the results and our treatment by the press. I was saying only what all the players felt. I never played for my country again.

14

CLUELESS OF SWINDON

I CAN'T REMEMBER WHERE I SAW THE SWINDON JOB advertised, I just recall thinking, 'Swindon Town, Don Rogers, beat Arsenal at Wembley in the 1969 League Cup Final, I'll have a little look at that.' Contact was made on my behalf: a pal rang to see if there was any interest. I got a positive response so I headed down for an interview.

There were a few people around the boardroom table when I went in – a similar situation to the one I had encountered at Derby County. Questions came at me from all angles. They wanted to know how I would be able to adjust to life at Swindon after Manchester United, how I would cope with fish and chips on a bus instead of steak and chips in a restaurant. At United, whenever we went to London we travelled first class on the train and booked into a top hotel; but they didn't consider that before I joined United I was a player at Celtic, going back to Largs in the back of my father's Ford Anglia, and I didn't tell them. I could cope. Fish and chips were a staple of my time at Celtic. I even bought a fish and chip shop at Old Trafford. Fish and chips on the bus would do me fine.

The details of my responses long ago have left my memory. All I know is that I spoke my mind. I did not tailor my answers according to what they wanted to hear, I just told it as I saw it, for better or worse. I left with no idea as to how I'd been received, but a couple of days after the interview I got word that they were happy in the main. Only one board member had some reservations. He thought I might be difficult to handle.

Swindon were struggling at the wrong end of the old Fourth Division, but I was not the only one in for the job. Phil Thompson, the former Liverpool centre-back who had also finished his glittering playing career in the summer of 1984, had been interviewed too and had obviously made a better impression than I had: he was invited for a second sitting before the panel. That was enough for Swindon to offer him the job. Luckily for me, he turned it down. So, just weeks after kicking my last ball for Manchester United, I became a manager.

Believe me, when you start life as a manager, you start off in the dark. I had no experience whatsoever. Swindon were taking a punt on my name as much as anything else, and on my performance in an interview. I hadn't a clue how to manage a football club. I'd played under a few managers, but I'd only ever looked at the game as a player. I'd paid next to no attention to what the manager did, unless I was out of the team, which was not very often, until the end of my career.

Out of the blue I got an unsolicited knock on my door from

Harry Gregg, who had read about my appointment in the newspapers. I knew Harry from United, where he was a goal-keeping coach. Before that he was a great player, the goalkeeper in the Busby Babes side and a hero of Munich. He'd been given the boot by Big Ron and was looking for a job. Casually, he said I should give him a shout if I was look-ing for somebody to help out. All things considered, it wasn't a bad idea. I could do Harry a bit of a turn, and he could provide a bit of back-up for me. So off we went, Macari and Gregg, into the unknown.

My physio at Swindon was a lad called Kevin Morris. I think he was there when the first brick was laid. He certainly knew the club inside out. Kevin was a lovely fella. He had silver hair, which prompted away fans to shout every time he ran on to the pitch to treat a player, 'There's only one Jimmy Savile!' Kevin made me feel welcome from the off. He was invaluable as a guide, giving me a good idea of how the club ran. He quickly made it clear that only one person was in charge, of the day-to-day running of the club and that was Bob Jeffries. Anything you wanted you had to run it past Bob.

We were all in the dark in those first few weeks. Swindon didn't know what I was going to do, I didn't know what they were going to do, Harry didn't know what I or the club was going to do, and so on. There were no words of wisdom from me, no miracle cures, just trial and error.

The training ground was just up the road from the County Ground, as far removed from The Cliff with its canteen and sauna as you could get. Apart from the pitch, it didn't have any facilities. You couldn't even get changed there. The players had to get changed at the County Ground, run down the road in their trainers and change into their boots at the side of the pitch. The balls followed in the back of a car. It was no great surprise, though. This was lower-division football after all. On the first day I introduced myself to the players. They all knew who I was, obviously, so the introductions didn't take long. Young Jimmy Quinn was the only player most of you would have heard of. The squad was full of people I knew nothing about. They were all very excited.

There were no real shocks in terms of the players, once I had adjusted my mind to the fact that it was a club in the Fourth Division. The difficulty at first was recognizing that they were not capable of playing the way I wanted to play. I was always a couple of moves in front of them. I would go for a one-two and the ball wouldn't come back. It's not that they were incapable of executing a one-two, of course they were; they just didn't necessarily see it. Players in the lower divisions don't see things quickly enough, so they don't make the necessary adjustments, and moves break down. It is all about anticipation. If you wait to see what your team-mate is going to do with the ball, you can forget it. You have to know intuitively so that you are already in a position to receive the ball almost before he has kicked it. That is how it works the higher you go in sport. The best players anticipate actions and are always a step ahead. Everything becomes automatic. In the lower divisions very little is automatic. Players wait until the ball is kicked, then they react. We are only talking fractions of a second here, but at the highest level that's all you need to beat your man and score.

Fitness was also an issue. I arrived at Swindon at the age of thirty-five and was the fittest player there. Actually, I was the second fittest, behind John Trollope, and he was even older than me. Again, though, everything was pretty much as I'd expected it to be in terms of technique and fitness. Things were done a degree or two more slowly in Division Four. Speed of thought and fitness were not what they were in the First Division, where you got less time to make your mind up about what you wanted to do. It was four or five games into the season before I realized that I would have to adjust down rather than expect them to adjust up. I was getting a bit frustrated, blasting them for not doing this and that, but I soon learned to appreciate that they were not capable of doing things the way I had been used to doing them at United. I scored on my debut as player-manager against Wrexham, but over time I understood that it would be better if I were not on the pitch at all. I wasn't helping in that environment. I eventually hung up my boots in 1986.

Changing my approach and attitude towards the players was the first good decision I made. But handling the players was only part of the new experience. Dealing with the board was another. The kit man brought it to my attention that we needed some new items. This kit man was none other than my favourite person at the club, Kevin the physio. Yes, people multi-tasked in those days too; the only difference was they didn't call it multi-tasking. The state of the jockstraps was a particular concern for Kevin. He showed them to me. They were full of holes.

It was probably one of the first stupid things I did early in my managerial career, but I stuck one of Kevin's jockstraps in my pocket and took it to the board meeting. There was a bit of preamble around the table, then the chairman, Brian Hillier, addressed me.

'Well, Lou, what are your first impressions of the club?'

I started off with a few positive remarks, praised the lads and what have you, then reached for the jockstrap in my pocket and put it on the table. 'But that ain't good enough no matter who you are,' I concluded.

The jockstrap sat there in the middle of the table as though a thousand mice had been nibbling at it. Everybody looked a bit embarrassed.

'Erm . . . yes, Lou, we see what you mean.'

I came out of there thinking, 'Fuck me, I wish I hadn't done that.' It was just an attempt to try to smarten things up a bit. I was never one for perfection, but when Kevin brought it to my attention I thought it was worth pointing out. It was probably a bit over the top, though, a bit unnecessary. Nevertheless, Brian very kindly said to Bob Jeffries, the secretary, that any kit that was needed I was to get. Bob was in the habit of keeping things on a tight budget – nothing for this, nothing for that – but he relented. The Swindon Town secretary signing a cheque for new jockstraps was the first sign of change at the club in years. It was a triumph. Onwards and upwards.

I learned not to rush into judgements. Not so much about a player's ability, but his attitude, his character. Was he going to be of any use to me? Was he a winner? What's his response to a change of regime? What's his response to a tougher regime? All these answers would come over time. And for most managers when they join new clubs, the players are not the only people they have to make a judgement about. From day one members of staff belonging to the previous regime will be wondering if they are going to be called into the manager's office to be told they are down the road. When Kevin Keegan returned to Newcastle as manager after Sam Allardyce, he discovered that he had a support staff of forty-two. That's precisely forty more than I inherited. I had Kevin Morris and John Trollope. Before I was appointed, John was the caretaker manager. He was a Swindon legend, having played a massive 770 games for the club – a record in English football for a player at one club. He had also had a three-year spell in the same hot seat I now occupied, before Ken Beamish took over. Kevin, too, was a fixture of the scene so there wasn't much of a decision to make. It never even crossed my mind to sack them. I simply brought in Harry Gregg. The club basically revolved around the four of us and Bob Jeffries. We were the staff.

The first thing I did was make training tougher. Swindon had been through a nightmare time the season before, 1983–84, finishing seventeenth in the Fourth Division – the lowest position in the club's history. It was fairly obvious that something was wrong. At United we would warm up for about twenty minutes. You wouldn't see any balls at that point, just a fair amount of running. We'd then do ball work – shooting, crossing, etc. It was a similar sort of format at Swindon, but it lacked intensity. John was fine. He could have run two marathons a day. Others needed some fitness work badly. I was pleased with the response I got when I stepped things up. I'd get them in for ten o'clock until one. In the afternoon I would be out watching a reserve game before going to another game at night. It was labour intensive.

As the months went by, my friendship with the physio-cum-kit man Kevin grew stronger and stronger, not only because he knew everyone and everything at the club inside out, but because he was a very funny fella. It was not long before I was taking Kevin to matches with me. Harry covered the games we couldn't get to. I soon learned to trust Kevin's judgement on players. On everything, really. One day he said to me out of the blue, 'Lou, you've got a problem.'

'What do you mean I've got a problem?'

'You've got a problem with your assistant,' he said, meaning Harry. 'He's up to no good. He's hanging around the directors, trying to influence them too much. He talks to them as though he is the manager. He has too much to say for himself.' I hadn't paid that much attention. I was new to the management game. I didn't read anything into Harry's habits. But it had hit Kevin like a bullet between the eyes. In the weeks and months that followed I began to build a completely different picture of Harry. I understood his behaviour and his motives differently. Kevin would point out one or two things, but over time he wouldn't need to. Everything was beginning to make sense to me. I could only assume he was feathering his own nest, that he wanted the manager's job – having always been a manager himself, that was understandable. Obviously I wasn't happy about the situation and at the next board meeting I brought my concerns to the attention of the chairman, Brian Hillier. Three days later, on the Sunday, I received a call at home asking if I would come down to the County Ground for a meeting. When I got there the chairman explained it was about the situation with Harry.

Unbeknown to me Harry had been tipped off about the meeting. About an hour after I arrived Harry turned up with his ducks in a row. Harry was an aggressive fella. He didn't so much speak as growl. He'd often frighten people with his manner. Harry said his piece, I said mine and away we went.

The meeting ended there – so far as Harry and I were concerned anyway. A few days later, on 5 April 1985 – Good

Friday in fact – the club sacked us both. There is some excellent footage on YouTube of Brian Hillier's statement. He told the world we were sacked because of our inability to work together.

I was stunned. So were the fans and the players. In fact, I had no idea how highly I was regarded by the supporters or the players until that moment. The fans staged a demonstration across the Easter weekend in protest, and a group of players led by the captain Andy Rowland turned up at my house. I was overwhelmed by the response. It was genuinely uplifting. To have players pledging their support at your house at a time like that is a huge morale boost. I said at the time that it felt as good as running around the pitch at Wembley celebrating victory in the FA Cup. That is how much it meant.

Their voices were heard, and I was reinstated. Harry wasn't. It was a strange turn of events.

There was another incident that put my nose out of joint. Swindon is close to the racing fraternity at Lambourn. I knew Johnny Francombe well, and Julian Wilson, the BBC racing correspondent. Julian is Swindon mad; because of his close links with the club and with me he played a part in recommending me for the job. A lot of the racing lads would come to the matches. Simon Whitworth, a flat jockey, was a big Manchester United supporter. He used to come up to Swindon as a youngster. We formed quite an attachment. On one occasion I invited him down to Exeter with us on the team coach. I was playing that night. Simon was in the corridor before the game, then he disappeared for a while. Shortly before kick-off I saw him and asked him where he had been. 'I went up to the off-licence to get a bottle of whisky for Harry,' he said. Being a non-drinker,

I was seething. The thought of drink in the dressing room before a game was a non-starter for me. Zero tolerance for that.

Harry spent most of the game bawling and shouting. We battered Exeter but managed only a draw. At the end of the game he was going around the dressing room patting the players on the back. 'Well done, lads, brilliant.' It wasn't brilliant. We'd played well but got no more out of the game than Exeter. That didn't feel brilliant to me. So I jumped in, as you would, being the manager.

'Wait a minute, there's not a lot to praise here, lads,' I said. 'We've battered them and dropped two points.'

Harry started arguing with me. That pissed me off. This was the start of a new chapter in my football life. I was trying to get something going here, and not drinking was a big part of that. Everybody had bought into it. No drink on the team bus, no getting leathered in the players' lounge after games. I don't know what he intended to do with the whisky. I was not interested. He said it was for the players, which was even worse, given my stance. Discipline was my big thing, and Harry was out of line. I pulled him about it the next day and that ended in another argument. He had no defence, but that didn't stop him trying. I tucked it away for a rainy day, which of course was not long in coming. I mentioned it at that fateful board meeting.

To many Harry is a hero. He was brilliant in goal for Manchester United and distinguished himself with his bravery at Munich, sacred ground which was revisited during the fiftieth anniversary commemorations.

15

THE HEIGHTS IN OUR SIGHTS

WITH HARRY GONE, IT WAS TIME TO MOVE ON. I FELT WE WERE making progress even though we were not getting the results to prove it, but if I'm honest, I could not really see how things were going to change much in the short term. I certainly did not see my second season as a title-winning year with a record number of points. What I would say is that the players were responding to me, and that the supporters seemed to believe that somehow 1985–86 was going to be special.

Maybe the fans, who had been used to failure and mediocrity for so long, had picked up on one or two changes in the players. Lee Barnard was getting dog's abuse from the crowd when I arrived. I pulled him aside and told him that if he lost a bit of weight and got himself in good condition his game might improve and he might enjoy his time at the club more. Lee was a nice lad and a good player. He just couldn't get around the pitch effectively enough, which for a midfielder is a problem. His response was fantastic. Lee lost a lot of weight, got himself fitter, and come the end of my first season was in the running for Player of the Year. Years later, Lee and I were involved in a charity event at the club. He thanked me for my advice, admitting that it turned his career around.

And he wasn't the only one. Charlie Henry was a local lad. He was a good attacking midfielder, he got in the box and scored valuable goals – a Paul Scholes prototype, if you like. He was in and out of the team when I arrived. I liked his attitude straight away. He always had a big smile on his face and was desperate to do well for his local team. I liked that about him. Like Lee, however, he needed to be fitter. There is no guarantee that players will respond to direction like that; some could just as easily resent what you tell them and rebel. Lee and Charlie were examples of two lads going nowhere at the club who responded positively and turned their fortunes around by changing their habits. Charlie ended up with eighteen goals in our first promotion year, which was incredible.

I can't tell you the secret. I was simply doing things the way I believed things should be done. I was obviously doing something right, though. Apart from the promotions and the great nights at Swindon over my time there, the club made more than £8 million on players. All those trips to reserve games paid off. That's the only way you can really drop on to players. I know managers, then and now, who never go to games. I don't know how they can manage without getting about the country. They don't seem to regard it as part of the job. But at lower-division clubs it's essential.

My first signing was a young lad called Colin Calderwood, who I nicked from Mansfield at the end of my first season. They were desperate to keep him on and were on the point of signing him when I jumped in with a £15,000 bid. That was not accepted. I ended up paying £25,000 at a tribunal. He was eighteen years old, a lovely raw Scots boy with a great attitude. He went on to captain the side, and to play for Spurs and Scotland.

I took Fitzroy Simpson from amateur football. I spotted him in a parks game one Sunday morning in 1987, a young kid kicking shit out of established grown men. He went on to play for Manchester City. No game was off limits to me. If a football was being kicked, I would be there. I didn't go to watch Simpson deliberately; it was just a random visit to Chippenham. It could have been anywhere in the Swindon area. Luckily for Fitzroy, me and the club, it was Chippenham.

Phil King was another great signing, from Torquay. The fee was ten grand and a cheeseburger. He was in the office and said he was starving. 'Would you like a cheeseburger?' I asked, and he said yes. I used to joke with him later that I'd paid too much for him. He wasn't worth that cheeseburger. Phil used to put on weight easily. We called him Fat Phil. Terrific attitude and good character, though. When you can call someone Fat Phil and they don't take offence, you know you are on to a winner. Big Ron eventually signed him for Sheffield Wednesday. He now runs a pub in Swindon.

I brought in Peter Coyne from Hyde United on a free. Peter started out at Manchester United. He scored a few goals as a kid and had this great knack of falling over in the box and getting a penalty. Always helpful. He'd then get up and stick the penalty away, which was even better.

Six-foot-four-inch Dave Bamber joined as a centre-forward from Portsmouth. I played him on the right wing. I took the view that his decision-making in the box was not his strong point. You only get a second to act in that part of the pitch. But he was very quick, much better on the wing running at people, running at pace into the box. He had these big long legs. If you blew on them he went down. Think of a Zlatan Ibrahimovic at outside-right for Inter Milan and you get some idea of what Bamber was like.

When Dave started on a run it was a bit like going back to my Celtic days when we had John 'Yogi' Hughes on the right wing. The crowd used to chant 'Feed the bear, feed the bear!' because John looked like one (hence the nickname). When Yogi got the ball and started running at defenders wide on the left, the place went wild. I wondered if I could do the same with Dave down the right. When Yogi arrived at Celtic he too was a striker. Putting him out wide was another demonstration of Jock Stein's genius. At centre-forward he was a little too slow to react; he would miss chances and the crowd would get on his back. On the wing he was a hero. He and Celtic never looked back.

So I put Dave Bamber at outside-right, and the change was incredible. He'd get the ball on the halfway line, start running, and immediately the noise would get louder and louder. After five or six strides he was in the box. You were praying for someone to breathe on him in the area. As soon as anyone came near him I'd be screaming, 'Penalty!' More often than not the referee would be pointing to the spot. What an asset to have in your team.

That said, we had gained assets all over the pitch.

I signed Chris Kamara. He had an unbelievable engine – a throwback to my United days this time, first with Bobby Charlton and then with Gerry Daly. Chris could run all day and all night. The team I was starting to build would run any team we faced into the ground. Chris was at the heart of that.

Chris Ramsay, at right-back, was another gem. Most people remember Chris for his performance for Brighton against Manchester United in the 1983 FA Cup Final. After that he was with me. Chris used to travel in every day on the train from London. He didn't have a care in the world. He'd arrive with a cup of coffee in one hand and a bacon sandwich in the other. Every day was the same, and this was fifteen minutes before the start of training. But he was a character. We had a team of characters. We had a team of warriors in every position, exemplified by men like Andy Rowland, the club captain when I arrived. When people ask me who my most important player was at that time, I tell them I did not have one. They were all equally important to me and the team. I wouldn't have wanted to be without any one of them.

It's a cliché, but that is what this game is all about: eleven blokes battling for one another. It is not about managers plotting and planning the downfall of the opposition. It isn't about formations and tactics. It's about players; it's about attitude and determination. I listened to so much rubbish being talked about England's failure to qualify for the 2008 European Championship. It was a failure of organization, a failure of the coach to get the best out of a talented group, blah, blah, blah. These days money has changed everything. It has taken the players' hunger away. Again, we are only talking fractions, but that's enough at the highest level. It is harder for managers in today's game to get that little bit extra you need out of players. At Swindon I never had a problem urging the lads on to bigger and better things. They knew that then they would all be winners. How can you say that to the modern-day player, who is a winner before he starts, with millions in the bank and a Baby Bentley on the driveway? In their eyes, how much better can it get? When I sent those lads out in their Swindon Town shirts they did not want the opposition to deny them their win bonus. The boys had the right attitude, they wanted to get better.

My job was simply to get everybody in shape and singing from the same song sheet. There were issues from time to time, of course. Routine stuff. I remember Steven Foley, a tough little Scouser I signed from Sheffield United. You'd want him in the trenches with you. The only downside was that he could be a little too aggressive at times. One week I left him out of the side. I was in the toilet having a pee when Steve came in beside me.

'Why am I not playing?' he asked.

'Because I pick the team and you are not in it,' I replied.

He started ranting and raving. I ended up grabbing him by the throat, which as you might imagine in the circumstances was a bit tricky. But it was an hour before kick-off. You don't want rebellion in the dressing room at any time, but an hour before kick-off, forget it.

The following day I got a knock on the office door. It was Foley.

'Sorry about yesterday, boss.'

'No problem, Steve. Let's crack on.'

That was how it was with me. He came out with a load of crap I did not appreciate, and I let him know it. The following day it was back to work. I can't say I had a particular technique. I was simply falling back on footballing instincts honed over time. Jock Stein used to walk into the dressing room and not say a word. He did not need to. Can you coach that? Did Jock have a FIFA coaching licence? Does Sir Alex Ferguson? I didn't at Swindon.

Eventually we started to win. I say eventually, because at the start of my second season in charge, 1985–86, things did not begin well. A couple of months in we were still in single figures, five points from eight games. There was no talk of promotion at that point. We were not getting hammered, it was just a case of having to up the tempo a little and get fitter. We used to have three sessions a week at a running track close to the ground. Every one of them was serious, man against man, team against team. The new players coming in responded. Once we started winning, we seemed to get stronger and quicker. Eventually we built real momentum, sweeping all before us.

I hadn't been in such a position before so I didn't recognize the signs. An experienced manager might have twigged that we were on our way. At no stage in the campaign did I feel that. I certainly did not believe 102 points were on the cards, that we would be the first Football League team to reach that number in a season. On the way we shattered a sixty-two-year-old Swindon record when we beat Burnley for a fourteenth straight home win. We had twenty home League victories that year. Fortress Swindon. We also nailed some big scalps in cup competitions: Sunderland 3–1, and Sheffield Wednesday 1–0 in front of twelve thousand fans – unheard of at Swindon.

As fate would have it, we ended up clinching the title away from the County Ground. I'll never forget the date: Saturday, 19 April 1986. A draw at Mansfield was enough. Lee Barnard scored the equalizer. It was Swindon's first title in sixty-six years of League membership. We came from twenty-third spot and won the championship with four games remaining. At the end, the gap to second place was eighteen points. The achievement livened up the whole town, which at that time was growing quickly with lots of companies relocating from London along the M4 corridor.

As a manager, my mind turned immediately to the business of playing in Division Three. Again, I had no grand design. I would have settled just for staying up. I never imagined that we would gain promotion for a second successive season in 1987, albeit via the play-offs after finishing third. The play-offs were a new idea, and the final was over two legs in those days rather than a Wembley showpiece. We faced Gillingham, and the score stood at 2–2 on aggregate after we had at one stage been 2–0 down; Peter Coyne and Charlie Henry, with twelve minutes to go, forced the replay, at Selhurst Park. When we beat Gillingham 2–0 in that replay – Steve White scored both goals – it was our sixty-fourth match of the season. I signed Steve from Bristol Rovers in a double swoop with centre-half Tim Parkin. I paid £25,000 for the pair. Bobby Gould was not very happy. Because of the local rivalry it was unusual for Swindon to recruit players from Bristol. They were fantastic buys for me. The asset that had proved so valuable in Division Four, our fitness, was decisive again. We ran into the ground and outplayed the likes of Fulham, Wigan, Middlesbrough and Bolton during that Division Three campaign with the same group of players. We were now just one step away from the big league, and up against sides like Birmingham, Aston Villa, Manchester City, Blackburn, Leeds United, West Bromwich Albion and Sheffield United.

I didn't feel the need to make wholesale changes for the Division Two campaign. I was prepared to carry on operating in the same way, and give the lads who got us up an opportunity to prove themselves in more exalted company. I saw no point in denying them that chance when from the start I was selling them the idea of improving themselves as players. I was not about to chop the legs from under them, so we soldiered on. The games were tougher and the standard was better. And we rose to the challenge. Jimmy Quinn scored thirty-one goals in all competitions and we finished that 1987–88 season respectably in mid-table.

Despite those successive promotions, some things did not change that much. The fish and chip order on the bus was still one of the more important considerations for the players. We would size up the nearest chip shop at away grounds and on the way to the game send someone out with the order so that it'd be ready to pick up on the way home. That's the way it was, all very simple and low key. Hopefully we had collected three points because the chips always tasted better after a win. All this diet nonsense you get now – you can't eat this, you can't eat that. It's a load of bollocks. And anyway, what's the point of the modern-day pro following his elaborate dietary regime then staggering about London at four in the morning pissed out of his head? The point is this: if you have the level of fitness my lads had at Swindon, then fish and chips, chicken and chips, a sackful of potatoes is not going to get in your way. The dreaded booze can.

Speaking of chips and booze, reflections on my time at Swindon cannot pass without mention of the club's greatest fan, a fella called John Menham. John had cerebral palsy. When I arrived at the club I was told he was not in the best of health. He'd not missed a game since he started following the team. His mother and father used to take him to matches on the supporters' club bus. After home games they would wheel him into my office. John could drink for England. He was the only person at the club allowed to drink in my office. I would go down to the boardroom and stock up with beers just for him. At six o'clock his parents would collect him and wheel him down to the local at the end of the road – where he went most nights, incidentally – and leave him there until closing time. He could shift eight or nine pints no trouble. On the odd occasion we took John with us on the bus to away games. He loved it. His order was sausage and chips. He had a great sense of humour. I used to pick up his sausage and say, 'Here, John, stick this in your mouth.' He would get his own back by mistaking my finger for the sausage. Wonderful lad. Swindon without John Menham would not be the same. John and people like that are a club's lifeblood. He is still there now, as far as I know, and still going strong.

The one aspect of the beautiful game that proved problematic for the club, and ultimately for me, as we rose through the ranks was the financial side of things. I was never one for the boardroom. I never went there after games. I tried to keep my involvement with boardroom matters to a minimum. If members of the board wanted to see me or have a chat after a game, they would tend to come to my office. I am, first and foremost, a football man; the boys in the boardroom tend to be businessmen. I approached all matters at the club from a playing perspective. There was no degree course or apprenticeship entitled Football Management. You learned as you went along. I was just a baby in management terms at Swindon. I got the football side of it right, achieving way beyond my own expectations, and the club's. But I perhaps did not pay enough attention to other aspects of the way the club was run. I didn't know how to. That cost me dearly.

Though even now, looking back, I don't believe the club acted criminally. Swindon Town FC made mistakes, but not in a malicious way. And as far as my own involvement in what happened is concerned, I can sleep soundly in my bed at night.

At the beginning of each season clubs were required to produce a bonus scheme which would be sent off to the Football League. That bonus sheet provided the framework for payments throughout the season. Now, as Swindon had not been very successful in the period before my arrival, bonus schemes had not demanded that much attention. The team wasn't winning so players didn't get bonuses. Things started to change when we began to draw big names in the cup competitions and beat them. The club was generating more money as a result of the bigger crowds but the players were still governed by the bonus sheet put in at the start of the season, which took no account of who you beat. Whether it be Torquay or Mansfield in the League or Chelsea or Sheffield Wednesday in a cup competition, it was still £15 for a win.

Unsurprisingly it wasn't long before a deputation of players led by the captain, Colin Calderwood, came knocking at my door. After a victory or two in front of five-figure crowds they worked out how much extra revenue they had generated for the club. They were of the opinion that the bonus was not fair, that the rules were restrictive. They asked me to speak to the chairman, which did not seem unreasonable to me. Why shouldn't a club be able to reward its employees (within reason) for improved performance? I approached Brian Hillier and the club agreed payments of an extra £30 or £40 per man. That kept them happy. And when you are bombing along on all fronts a club needs to keep its players happy. They were not getting massive signing-on fees or huge wages. We were making them play for every penny they earned, and getting maximum returns. The problem was, those extra payments were handed over in cash. They could not go through the books because of the restrictive nature of that ridiculous bonus sheet. They had to be given as perks.

The first match concerned was a Simod Cup match at Blackburn in November 1987. I was approached by Colin Calderwood before the game, and he informed me that there was no Simod Cup bonus on the bonus sheet. I immediately mentioned Colin's concerns to the board members who had travelled with us to Blackburn. They held a board meeting on the coach and agreed that the players could have a proportion of the gate money and that is how it all started. A few years later the issue came to the surface. My interest was only in the players, doing right by them. How the club managed that was not my problem. I had no interest in accounting, in how the books were presented, in that side of club affairs. By the time the club went to court a year after my departure, the Inland Revenue presented the case in a way I thought was completely distorting the picture. The figures were hugely inflated. It was all hype. Swindon were used as whipping boys. The real targets for the Revenue were the big clubs, through which millions of pounds were passing each year.

And it was not only bonus payments that the League did not like. There were other trivial practices that offended. When we were trying to bring Steve Foley to the club from Yorkshire, he wanted to sign but the high cost of property in the south became a stumbling block, even though we were paying him an extra £20 a week. To get around the problem he asked for his signing-on fee to be paid up front so that he could put a deposit down on a house (standard practice was to pay signing-on fees over the terms of a contract). We were only talking £12,000, so instead of paying him £4,000 a year over three years, the club paid in full. That was against the rules apparently. It became a big issue when the shit hit the fan. But we could not have attracted a player like Steve from Sheffield United to Swindon without offering him some sort of deal. In my view we did nothing wrong. We were simply trying to improve the standing of Swindon Town. Today it would not be an issue. Sadly, that was not the case back then.

It took a couple of years for this to surface. I had left the club by then, but it would still have a profound effect on my management career. At the time I was just happy to have sorted out the situation to the players' satisfaction. They paid me back with another promotion push in 1988–89 after a year of consolidation in Division Two. I brought in Duncan Shearer from Huddersfield to play up front with Steve White. Together they scored bundles of goals and we made the play-offs with a fantastic late run that saw us lose just two of our last nineteen games.

Crystal Palace stood in the way of progress to the top flight of English football. And this was the Palace of Wright and Bright – all pace and power. We battered them at Swindon, but won only 1–0, and that was an own goal scored by Jeff Hopkins. I had a feeling it might not be enough. It was just one of those games. We had a goal disallowed and should have won by two or three. We paid the price at Selhurst Park, where Wright and Bright caused all the problems. The 2–0 loss was a huge disappointment, and it turned out to be my last game in charge of Swindon.

At the end of the previous season Chelsea had come in for me. Ken Bates made contact and invited me over to his house.

We spent an hour in conversation. I liked what he had to say. We were not talking José Mourinho money, but it was a welcome step up and I agreed to take the job. I left believing I was the next Chelsea manager. The next day I got a call from Ken. He said he would like me to take Bobby Campbell as my number two. The night before I'd had no knowledge of Bobby Campbell being part of the scheme of things. I didn't even know Bobby. Ken Bates does things his way. He wasn't asking me to take Bobby on, he was telling me. 'Sorry, Ken,' I said, 'if those are the terms I don't think I'll be taking the job.' I can't really explain why I took that stance. I had no reason to doubt Bobby; I had no particular objection to him. I just felt a little uncomfortable having a major condition like that sprung on me at the last minute. Looking back, I probably acted too hastily. I should have taken the job. But at the time I was a young manager on the up. I felt another opportunity would come along.

Sure enough, twelve months later one did. This time I did not make the same error. I agreed to go to West Ham on my own, working with the existing staff. Little did I know that my world was about to turn upside down.

There was no real opportunity to say goodbye to the staff or the players at Swindon. People come and go in football. I was along the road to my next appointment. Ossie Ardiles followed me into the County Ground – a terrific signing for the club. The fans had a new name to cheer.

Swindon will always have a place in my heart. Like a first girlfriend, you never forget your first club as a player or as a manager. Brian Hillier took a chance with me. I believe I served the club well. I'm proud of my achievements there.

The text that follows appeared in a pre-season pull-out in

the *Swindon Advertiser* before our first campaign in Division Two. It was written by Clive King, a local journalist and friend who died way before his time. I include it only because it gives a flavour of the atmosphere during my time at the club, and because Clive sums me up as a person well enough. And it is true what he says about the phones. I would answer them right enough. If it started raining, people would ring up and ask if the game was still on. Yes, it's definitely on. No problem. Thank you. They never knew they were talking to the manager. The beautiful game . . .

To go from the Fourth Division to the Second in successive seasons is a tremendous feat for all concerned. It has also got the Town fans wondering if the fairytale can continue. First Division next stop? Who knows? I would not bet against it while Macari is still at the County Ground. All we have to do is get off to a bad start as we have in the past two seasons . . . It is hard to remember just how dismal things had got until the emergence of Macari. Ask him what his recipe for success has been and he tells you a good appetite for the game and fitness. Just as he does not suffer fools off the pitch he does not tolerate players who are not totally committed. Everything has to take second place to football. He is a total professional. It's as simple as that. Do not run away with the idea that he is any boring workaholic. Far from it. He has an impish sense of humour and loves nothing better than sending people up, especially ageing journalists.

The only time he had to admit defeat was when he had a confrontation with the family Labrador called Rocky. The dog had a passion for socks, Macari's socks, and he can sniff out Lou's from anything up to 30 other pairs in the dressing room. Unfortunately for Lou, he takes the socks and buries them somewhere in the County Ground. The Town manager has at least three or four odd socks in his room at any one time. He keeps them just in case Rocky decides to dig up any of his buried treasure.

That apart, Lou is fully at home at the County Ground. As the fans have grown to love him he has become attached to them and the club. It is nothing to hear his voice at the end of the phone if you are at the County Ground. He often helps out answering phones, or in the secretary's office, the ticket office, the treatment room. He wears the first kit that comes to hand for training. It is quite common to see him running round with Andy Rowland's top on, John Trollope's shorts and of course any kind of socks Rocky may have left him.

He is in short a free spirit, and there is nothing he hates more than to be tied down. Fortunately the board at the County Ground have grown to understand this, and that is not easy for some directors who like a place for everything and everything in its place. Since his sacking and reinstatement two years ago they have given him a free hand. They don't tie him down to attending board meetings or want to know what players he is currently watching or wanting to buy. They are interested, naturally, but know he will tell them in good time. Life at the County Ground is fantastic, a very pleasant place to go. That is due mainly to one person.

Bobby Moore watches from the floor as I celebrate my first goal for Manchester United on my debut against West Ham at Old Trafford, January 1973.

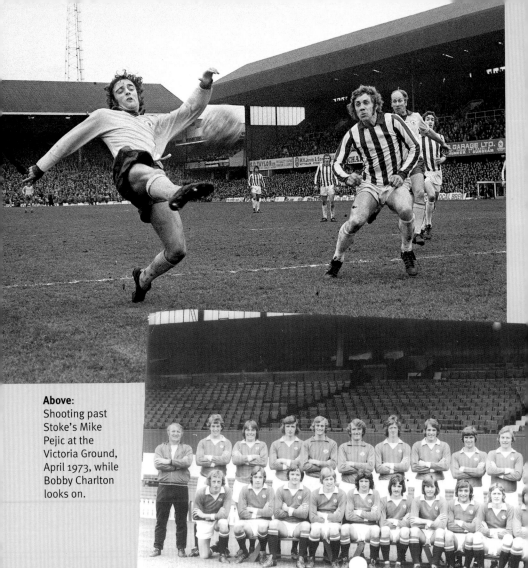

Above: Shooting past Stoke's Mike Pejic at the Victoria Ground, April 1973, while Bobby Charlton looks on.

Above: Manchester United team photo (I'm seated third from right).

Left: Receiving an award from Sir Matt Busby.

Take that, and that. Watching my first go in **(main picture)** against Carlisle and hooking in the second, United's fourth (**inset**).

Above: On the couch – starring in a football quiz show with (*from left*) the Saint, Andy King, me, Tommy Smith and Mick Channon.

Above: Young guns at the 1974 office Christmas party. Only the players were loaded! (*From left*) Sammy McIlroy, Willie Morgan, Stuart Pearson, Gerry Daly and me.

Left: Celebrating the Division Two Championship in April 1975 after the 4–0 win over Blackpool. (*Left to right*) Alex Forsyth, Stuart Houston, Brian Greenhoff, Pearson, Steve Coppell, me, Steve James.

Below: Celebrating one of my two goals against Wolves at Molineux on the opening day of the 1975–76 season.

Left: The 1977 FA Cup winners: (*back row, left to right*) J Greenhoff, McIlroy, B Greenhoff, Stepney, Nicholl, McCreery (sub); (*front row, left to right*) me, Pearson, Buchan, Hill, Albiston, Coppell.

Above: Celebrating Jimmy Greenhoff's winner in the semi-final against Leeds.

Below: The two goalscorers. Stuart Pearson and me with the Doc, following the final against Liverpool.

That goal. Watching it go in (**inset**). Leaping into Gordon Hill's arms.

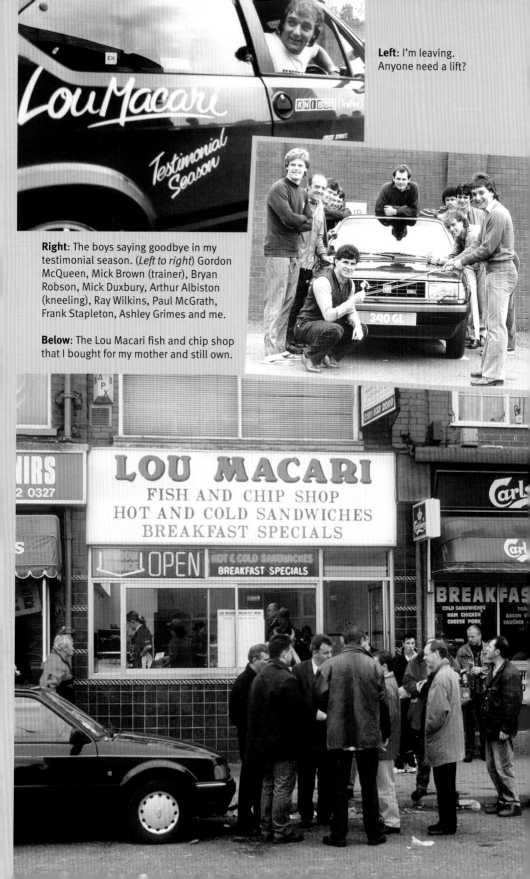

Left: I'm leaving. Anyone need a lift?

Right: The boys saying goodbye in my testimonial season. (*Left to right*) Gordon McQueen, Mick Brown (trainer), Bryan Robson, Mick Duxbury, Arthur Albiston (kneeling), Ray Wilkins, Paul McGrath, Frank Stapleton, Ashley Grimes and me.

Below: The Lou Macari fish and chip shop that I bought for my mother and still own.

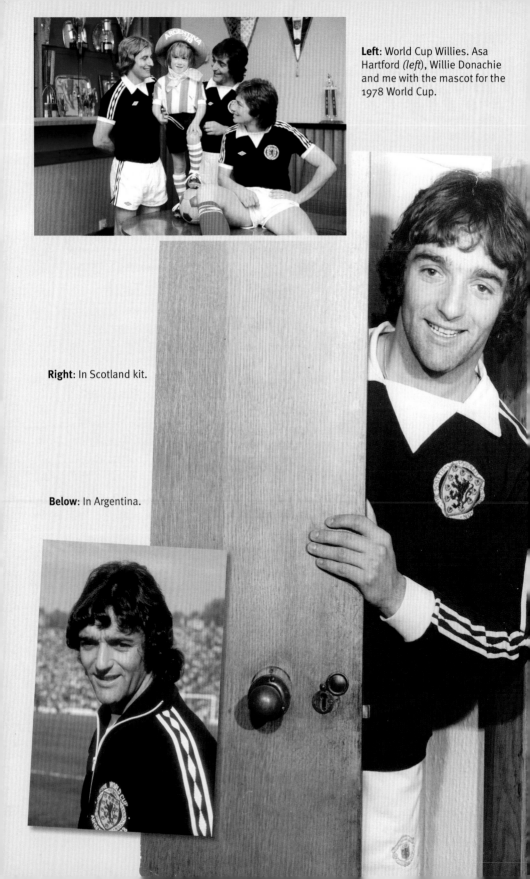

Left: World Cup Willies. Asa Hartford (*left*), Willie Donachie and me with the mascot for the 1978 World Cup.

Right: In Scotland kit.

Below: In Argentina.

16

LONDON CALLING

I DIDN'T KNOW MUCH ABOUT PAUL INCE BEFORE I WALKED through the doors at Upton Park, but it did not take long to get acquainted. Within a week of my arrival I was told he was off to Manchester United. Not only that, I was threatened by his agent, Ambrose Mendy. Agents were still in their infancy in the late eighties. I couldn't remember having dealt with one before. Let's just say Mendy was a bit of a lad.

'I think it would be in your interests if you did not stand in his way,' he said. 'If you do, it could be a problem for you.'

I may have misunderstood the message, but it seemed menacing enough to me. What else could he have meant? I wasn't going to take any chances. I knew someone who moved in the same boxing circles as Mendy. I asked him to have a little word. I wanted him to understand that as far as I was concerned Paul Ince was going nowhere. It was not the greatest of starts. I had just arrived. I was desperate to establish myself in my new surroundings, and before I had hung my coat behind the door I had someone trying to take one of my best young players away, saying there was nothing I could do to stop it. I wasn't having that.

Matters quickly came to a head. The players arrived at the ground ready to leave for a pre-season tour of Norway. Ince did not turn up. OK, fine. We went without him. While we were away I got a call from one of the press lads covering our tour. 'Got a minute?' he said. 'I think you had better come down to reception and have a look at this.' I went down to find Ince pictured in the newspapers with a Manchester United shirt on. No one from United had been in touch with me. And I had no intention of speaking to Sir Alex.

Now I had a problem. I was determined not to let Ince leave. No matter what Mendy said, I was ready to dig my heels in. Quite apart from anything else, I knew the fans were not going to stand for any of that crap. The West Ham support is fiercely loyal. They saw it as a betrayal. I couldn't disagree with them. The moment I got back I was in with the chairman and other board members to see what could be done. But that picture changed everything. United had already been in touch. There was a £2 million bid on the table. The fee was agreed, and Ince went up to Manchester for the medical. He failed it. The staff at West Ham were amazed. There had never been a problem with him at Upton Park. Sir Alex then started talking about a restructured deal conditional on appearances. West Ham settled for £1 million up front with the rest payable over a certain term. Ince was gone.

The club still had some top players, lads like Liam Brady, Frank McAvennie, Alan Devonshire, Julian Dicks, Alvin Martin, Tony Gale, Phil Parkes and Mark Ward, but something was obviously not right at the club. West Ham had been relegated from the old First Division the season before, 1988–89. John Lyall paid for that with his job. He had been the longest-serving manager in the Football League until that point, with two FA Cup wins to his name, including the victory over Arsenal in 1980 courtesy of Trevor Brooking's goal. As recently as 1986 he had taken West Ham to third in the First Division. He was some act to follow, and what nobody wants to be doing in such situations is selling their best players. I didn't rush to judge anybody, and I canvassed opinion widely. When you arrive at a club, everybody's views are worthwhile. As the days ticked by I felt the problem was a lack of discipline, a lack of respect for the staff. And now my best young player was up the road.

A week or so later I got a call from Terry Venables, the manager of Tottenham Hotspur. He wanted to buy Julian Dicks. Interestingly, before I joined West Ham I had been on holiday in Spain. I bumped into Terry over there and was in his company for a few days. We got on really well. He obviously felt comfortable enough with me to pick up the phone and try to do some business. 'Do me a favour, Terry,' I said, 'the last thing I want to hear is you, or anybody else for that matter, coming in for Julian Dicks.' But Terry was desperate for him. And he was persistent. Over the length of the negotiation he doubled his bid every time we spoke. It started off at a million and ended up at name your price. As far as I'm aware, Dicks never knew about Tottenham's interest. I never told him. There was no way I was going to let him follow Ince out of the door. He could have knocked my office door down and it would not have made any difference. I felt I had to take a stance. The new kid on the block, getting treated like a mug, people running right over the top of you. That wasn't going to happen to me. I'd been stuffed once. Besides, if I was going to get the club back into the First Division I needed players like Dicks in my side, not Tottenham's.

Terry had seen a lot more of Dicks than I had. I felt from what I had seen that I was looking at a top player. In a way, Terry's bid reassured me that I was right. Sure enough, Dicks turned out to be a brilliant player. What stopped his brilliance shining through as much as it should have done was his aggression. He was too confrontational, particularly with referees. People thought Julian was a nutter. He wasn't. He was a nice lad. But for some reason he developed this reputation for being the hard man. He felt he had to take this identity with him on to the pitch every game. It took the emphasis away from his qualities as a footballer. He had excellent technique, a great left foot and a thunderous shot. Sadly for him, that was not the first thing people saw. I believe that hurt his England prospects badly. It was a great shame that a talent like his was not taken to the international stage. Even today he is remembered as a rough, tough lad always involved in skirmishes.

He was the same in the gym. He used to like kicking me. To be fair to Julian, he was indiscriminate, but I do think he took a particular delight in taking me on. I used to make sure I was on the opposite side. I was strong enough to go in there and compete against him. I saw it as a little challenge every day. He used to take great delight in tackling me against the wall. He liked to pin me against it and sort of squash me into it. I enjoyed it. It was part of the banter, a talking point afterwards, who kicked who. Stewart Robson was another who was very competitive, and Leroy Rosenior, a good pro. Sadly, both were injured for the majority of the time I was there.

We managed to get Robson fit for a League Cup tie at Derby in January 1990. We more or less threw him out on the pitch. We were so short of numbers I feared we were going to get a tonking. We drew before going on to win the replay, and Robson played like a man possessed. You could not tell he had been out for months. His fitness level was incredible, which was not necessarily the standard at the club. When I signed Ludek Miklosko from Banik Ostrava he was twenty yards in front of everybody in his first training session, and goalkeepers are notorious for trailing off at training. All you could hear was the lads in the chasing pack shouting, 'Get back here, you Czech bastard!' If I could have put out Robson and Rosenior in every match, West Ham might have gone straight back up. Then again, if that had been the case they might not have come down in the first place, and I might never have crossed the threshold at Upton Park. Ifs and buts.

The difference with Robson and Rosenior was this: being hard was not part of their identity. For Julian Dicks it was an issue. I tried to get it out of his game. It is enough just to be tough. Paul Reaney was tough at Leeds, but only in the line of duty. He did not feel the need to demonstrate how hard he was for the sake of it. Julian was too skilful a player for all that nonsense. There were plenty of occasions when I had to speak to him about diving in. I tried to calm him down so that he could concentrate on doing what he was exceptionally good at, playing football. He had everything you could want in a full-back. In fact he was better than that: quick, strong, with a great touch, a beautiful passer of the ball and a dead-ball expert. Whenever we got a penalty, I used to close my eyes – not for fear of Dicks missing, just to mentally clock the goal. He never missed. Dicks was the best left-back I ever had.

A few years later, when Terry Venables was manager of England, he sent Ray Clemence along to sound out Julian about playing for the national side. It was too late. Julian was angry at being overlooked for so long. He told Ray he could shove his England caps up his arse. Then a knee injury cut his career short. He took up golf and became good enough to turn professional. That's how good a sportsman Julian Dicks was. An exceptional talent, and misunderstood. He will look back on his career knowing he should have played for England. After reading this, he'll also be thinking he should have played for Spurs. Sorry, Julian. You were just too good.

Injuries were a blight at the club. They were also a delicate issue. It is hard to tell a player he might not be injured when he insists that he is. I had not encountered this phenomenon before. My players at Swindon were too embarrassed to admit to injuries. On the first day of the 1989–90 season I found myself wheeling Frank McAvennie into Stoke Royal Infirmary with a broken leg. I'd advised Frank long before that with the talent he had, if he could just add fitness to it he would be a real problem to teams every week. 'Without it,' I'd say, 'you'll end up getting injured.' I'd been on to him about this for several weeks since arriving at the club. But Frank was a talented player. He had done well at West Ham. He didn't want to hear about the fitness side of the game. In pre-season he did not train exceptionally hard. In fact he was last at most of the physical stuff. But he had a burst of speed when the urge took him, and an eye for goal. He was clever in the box, and that was getting him through. Or so he thought.

I was always mindful of my Celtic days when talking to Frank. I'd say to him, 'Your career won't be a long one, Frank, if you don't look after yourself, don't work hard, don't train hard.' He got fed up hearing me say this. Then, late in that game at Stoke, he went into a tackle with Chris Kamara. That was the last time I was able to pick Frank as West Ham manager. A great shame for him, me and the club. I'd had Chris at Swindon. It wasn't a nasty challenge, it was accidental. It wouldn't have happened if Frank had been super-duper fit – he'd have skipped away from Chris. Football would be great if you didn't have to train, but you do.

Frank's situation seemed symptomatic of the state of the club. The busiest person at West Ham was the physio, which was not good. Phil Parkes could not train at all because of a knee injury. I felt sorry for him. I used to watch him in matches thinking, 'Bloody hell, if he'd been training all week he would be some keeper.' He was a big, big presence in goal. No matter how good a keeper you are, if all you can do between games is sit on a bike, your days are numbered.

The problem with Parkes came to a head in the middle of February during the semi-final of the League Cup. We had conquered all before us at Upton Park, seeing off the likes of Aston Villa and Wimbledon. We drew Oldham in the semis, who at the time were flying. They had a plastic pitch, and the first leg was at Boundary Park. Phil on the astroturf was a disaster. He couldn't move. I'd had personal experience of this. Once, when I was touring with United, I picked up a niggling knee injury in Canada against Vancouver White Caps. We moved on to Dallas, where the Tornados played on an astroturf pitch. We had never seen astroturf before. I couldn't run on it with the bad knee, so I fully understood Phil's difficulties at Oldham. The ball bounces a lot higher. You have to be agile to cope. It was one game too many for Phil. He was too good a keeper to be picking the ball out of the net six times. There is a hospital that runs the length of Sheepfoot Lane right behind Boundary Park. Phil must have felt like limping straight into casualty. As a matter of fact, so did I.

Phil's knees led to the arrival of Miklosko, who turned out to be a great signing. I was in a hurry to bring a keeper to the club. On loan, Perry Suckling was Phil's deputy, and Allen McKnight was still at the club. He'd had a nightmare during the relegation season. Whenever he was named in the team the crowd was on to him straight away. That made it difficult to select him.

We paid Banik Ostrava three hundred grand for Ludek. The deal had been done prior to the 6–0 defeat at Oldham but we did not get the work permit through in time for Ludek to play. He was recommended to me. I only saw him once. Six foot two, built like a brick shithouse, he ran the game from his goalmouth. Ludek became a massive favourite with the supporters. He was easy to like. His work permit actually came through while I was with him at the Hilton Hotel in Prague. He was jumping up and down, kissing me. There was a lot hanging on it for him. Once the permit came through he was literally a free man. This was before the break-up of the Soviet Union, remember. Czechoslovakia was still one entity, a socialist state. Ludek was not permitted to leave the country until his work permit from Britain came through. I went out there knowing that a decision was due that day. It was not a foregone conclusion. We were hoping for the best. When we got it, the news changed his life. He deserved everything he got out of the game. After training the first day back in England he came up to me and asked what time he had to be back in the afternoon. That's the way it was in the Eastern bloc. He was stunned when I told him he was done for the day. Off he went back to the hotel at Waltham Abbey. Ludek is still at West Ham, eighteen years on, as goalkeeping coach.

Martin Allen was another I brought in. With Robson injured, I needed a warrior in midfield, someone with a bit of steel. Send for the Mad Dog. But there was nothing mad about Martin. I got him from QPR. He used to put himself about, which made him popular on the Chicken Run, where they appreciate a player who spills blood for the shirt. It was good to have a fit bloke to pick. Alan Devonshire, a cracking player at his peak, was constantly on the treatment table. Liam Brady was in the twilight of his career. He wasn't finished, but he was finding the going tough at times. Week after week I prayed for enough fit players to get a result.

With Frank McAvennie injured, I promoted Stuart Slater from the youth ranks. He did exceptionally well for us up front – a breath of fresh air ready to have a real go. We then added Ian Bishop and Trevor Morley in exchange for Mark Ward, who wanted away. That was one of those coincidences you sometimes get in football. Twenty-four hours after Ward told me he wanted to leave the club I had Manchester City manager Howard Kendall on the phone. He was after a right-sided player. I mentioned Ward's name and before I knew it I had two players coming in plus a million quid. Not a bad return. Bishop was a good footballer, Morley worked his socks off. They were quickly accepted by the fans, which is half the battle.

I was also having a look at Justin Fashanu. He was a nice lad. I wanted to give him a chance to resurrect his career. Justin was Britain's first million-pound black footballer when he joined Nottingham Forest in 1981. Since then he'd lost his way a bit. He hadn't come out of the closet at this stage, so clearly he had to be a bit careful about his private life. I returned to the hotel where I was staying one night and asked the receptionist if Mr Fashanu was back. He had come back but had gone out again. A car had picked him up and taken him to a nightclub in the West End, the Embassy, which is still a favourite among footballers in London. I wasn't happy with that. When he got back I had a word. 'Justin,' I said, 'if you are trying to get back on your feet in this game, forget about nightclubs.' In fairness to him, he wasn't a drinker. He was polite and apologetic. He said he was bored and just wanted something to do. It must have been hard for Justin. At the time he obviously felt he could not declare his hand at a football club and survive.

We picked Justin up from Manchester City, where he'd been since October 1989 after a period out in the States. I took him on in November. Justin was with us for about three months. In that time he played only a couple of games before moving on to the Orient. I was not convinced of his commitment. I know a Waltham Abbey hotel is not the centre of the universe, but I was a bit dismayed to learn of trips to central London to pass the time. It was not the best start for a bloke supposedly trying to restart his career. If I were fighting for mine I would put off London for a few weeks until I got myself established. He eventually left West Ham after me, in March 1990. Later that year he became the first high-profile player in English football to admit to being gay. A brave move. Eight years later he was dead after taking his own life.

By the time Justin arrived at the club I was beginning to stamp my personality on the job. I was about to move into a house in Loughton in Essex and felt like I was making progress, starting to establish myself. I'd encountered a different work ethic at West Ham from the one I'd left at Swindon, and a different atmosphere. The team had just been relegated. I had to cope with the loss of key players, either to injury or transfer. I had a big job on my hands. I couldn't dash straight into the transfer market to freshen things up, I had to keep things ticking over and try to work mostly with what I had. My knowledge of lower-division players was not of great value anyway. At West Ham a manager had to aim higher. The problem with that was the cost of bringing players in. A lot of them were already earning good money, around two grand a week. Wages were a major issue. Injured players still had to be paid even though they were not available for selection. That cost a lot of money, diminishing the potential to dip into the transfer market. So my aim was to get the club's existing players fit. If I could get Robson, Rosenior and Devonshire in my starting line-up they would be great assets. We'd probably go straight back up. The problem was, as time went on that wasn't happening.

What was happening was that I began to get a real feel for the place. West Ham is a homely club, right up my street in so many ways. By the time I left I had grown to love it. The support was unbelievable. The staff made me feel welcome. I was only the second manager to be appointed from outside the club fold since its inception in 1902. The other was Ron Greenwood, who joined from Arsenal in 1961. I was immensely proud of that. West Ham has its own identity. It has already made a real contribution to the English game, and has the potential to become even more influential. Like Newcastle, it has an amazing and extremely loyal fan base, though the club would probably have to extend Upton Park to fully tap into that. If it does, watch out Arsenal, Chelsea and Tottenham.

17

HAMMERED

WEST HAM WERE NOT EXACTLY SETTING THE SECOND DIVISION alight in 1989–90, but I was delighted to reach the semi-finals of the League Cup. I felt that given time I could turn a cup run into a championship challenge and promotion. The club owners were fantastic with me, very patient. The board was incredibly supportive. What could possibly go wrong?

I don't recall the exact date – early January some time. At first I didn't pay that much attention. I knew the stories were rubbish. But in the end I couldn't ignore them. A newspaper had got its teeth into my old club, Swindon. First of all it ran a story about the Swindon chairman Brian Hillier betting on the team to lose in a fourth-round FA Cup tie at Newcastle in 1988. It followed that up with more about illegal payments to players. The football authorities did not handle the allegations well in my view. The response to the sensationalist claims made by the newspaper was disproportionate and ultimately brought about the end of my reign at West Ham.

Let me give you the background. First the Newcastle issue. The newspaper presented this as a huge scandal, an attempt by the club to influence events so as to make a killing at the bookies. In effect, match fixing. It was nothing of the sort. This is what really happened.

I had established the habit at Swindon of taking the team away for a few days before big games. This involved using army camps, which were cheap and out of the way. The army did us a favour. The going rate was £6 per day per head, full board – your lodgings and all you could eat. This would allow us to stay for three or four days. We'd do this all over the country, staying at different camps. I'm not saying the players looked forward to it. They didn't have a choice. I wanted them out of the way, getting plenty of rest and a good night's sleep. In my view, proper preparation meant a better chance of winning those big games. This was the mentality of Celtic and United too: get away and prepare.

For the Newcastle game in question, I tried Catterick barracks. For some security reason they couldn't take us in. In the end we had to settle for a three-day hotel stay. Brian asked me to cost it and report back to the board. It was the Gosforth Park Hotel. The price was about £100 a scalp for the three days; all told it was going to cost nearly £4,000. The board weren't that keen on it. One of the board members worked for the insurance company that sponsored the team, Lowndes Lambert. The chairman asked him if the company would insure the club for that £4,000. Every penny was a prisoner at Swindon. Insuring the club in the event we got knocked out of the FA Cup seemed like good business. The board member promised to come back with a figure.

For whatever reason, that didn't happen. The game was by

this stage upon us, so we went to Newcastle and checked into the hotel without the insurance in place. Brian decided to cover himself with a wager at Ladbrokes. Obviously he didn't want Swindon to get knocked out of the FA Cup – there was real money to be earned from a run in the competition – all he was interested in was covering himself so that he got the expenses money back if we lost. It was a no-lose situation. In the event we were hammered, which is what most people expected. The chairman picked up his cheque from Ladbrokes and banked it. There was no question of us deliberately losing the game. There was more money to be had from a win. Besides, had the chairman been acting in a sinister manner as part of a betting ring, he would hardly be accepting a cheque and putting it in the bank. He'd want to hide that kind of activity. But there was nothing to hide because it was an innocent bet.

The journalist who reported the story was acting on a tip-off from within the club. There was a so-called consortium in Swindon desperate to get rid of Brian Hillier and take over the club. Some members of the consortium were on the board. They had a vested interest in forcing Brian out. The newspaper denied it was a board member who provided the information, but I believe the tip-off was politically motivated. The reporter screamed scandal, and everyone fell for it. He gave the impression that this was not an isolated incident, it was a deep-seated problem at the club, and many games were involved. Bunkum.

To add weight to his theory, he interviewed the players about the Newcastle match. He got hold of Colin Calderwood. 'What did you have for your pre-match meal? And what do you normally have?' Colin replied that at the army camp the players normally ate scrambled eggs and toast. That then got compared to the spaghetti Bolognese and steak and chips they'd had at the hotel. It was presented in a way that suggested the players had been stuffed with heavy food in order to compromise their efforts on the pitch, to slow them down. 'Did you feel different on the night, Colin?' 'Well, you'd have to say after getting beaten 5–0 I felt a lot different on the night.' He then moved on to another player, and asked the same questions. What did you have? Steak and chips? How many chips did you have? And so on. Utter bollocks. More stories followed, relating to the payments to players. The sums were pathetic anyway – an extra £20 a player, or whatever it was. It didn't feel like criminal activity to me. Not, as I said, that I had any involvement in how the club presented the payments or otherwise on the balance sheet. I was the manager, not the accountant. I was just concerned with doing right by my players. And believe me, they deserved every penny they earned, and more.

What happened next took the informant by surprise. He'd hoped the matter would stop with the FA; that way he could exert some influence, control events to a degree. He just wanted Hillier out of the club while at the same time distancing himself and other board members from the actions of the chairman. That way they could keep the reputation of the club lily-white. The board were victims of an errant chairman, so to speak. But as I understand it Graham Kelly, the FA chief executive at the time, passed the matter on to the Football League. That's when things began to spiral out of control for everybody at Swindon. The plot went badly wrong. The Football League had to act on it.

My initial response when the first story broke about the

betting incident was incredulity. I could have done without it, but I knew the circumstances behind it. There was nothing in it as far as I was concerned. It was not a problem for the owners at West Ham. I discussed it with them, of course. I mentioned that I might need a bit of help from the club lawyer to handle the situation. 'Whatever support you need, Lou, you've got it.' These were London people, sharp cookies, not tittle-tattle merchants whispering in the ears of journalists.

As a club, West Ham liked to keep a relatively low profile. There was never any scandal. The only news that came out of West Ham was about football. I was mindful of that tradition. I could handle the betting issue because it was so ridiculous, so wide of the mark. But as January wore on, the newspaper continued to publish stories. It was a big deal for them. Newspapers like nothing better than a big exclusive. It gives them a unique selling point. The journalist is gaining brownie points by the bucketload with his bosses, and the paper has a money-spinning headline. It was becoming tiresome having to read this bilge week after week. It was all very puzzling to me. Not only were the sums pathetically small, Swindon were not the only club that paid their players in this way. There were far bigger fish in the sea, distributing much larger sums.

In this heightened emotional state, I offered my resignation to West Ham. I should not have done it. West Ham were not looking for a way out of our association. Tom Finn, the club secretary, advised me that I had no need to act. 'Don't be daft, it's not a resigning matter.' I can see that now, but in the heat of the crisis I felt it was becoming a bit of an embarrassment to the club. There were all sorts of documents appearing in the papers detailing payments and signing-on fees. If you believed what you read in the newspapers you'd have thought they had a bigger story than Watergate on their hands. They offered one reality, but not one that I recognized.

I just wasn't able to put all the pieces of the jigsaw together as I am now. I let the heat of the moment sway my thinking. So I was gunning for people. I couldn't concentrate on anything else. It became all-consuming.

I wish I had acted differently though. Leaving West Ham is the biggest regret of my managerial career.

18

A KNOCK AT THE DOOR

WHEN I WALKED OUT THE DOOR AT UPTON PARK I WAS ANGRY. I didn't have a plan. At that point there was no legal case to answer. I just needed to clear my head. I went home to Loughton and stewed for a few days. The newspaper moved on to their next victim. They had got their story and were not interested in me any more.

Eventually I came up for air and started to get out and about again. Towards the end of that 1989–90 season I agreed to take part in a Granada TV sports programme in Manchester, looking at the week's football events. It finished about one in the morning. I returned to the hotel afterwards and eventually got to sleep at about two.

I had booked myself on the 7.45 a.m. train to Watford. At about seven there was a knock on my hotel door. I was startled. When you are late to your bed the night before every minute is precious. I was trying to get as much sleep as I could before leaving to catch my train. I went to the door, but before opening it I looked through the little peephole. I saw three people on the other side.

'What do you want?'

The fella said he was from the hotel and he had two policemen with him who wanted to speak to me. I looked through the peephole again. The supposed policemen were dressed in T-shirts. They didn't look like any policemen I had ever seen. I wondered what was going on. I wasn't sure if it was a wind-up by some of my Manchester pals or whether someone was wanting to knock my head off for some reason. All these things were running through my mind.

I told them there was no way I was opening the door, so the fella said, 'Mr Macari, you have to open the door. These gentlemen have been sent to have a chat with you.'

Oh right.

'Show me your ID,' I said.

They stuck this thing up at the peephole. It looked like a badge but I wasn't convinced. I opened the door anyway.

Why does this stuff never happen at ten in the morning? It's a bit like the Harry Redknapp carry-on, people surrounding his house. They could have knocked on his front door at a civilized hour and asked to have a word with him about the transfers, or whatever. But they don't. They like to dramatize these things.

'Mr Macari,' one of the policemen said, 'we have been sent to pick you up with regard to a fraud.'

I started laughing. Fucking fraud? They didn't share the joke. Now I was starting to get concerned. I didn't have a clue what they were on about. I didn't know about any fraud.

'We just have to take you into Bootle Street Station. We don't know any more about it. We just have to take you in.'

I packed my bag and we left via a fire escape instead of the front door. That worried me even more. Why weren't we going through the front door? We went down the fire escape and out through a side door into an unmarked car. Now I was getting really spooked. I was expecting a police car outside. I don't mind admitting it was a relief when we turned into Bootle Street. At least I knew I was definitely going to the police station.

The station officer was a United supporter. He was very apologetic. 'I just have to book you in, Lou. There is someone coming to pick you up to take you to Bristol.'

'Bristol? Why am I going to Bristol?'

'I don't know,' he said. 'Don't worry, you can just sit there till they get here.'

He showed me to a seat. I was seriously confused now. A few minutes later he came back.

'OK,' he said, 'I'm going to have to put you in a cell. There has been a riot at Strangeways. We are bringing people in off the rooftop.'

So there I was banged up in a cell. I'd only come up to Manchester to appear on a TV show, now I was behind bars. Half an hour later, in they came, the inmates from Strangeways, kicking and screaming, fuck this, fuck that. You could hear the officers wrestling with them. At that point I was grateful to be in the cell. They banged up two blokes in the cell next to mine and they were shouting all sorts of abuse.

A couple of hours later I was let out to be escorted to a car by a policewoman and a fella from the Inland Revenue. They had been at my house in Loughton at six in the morning. The wife told them where I was. In turn she was instructed that she was not allowed to make any contact with me. Such dramatic stuff. So I got in the car and, being a daft ex-footballer, now a daft manager, I asked the guy sitting next to me, the fella from the Revenue, what this was all about. He just sat there mute. He wouldn't talk to me. The copper explained that as soon as he started to speak to me the clock would be ticking. What fucking clock? Apparently, they are allowed to question you only for so many hours. So it was a quiet journey the whole way to Bristol.

We arrived at the nick, and I handed over my wallet and personal belongings at the desk. I was then directed downstairs to the cells. The first thing I noticed was a big blackboard with a few names on it that I recognized: Colin Calderwood, Brian Hillier and the Swindon accountant Vince Farrar. That was the first I knew that all this must be something to do with Swindon. I was directed into a cell, and that was me for the next two days. Locked up, under arrest.

About six or seven hours into this ordeal I noticed Colin Calderwood walking past my cell on his way out of the door. I could not make head nor tail of what was going on. Then it was my turn to be interviewed. It was just me, a couple of police officers and a tape recorder.

'So, the players are getting money?'

'Yes, that's right.'

'Oh, so you know about it?'

'Of course I know about it. They asked me for the money. I spoke to the chairman about it and they got their money. What's the problem?'

This went on for two days. Interviews, questions, answers. I answered everything.

When I look back on the situation it's like I'm watching a movie. Back then I was in the movie, and I didn't know why.

I'm a football manager. Players want the best deal they can get. It's my job to keep them happy as best I can. In those days, managers not agents were the conduit between players and chairmen. As far as I was concerned I had done a good job. The intention was to reward the players, not to defraud the Revenue. Everybody at the club recognized the job the players had done in bringing a level of success to Swindon Town that was unprecedented. Nobody had seen it coming, therefore there was no way the club could commit in the short term to a financial strategy in terms of improved salaries. The payments were effectively a means of giving the players their due retrospectively. It was for the chairman, the club secretary and the accountant, not the manager, to make sure the money being paid was accounted for in the appropriate way.

So there I was in the middle of a criminal inquiry instigated by the Inland Revenue and I could not for the life of me understand why. I know better now. At the trial, which I'll come to later, they opened proceedings by talking about millions of pounds. It was ridiculous. The sum at issue turned out to be £80,000. But it all makes sense now. They were using me as an individual, and using Swindon as a club, to shake up every other club in the country. The Revenue had its eye on the money sloshing around football at the big clubs that was not properly accounted for. In that respect Swindon were a gift to the IR, who took full advantage by making an example of them.

After two days of this I was charged with conspiracy. I had to go from the nick in Bristol to Swindon Magistrates Court. That was a pantomime as well: the car driving you in, the photographers waiting for you – all part of the show. There were four or five hearings. More money spent on lawyers.

After the final hearing the general feeling was that the Revenue would not proceed with the case, spending time and money taking people to court over so little. My solicitor felt there was not a cat in hell's chance of me ending up in court. That turned out not to be the case, but at the time my attitude was 'Great, let's get back to work'.

At the end of the 1989–90 season Swindon finished fourth under my replacement Ossie Ardiles to secure a place in the Second Division play-offs. They beat Blackburn over two legs then met Sunderland in the final at Wembley. A 1–0 win should have seen them into the First Division for the first time, but ten days later the Football League demoted them two divisions for thirty-six breaches of League rules, thirty-five of which were related to payments to players. This was not what the new board had had in mind when they set the ball rolling with the help of the newspaper six months earlier. Of course the club launched an appeal in the High Court but could not afford to follow it through. An FA appeals panel later reduced the demotion to one division, which effectively left them in Division Two.

I might have gone, but I still felt the disappointment and hurt. I had given everything as a manager to help Swindon Town progress. It was a huge blow to me to see some of that work undone. Glenn Hoddle picked up the baton after Ossie moved on and in 1993 finally got Swindon across the line into the top flight of English football – the Premiership, as it now was. It was a proud moment for anybody who had an association with the County Ground. I still check for the club's results now.

19

ST ANDREW'S RESORT AND SPA

BIRMINGHAM IS A MYSTERY TO MANY PEOPLE IN THE GAME. There is a perception that they should have achieved more. Big-city club with an excellent, loyal fan base, yet no honours to speak of, save for the League Cup in 1963. I had a feeling for the place from my playing days. I scored my opening-day hat-trick at St Andrew's in Dave Sexton's first game as United manager. It was a really lively, hostile atmosphere. I liked the idea of that. It struck me as a proper old-style football place.

When I turned up in January 1991 to take over from Dave Mackay there was nothing like the investment the club has seen in recent years from the Gold family and David Sullivan. I was told there was no money to spend, no possibility of bringing any players to the club. I had to go with what I had. It was like being back at Swindon with less money to spend, if you can imagine that. Even staying in a hotel was an expense beyond the pocket of the chairman, Samesh Kumar. I had no contract. The club was paying me £600 a week until the end of the season, so I wasn't going to be paying hotel bills out of my own pocket.

Instead, I bedded down at the St Andrew's Resort and Spa Hotel – also known as the physio's room at the ground. The physio, Pete Henderson, had one treatment table, I had the other. I think Pete was grateful for the company. We got on fine. The only problem was the mail train, or whatever it was, that used to rattle past St Andrew's at six in the morning on its way into New Street Station. It came right past the bloody window. It sounded like it was coming down the players' tunnel. Every morning it was the same, and I'm a light sleeper. 'Pete,' I said, 'I'm not being funny. I can rough it, but I can't stay here.'

My plight became the *cause célèbre* of the Birmingham City match-day programme. Two weeks into my reign a sofa bed arrived at the ground courtesy of a sympathetic fan. It was a top-of-the-range number. I put that in my office and made camp there instead. I'd wake in the morning for my cup of tea and bacon sandwich feeling half refreshed. I could still hear the train, but it was more of a distant rumble. I no longer felt I was living through an earthquake. So that was me for the next three or four months. I kept my clothes in the office and shared the showers in the changing rooms with Pete. It did not bother me in the slightest. I was just happy to be back in work. Nearly a year earlier I'd quit West Ham in error. Now I had another chance to make a mark. The deal was this: prove yourself in the five months until the end of the 1990–91 season and we'll discuss a proper contract in the summer. Fair enough.

I took over at Birmingham just twenty-four hours after the latest adjournment in the Swindon affair. I was content in the knowledge that I had done nothing wrong and that the legal process would come to nothing. That was my intuition based on the advice I was being given by my solicitor. Birmingham City were in the old Third Division – familiar territory to me. I knew from my Swindon experience what was required to make progress. The difference here, of course, was that we were halfway through the season already with no chance of making any significant impact in the League. If I was going to shine it was going to have to be in a cup competition, and the only one available to me was the Leyland DAF Cup.

I was working with the team that got Dave Mackay the sack. As the League season wore on we were up a couple of places, down a couple of places. There was no real meaning to it. For the players, and for me, it was all on the cup. It was only the Leyland DAF, but in the circumstances, for a group of lads playing for their careers at a club under new ownership, it had taken on the importance of the European Cup. The public felt that way too. Birmingham had not been to Wembley for thirty-five years. That's thirty-five years of buying your season ticket without much of a return. After a run like that it doesn't really matter what competition comes along. The issue is, can you get there?

As fate would have it, the team we played in the regional semi-final was Cambridge United, the same team that had thrashed Birmingham 3–0 in the League, the result that saw Dave out the door. I can tell you, I did not enter that fixture full of confidence. But we beat them 3–1, which put us in the area final against Brentford. With twelve minutes of the second leg to go, Simon Sturridge, a good player for me, scored the goal that took us to Wembley.

After the game I was struck by the reaction of the fans. They didn't care about winning or losing at Wembley, it was enough that they were there, that they were contesting a final again. That sentiment did not register with me, though I understood it better when forty-five thousand blue noses bought tickets to the game. The attendance on the day was 58,756, and this against Tranmere, who won the competition the year before.

It is quite scary coming out of the tunnel when three-quarters of the fans in the stadium are yours. It took me back to the FA Cup Final against Southampton when it seemed United supporters outnumbered the opposition by five or six to one. In addition to that, Tranmere were on fire. They were going back to Wembley the following week to meet Bolton in the play-off final. The pressure was on.

Fortunately we got off to a great start. We came in at half-time leading 2–0, with goals from Sturridge and John Gayle. The majority of the stadium was going absolutely bananas. It could have been even better: Dean Peer missed a great chance to put us three up. It was a terrific header, to be fair to Dean, but Eric Nixon made a fantastic save to keep it out. As we came down the tunnel for the second half I wondered if that might prove a turning point. Football does that to you. Even when you are well ahead, you are always aware that at any moment something might go wrong.

Something did go wrong. Twice. Tranmere pegged us back in the second half to two apiece. All I could think about when their second went in was that header. Then John Gayle scored what was probably the greatest goal of his career with six minutes to go. No, forget that 'probably'. It was the greatest goal of his career. Wembley went crazy, mostly with surprise at what they had just witnessed. John was a six-foot-four-inch big lump of a centre-forward. He had a Mike Tyson-type frame but was six inches taller. His fearsome appearance belied a gentle giant, but if you were a centre-half and didn't know him you would be wanting to run a mile if you had any sense. He was the kind of player who as a kid you would look at and hope you weren't marking.

Gayle started his career at Mile Oak Rovers before moving on to Burton Albion and, more famously, Wimbledon as part of the Crazy Gang. Birmingham had paid £175,000 to bring him to St Andrew's the season before. He was the kind of player who had either a blinder or a nightmare. This final just happened to be the former. His first goal was marvellous enough, finishing off a lovely passing move with a rocket from fully thirty yards. I was sitting on the bench when I saw him pull his right leg back and thought, 'Surely he's not going to hit it from there?' I'd never seen him hit a ball thirty yards in any direction before, never mind shoot. He then followed it up with this incredible bicycle kick. It was as if he'd turned Brazilian overnight. Jack Charlton later remarked that Gayle's two goals that day were among the best ever scored at Wembley. Afterwards, in a TV interview, John set another landmark, beating Frank Bruno's record for the number of times he said 'You know what I mean?' in a minute.

Ron Atkinson, who was the manager of Aston Villa at the time, was part of the TV commentary team. He made a point of saying that he'd had no idea John had that kind of ability. Like most people, Ron thought Gayle was good for getting on the end of long balls, knocking people about and not much more. I couldn't have disagreed with that after watching him at close quarters. He never gave any indication he was capable of goals like that. He was like Julian Dicks at West Ham: he liked knocking me about more than scoring goals. His performance became the big joke at the end of the game at

Wembley. 'Hey, Gayley, what have you been taking? You'd better go and get yourself drug-tested.'

Big Ron was impressed enough to put together a bid of £900,000 for the unlikely hero. John went down to his cousin's caravan in Weymouth for a couple of days' rest and recuperation to think about it. While he was there he did his Achilles when he was out running. Negotiations never progressed, though John did say that he could never have crossed the border from St Andrew's to Villa Park anyway. We'll never know.

At the end of the week after the final I asked the lads to report back in before going away on holiday. We had contracts to sort out. This was their chance to make hay. They had been part of a special moment in Birmingham's history, a first trophy for twenty-eight years. Forget about its status. That particular cup run had put money in the bank and given the owners a glimpse of what might be possible. I wanted to tie everything up with the players and sort out my own future so that I could start planning for the next campaign.

We had a decent squad, players like Martin Thomas in goal, Ian Clarkson (now a journalist and who later played for me at Stoke), John Frain, Mark Yates, Vince Overson, Trevor Matthewson, Phil Robinson and Nigel Gleghorn. The big-man-little-man combination of Sturridge and Gayle worked well. Behind them, Gleghorn was dynamic in midfield, even though he lacked a bit of pace. Once I had spelled out the rules and regulations to them, a bit like Fabio Capello putting his stamp on England, there were never any problems with any of the players. It was just them and me, Pete Henderson and Chic Bates, who had been my assistant at Swindon after Harry Gregg. There were no dieticians, masseurs or psychologists.

This was football in the raw, lower-division football existing on a shoestring. We were all in this together. There was a real collective spirit. It was explained to the players that there was no money to throw around. If they were to get a better deal, it would be on the back of results. And they were the only ones who could get them.

After the final, my only thought was tying up the loose ends ahead of the coming season. I was optimistic. The players had been given a civic reception. It was a terrific event, with the lads gathered on the balcony of the Town Hall while below thousands of blue noses gathered to cheer on their heroes. A couple of days later I sat down with the players, about eleven in total, who were at the end of their contracts. At that level of the game a manager has two jobs to do: his best for the club, and his best for the players. It is a tricky balance, but I believed I had a pretty good handle on a player's worth. Most of the boys were earning about £350 a week. We discussed terms and I went back to the chairman with their demands.

I would not have approached Samesh Kumar with anything unreasonable. One player asked for a signing-on fee of £25,000, which he was entitled to do at the beginning of a new deal. I said it was too much. We eventually settled on £15,000. I took that to the chairman and he changed it to £5,000. I thought, 'Bloody hell, I've got trouble here.' I offered a couple of players the same terms as they were already on. The chairman knocked that back. The Wembley achievement was souring rapidly, and I still had my own terms to settle. I felt I had demonstrated what I was capable of, so what he offered me was ridiculous, in the order of half a million pounds for winning the FA Cup, more if I took Birmingham all the way to the First Division Championship. But what I was looking for was a decent wage, a proper contract. We'd just won the Leyland DAF. We were in the Third Division. We weren't about to go up to Old Trafford and knock Manchester United out of the FA Cup. The contract he was offering me was ludicrous. Furthermore, I was expecting something in the region of £25,000 for the Wembley success. I'd done my homework. That was the going rate. The chairman had said he would look after me if I won trophies. We had given them a lottery win, a Klondike moment. I waited until I was out of his office before I looked at the amount on the cheque he had given me – £1,200. I was not happy.

I should have known what was coming. There had been a major row before the cup final over bonuses. I'd had a bellyfull of that at Swindon. At the lower level, when you can't go into the transfer market and you are so reliant on the players you have, you have to pay attention to what the players are saying if you are going to keep them. It said on the Birmingham bonus sheet that for winning the area final and getting to Wembley there was a £1,000 bonus. But when the players went to collect on pay day each had an extra £77 in his wages. The chairman had decided that the £1,000 was between them. It was here-we-go-again time. I had the whole Birmingham team knocking on my office door. At least I was out of bed at the time. It took a fair amount of negotiation on my part to get the chairman to agree to part with £1,000 a man.

I went back into his office with the £1,200 cheque to argue the toss. He put his chequebook in front of me and invited me to write out a cheque for any sum I wanted. I wasn't interested. I can't work like that. It was clear the reward the players and I were expecting after our Leyland DAF win would not be forthcoming. I would now have a bunch of unhappy players on my hands. There was no future in that as far as I could see. As a manager I was relying on those players to put their hands in the fire for me. I couldn't see that happening.

I'm not sure the chairman properly understood the game he was in. The Kumar brothers had a clothing business in Manchester. They were new to football. They thought they could treat the players like commodities, not as people with mortgages to pay. Samesh thought he could wheel and deal like he did in business. I tried to explain to him that it was legitimate to do that only if the players' demands were unrealistic. In truth, Samesh was the one being unrealistic. He was a nice fella, a good fella. I got on well with him, still do to this day. But I could not work with him on that basis.

I was gobsmacked by the turn of events. I wanted it to work for me at Birmingham. I thought I was on my way. And I was, up the road again, after just five months.

20

NO. 1 CAMPBELL ROAD

HARDLY WAS I OUT OF THE CAR PARK AT BIRMINGHAM THAN another bombshell exploded on my doormat: the Inland Revenue case against Swindon would be going to court after all. I was given notice that the following summer I would be judged by a jury of my peers at the Crown Court in Winchester.

I could not believe that it had come to this. We thought the monies involved were far too insignificant. I did the maths myself, and that didn't take long. Despite the notification I still thought it more likely that the case would not go ahead. When I was approached by Stoke a week or so later I had no hesitation in making that point. Stoke were very supportive. As the case would not be heard for a year, I put it to the back of my mind and cracked on.

When I left Birmingham there was no hint of another job, so Stoke came as a very pleasant surprise. Like Birmingham, I had a good feeling about the place. I knew the old Victoria Ground from my days as a player. It was never an easy place to visit. I met the chairman. It was all pretty straightforward. I remained in Division Three, lower-division territory that I knew well. My track record spoke for itself. It was a case of mixing, matching and making do.

Stoke was not quite as bad as Birmingham in terms of cash flow, but there were still no hotels for newcomers. For the first couple of weeks I stayed at Keele University. I had a room in a hall of residence there. Ken Walshaw, who ran the accommodation set-up, was a big Stoke supporter. He sorted me out with a decent pad – en suite, the lot. After that I stayed in a terraced house just fifty yards from the old Victoria Ground, No. 1 Campbell Road. I'll never forget that address. Ask anybody in Stoke, they can all find Campbell Road. It was another no-frills operation. The club owned the house and used to put players up there. I was just one of the lads – head chef in fact. I'd buy the food, of course. I liked to get the steaks on the grill when I had the chance. Footballers were big meat eaters in those days. Those boys in that house were huge, not the frail low-body-fat creatures you see today. This lot could have eaten for England. I also used to cook for the youth team every Friday, baked potatoes and pasta. I liked mixing with the kids. It was a good opportunity to mingle, to get a feel for the players coming through.

Chic Bates and Pete Henderson came with me. I took Vince Overson too, pretty much straight away. I like to build teams from the back, and I like strong, reliable defenders, so Big Vince was perfect. I trained him hard, knocked him into shape, and he was a giant for me. Then, pretty early on, I made my best signing ever in football – Neil Baldwin, aka

Nello the clown. Nello was twenty-five stone if he was an ounce. I met him at a 'meet the manager' evening at the club. For £2 a head the fans got to see you in the flesh and ask a load of questions. Every penny counts in the lower divisions, remember.

'Hey you, I wish you all the best at Stoke,' he said, in a kind of flat nasal accent reminiscent of Brian Clough.

'Thanks very much,' I said. 'What do you do?'

'I'm a circus clown.'

'Oh, really? And what do you do in your act?'

'They throw me off the back of the fire engine.'

'What, every night?'

'Yes.'

Of course I was in stitches at this point. After that Nello would be waiting at the front door of the Victoria Ground on match days. I detected a character in my midst. I decided he was the man for me, and Nello eventually became the kit man. That was a promotion. Before that his role was to make me laugh, and the players.

Nello had a heart of gold. The club did not pay him a penny. He did it all for love, and we loved having him around. His real value was in helping the players relax before games. No chemist ever produced a drug that could reduce stress levels like Nello. I'm convinced that gave us an edge in matches. Nello bonded the group.

One season we started with a pre-season game at Bournemouth. 'Hey Nello, I want you in fancy dress,' I said.

'What do you want me to dress up as?'

'A chicken,' I said.

We went together to get the outfit. It weighed a ton. We put him in it as we got on the bus. He was under strict instructions not to remove any element of the costume, including the massive head, until we returned to the Victoria Ground later that night. It was August. Hot would be an understatement.

We arrived at Bournemouth.

'Gaffer,' he asked, 'can I take this chicken head off?'

'No,' I said, 'you have to keep it on.'

About fifteen minutes before kick-off he said, 'Gaffer, I think I'm going to faint.' 'OK, Nello, you can take the chicken head off.'

The sweat was running down the side of his face like a river. The players fell about. The laughter in the dressing room just a quarter of an hour before the game released the tension. It was an accidental masterstroke on my part. We won, and everybody was happy.

Fast forward to an end-of-season testimonial at Villa Park. I made Nello sub. For him to be on the bench was a dream come true. All day he kept asking me, 'Hey boss, are you going to put me on?'

'No fucking chance, Nello. You are just there to please the punters behind the goal.'

As the game progressed, our fans started chanting 'We want Nello, we want Nello!'

'Neil,' I said, 'do me a favour, the crowd want you, go behind the goals and entertain them.'

Out he went. As he was doing this warm-up routine, all twenty-five stone of him in his full Stoke kit, the crowd started going crazy. I sent him out three or four times. They loved it. 'Fuck it,' I thought, 'I'm going to put him on.' Up came the number fifteen on the electric scoreboard – Neil Baldwin.

He had all the mobility of a container ship. He could barely move. We won a corner kick. I called Vince Overson over.

'Vince, have a word with all the players. Get them to come out of the box and leave Nello in there on his own.' Soon there wasn't a red shirt in the box. The Villa players caught on to what was happening. There was no one marking Nello because he represented absolutely no danger. The ball came over. Nello tried to control it but it just broke away from him. He followed it up. He was going to try a shot at goal. Then one of our players, Tony Kelly, who for some reason was not aware of what was happening, ran on to it and smashed the ball wide of the target. Nello went mad. Villa Park erupted. All I heard from Nello for the remainder of my time at Stoke was about the day at Villa Park when Tony Kelly cocked it up for him.

I could fill a book with Nello anecdotes alone. Though he was the butt of jokes, it was affectionate stuff, not malicious. He understood his role and played it beautifully. We were up at Tranmere once for a night match. At a quarter to seven in the dressing room, Martin Carruthers stripped off. 'See these, they cost me sixty quid,' he said. Martin thought he was a bit of a big-timer, not unusually for a striker. When the teams went out at a quarter past for the warm-up, I said to Nello, 'Here, when the players go out for the kick-off you are going to put on Martin's sixty-quid underpants, right next to your arse.' Before long, the teams were whistled out. 'Right,' I said, 'get those pants on.'

He was a big heavy fella and he tended to sweat a lot. It was a bit of a squeeze, but Nello managed to slide into Martin's silk underpants. 'I tell you what, Neil, put everybody's underpants on,' I said. For an hour and a half that evening Nello had thirteen pairs of underpants on.

We came back into the dressing room having won the game. Carruthers might even have scored the winner that night. The boys were as happy as Larry. The first out of the bath just happened to be Carruthers – first at everything. He went to get his underpants and shouted out, 'Some Scouse bastard has nicked my silk pants!' The staff, who were all in on it, pissed themselves.

'They didn't last long, Martin, those sixty-quid pants of yours,' I said.

One by one the rest of the lads climbed out of the bath, only to find that 'the same fucking bastard' had had theirs too. Their cries echoed around the dressing room. The players genuinely thought some weirdo had been through their things looking for footballers' pants.

I followed Nello into the toilet. We took his tracksuit top and bottoms off to reveal his Stoke strip and the thirteen pairs of pants. The boys clocked him. One by one they started ripping the underwear off him.

'You smelly bastard, Nello, give me back my pants!'

The pants came off a pair at a time, and eventually only Martin's silk boxers were left.

'Fuck me, Nello, I wouldn't get sixty pence for them now.'

Martin hauled him over to the bath and shoved him in. Top drawer.

One more Nello story for the road. We were up at Hartlepool one Saturday – a long old trip from Stoke. It didn't happen too often but on this occasion we were staying in a posh hotel. So I told Nello he had to travel in a dinner suit, bow tie and top hat. We arrived at the hotel, did a bit of training, then went into the restaurant for a meal. The players and staff were all in tracksuits. Nello sat down at the table in the full gear.

A waiter wandered up. 'What's the story with him then?

How come he's in a top hat and you lot are wearing tracksuits?'

'He's special,' I replied. 'Lord Baldwin from Keele.'

The waiters spent the night fussing about Nello. They even gave him a cigar at the end of the meal. Nello was in his element. He was a showman after all. There he was giving it the big one with the cigar. He looked like Oliver Hardy, only Nello was twice as big and twice as funny.

He came down to breakfast the next day in his tracksuit. 'No,' I said, 'you have to wear all the gear to the game.' So Nello became the first kit man to carry the bag in wearing a top hat.

You always get a bit of stick at places like Hartlepool, especially as an ex-Manchester United player, and they are not big grounds. As we made our way to the dugout there was all the usual banter. Then I heard this fella saying, 'What the fuck's that?' It was Nello in top hat and tails lumping the kit bag behind him. The players were cracking up as they made their way to the pitch. Another fine mess I had got him into. I think we won that game too.

Stoke was a fun place to work. Nello became a fixture, as big a part of the club's identity during my time as Stanley Matthews in days gone by. When you are happy in your work, you tend to do better. We had a decent squad of players and I was able to freshen things up with a few additions. Mark Stein was a terrific signing, and another who I plucked from obscurity. I'd first noticed him at a reserve game at Luton when I was still manager at Swindon. Oddly enough, West Ham were the visitors that day. It was a Saturday morning. I'd gone because Ashley Grimes, a big pal of mine, was playing in the Luton reserve side. The conditions were atrocious, the pitch little better than a bog. In among the muck and bullets was a little fella up front for Luton. His big brother, Brian, was a legend at the club. That day Mark looked just as good to me. After the game I handed a twenty-pound note to Ashley. 'Give that to the little kid, would you,' I said. 'It's one of the best performances I've enjoyed for a long, long time, especially from a kid his size, ploughing through the mud.'

A couple of years later I came across him playing for Oxford reserves. My mind went back to that wet morning at Luton. 'Right,' I thought, 'if that kid could do what he did that day, he can do it again, no matter what's happening at Oxford.' I signed him for £90,000.

Normally when you take someone who has not made it at a couple of clubs you are waiting to find out the reason why – suspect temperament, dodgy character, arsehole, whatever. Steino was brilliant. A nice boy, very polite. He had to get a lot, lot fitter though. He took that on board and responded well. He took to the club too, and the supporters took to him. In fact he was the most popular player in my time at Stoke.

The back four were rock solid, all big lads and quick. Ian Cranson was already there, bought for a club record £450,000. Ian was a terrific player. Had he not been plagued by injuries he would have gone on to have a stellar career. Actually, with the injuries he had it was a miracle he ever took to the pitch. Before I arrived he would play two then miss five, come back for three then miss four. His knees were shocking. Sometimes he could barely move in training, but he was a strong character and he wanted to play, and that's half the battle. Lee Sanford was my left-back, brought in under the Alan Ball regime before my arrival for £125,000. I paid £50,000 to bring in Vince Overson and took John Butler on a free from Wigan at right-back. That back four was the platform for the team, and behind them I had Peter Fox in goal.

In midfield I had a lad called Carl Beeston, who I think is the only Stoke player to appear for England Under-21s. He had tremendous ability. Like Cranson, though, he was susceptible to injury. I took the view that if I could get him fit then I would have a real midfielder on my hands. His stamina was astonishing. Sadly I never quite overcame the injury issue with Carl, which was perhaps my greatest disappointment during my time at the club. He had the ability to go right to the top, an exceptional passer with good aggression, a player who ticked a box somewhere between Glenn Hoddle and Bryan Robson. Alongside him I brought in Steve Foley from Swindon and Nigel Gleghorn from Birmingham. This time the signing-on fees were not an issue.

At outside-right I had Kevin Russell, who was quickly given the nickname Rooster Russell because of his bald head. I paid Leicester £85,000 for him. The crowd loved his direct running style. He gave us the width I was looking for, which brought Steino and his strike partner Wayne Biggins into the game. Wayne was a cracking player and a lovely lad. When he struck the ball he hit the target with good power. He had reasonable pace and was good in the air. Considering his lifestyle, Biggins should have been a bit of a wreck. If I said he liked a night out I'd be under-selling him. A night in would have been nice now and again. Incredibly, it didn't affect his training so I couldn't really criticize him. I didn't approve, though. It ran counter to my beliefs. He knew what I thought about it, but he was a difficult bloke to dislike, and as he wasn't disruptive and scored a goal every other game it was worth the gamble. Early in my second season, 1992–93, Barnsley came in with a £200,000 bid. I didn't want to lose him, but the club could not afford to say no.

Wayne's goals took us to the Third Division play-offs at the end of my first season, 1991–92. But after losing the first leg at Stockport we could only draw the return – very frustrating after finishing fourth, one place above them in the League. I also made it back to Wembley just twelve months after taking Birmingham to the Leyland DAF final. It was only the second time Stoke had been to the home of football. The previous time was for the League Cup Final twenty years earlier when a fellow called George Eastham scored to beat Chelsea. As with Birmingham, it didn't matter that it was only the Autoglass Trophy. It was a final under those twin towers. And we won, beating Stockport. Stoke were up and running again, and quickly too, which no one had expected when I walked through the door nine months earlier.

The day was similar in some respects to the Birmingham experience. About forty thousand made the trip south and a striker, Steino, scored the winner. It was only marginally less spectacular than John Gayle's, and I celebrated just as hard when the ball hit the back of the net. As did the fans when we paraded the trophy on the pitch accompanied, of course, by the best rendition of 'Delilah' I've ever heard. Or at least that's how it sounded. When we got back to Stoke for the open-top bus ride the fans lined the streets of a packed city centre. The bus was given the full motorcycle escort. Stoke is a proper footballing town. The red and white striped shirt is one of the oldest in the game. The club was one of the twelve founding fathers of the Football League way back in 1888. When we rode in on that bus it felt as if Stoke was the centre of the football universe. I was proud to have played a small part in the club's history.

I felt I was beginning to get the hang of this management lark. My and the players' confidence for the 1992–93 campaign was high. But before then I had another chapter to close, in Winchester Crown Court.

21

IN THE DOCK

FROM 22 JUNE UNTIL THE LAST WEEK OF JULY – FIVE WEEKS OF hell in 1992. I had never set foot in a court like that before. I didn't know what to feel as I left my home in Swindon heading for Winchester on that first morning. I still could not see what all the fuss was about. Before we left Bristol nick after our arrest one of the Revenue's top fellas said in a casual aside to Brian Hillier that he could not see that he had done that much wrong, which backed up what we had thought all along. OK, Brian had not done things by the book, but we were talking less than £100,000, not even £20,000 a year over the five-year period. It cost more in legal fees to bring the case to court. And more than forty officers from the Revenue raided the County Ground in Swindon on the morning of our arrest. What was all that about? Swindon is not a Manchester United, an Arsenal or a Spurs.

I spent the first few days of the hearing in a state of shock. I was completely overwhelmed by what was going on around me. First of all I was greeted by a huge bank of cameramen lined up along a wall. As soon as I arrived they started clicking away. I recognized a chap from Sky, Gary Cotterill. 'Best of luck,' he shouted. 'I'll be speaking to you later.'

'Best of luck?' I said. 'You don't mean that. If I don't get banged up here there's no story for you.'

I was a bit aggressive, which surprised me. It was not like me to overreact with journalists. I felt ashamed afterwards. I knew Gary well. He is a big United fan. I apologized to him afterwards. But that was an indication that the whole experience might be more unnerving than I had been expecting.

I was sat with Brian Hillier, Swindon's ex-chairman, and the club accountant, Vince Farrar, in the dock. It was a very uncomfortable feeling. I had not expected the formalities of the occasion to weigh so heavily on me. As the jury came in I remember looking at them, trying to weigh them up, trying to establish whether or not they were decent people. It's crazy the things that go through your mind.

The Revenue kicked off by outlining their case against us. I wanted to jump up and scream at the barrister. 'This is a case,' he said, 'that represents millions of pounds.' To me that seemed unfair. I was just so shocked that he was allowed to say that. As far as I understood it the sums involved at Swindon were around £80,000. I know – I was the one asking the board for the money. I was raging.

During the lunch break I collared my solicitor and barrister and demanded to know what was going on. I wanted to know why he was allowed to paint a picture to a jury that did not reflect what went on at Swindon Town. I was told that it was all part of the process, that I was not to worry. I would get a chance to put my side of the story later on. But to me, that process did not appear to be worth a great deal if you were allowed to carry on like that. I was severely disheartened on that first morning. Everything seemed to be caving in around me. In my innocence I thought we'd all turn up, the facts would be spelled out clearly in court, and a judgement would be made the same day. Job done. I didn't realize the scale of things; that I would be in a theatre; that grave speeches delivered by men in black gowns and wigs would be used to persuade the jury one way or the other. It was all a huge shock to me. As the case proceeded I began to adjust, but it was still painful. I never got used to the feeling of frustration at sitting mute, unable to speak out when others were not telling it as I understood the situation to be.

Winchester is not the biggest city in the world. Options at lunchtime were limited. We'd go for lunch and it would not be unusual to have a couple of jurors eating in the same place. The judge tells the jury on day one that they are not allowed to make contact with anyone in the dock. 'Am I allowed to look at them?' I asked my lawyer. It was all a bit bizarre, eating in the same restaurant with people who were going to make a decision that would affect your life. The whole experience was weird. I'd drive home in the evening in a daze, my mind a whirl of possibilities. I was staying in my own bed but there wasn't much sleep to be had. It is hard to switch off when you have a date in court the following day. I had five weeks of this to look forward to. And by the first week of July the players at Stoke had returned for pre-season training, so as well as fighting for my reputation in court I had that on my mind. I rang the club every day to ask how training had gone. Chic Bates was running the ship, but it was awkward for me.

My barrister was Stephen Pollard, who has since been

involved in some high-profile cases. I was totally reliant on him. He did his best to talk me through things, to keep me calm until I took to the witness box. What did distress me was listening to the evidence given by the Swindon directors. That really alarmed me. They painted this picture where Brian Hillier ran everything like a despot, made every decision and to hell with everyone else on the board. I had been at board meetings. I did not stay all night but that is not how it appeared to me.

We had given players extra money for doing a job on the pitch, extra money that in the football world was insignificant. But the case no longer seemed to be about that simple issue. It had grown out of proportion like a story being passed down the line by a thousand different people: it becomes something at the end of the telling that it wasn't in the beginning. Goodness knows what my old chairman was making of it all. I could not understand how these people who had sat alongside him and shared in the decision-making with him could be so disloyal to him now.

The prosecution also tried to argue that we had gained a competitive advantage through the club's financial practices. Garbage. We did not sign one player for any amount of money that another club wanted. There was never an auction. We did not offer a player money to choose Swindon over another club. There were no other clubs. We were not in the market for the Ronaldos and Rooneys of this world. All we did was help people like Steve Foley to make the move to Swindon by paying him his signing-on fee up front instead of over the three years of his contract. Where was the advantage in that?

Eventually I got my chance in the witness box. I was so naive that before I actually formally opened my mouth and said anything I wanted to stand there and say to the jury, 'Before we go any further, can I just say something to you? What you have heard over the last ten days is a load of fucking shite. And that bloke there in the wig representing the prosecution is the biggest liar I have ever met.' Of course I couldn't do that, and of course it was the objective of the prosecution to present questions to me in such a way as to elicit a response that would help prove guilt, or help create an impression that might lead the jury to a guilty verdict.

I was in the box for a couple of days overall. The court was packed. It was like one of those old Westerns where every seat in the house is taken. The Revenue had had their say. It was now my man's job to present things in a completely different way – as far as I was concerned in the right way, the proper way. After that it was down to the jury.

In all, about seven directors appeared in the witness box and as many as fourteen players. I wouldn't say my man ripped the directors to pieces, he just got enough out of them to make it clear that everybody at Swindon was aware of the payments. The whole of Swindon knew about it. For my part, I gave a true account of what happened. It was corroborated by the testimony of the players. We were all singing from the same song sheet because it was the truth. They wanted more money because the bonus scheme was ridiculous. I could not disagree with them. They told the court that they thought £25 for beating another team when there were only 1,500 people in the ground was about right. The club wouldn't have had any extra revenue to pay them anyway. But when there were twelve thousand in the ground, they felt they were entitled to more money. They'd approached me politely and I'd gone to the board on their behalf, and happily so. If that made me guilty of an

Below: Tracksuit management. Ordering the fish and chips from behind my desk.

Above: Arriving at Swindon.

Below: In the snow at the County Ground with Rocky – that's me on the chair.

Above: Showing the Swindon lads how it's done.

Above and left: Happy days with the board, and with the team, sharing the Bell's Manager of the Month Award.

Flying the flag with my sons Paul and Jon, **above**.
Receiving the 1986 Manager of the Year Award,
above right.

Above: Celebrating the 1985 Manager of the
Year award with (*left to right*) Paul, Michael
and Jon.

Right: Celebrating the Fourth Division
Championship in 1985.

Clockwise from above: More whisky – not much use to me – and more awards as the good times continue to roll at Swindon. Proof that a bad haircut is no impediment to success.

The Midas touch continues. The family celebrate Stoke's win in the Autoglass Trophy, 1992 (**above**). The legendary Nello the Clown (**right**). The Leyland DAF triumph with Birmingham the previous year – again with the family (**below**).

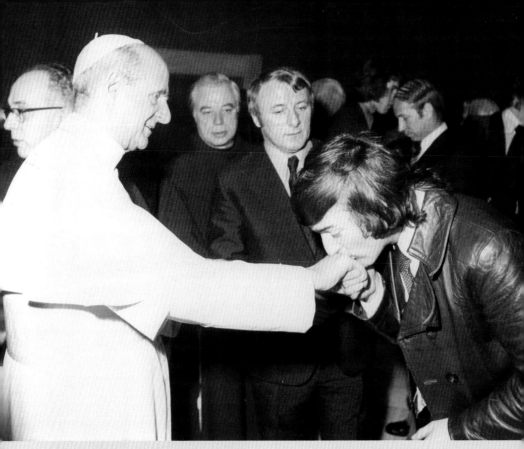

Above: The boy done good. Presented to the Pope with the Doc and the rest of the United players. Bobby Charlton waits patiently in the background.

Right: On Dualin at Ayr while still at Celtic.

Facing page: Macari and sons in the Swindon dugout.

At home with the Macaris.

offence, then so be it. I could not have answered any other way.

'Mr Macari, did you seek more money on behalf of the players?'

'Yes.'

'Did you one day give Colin Calderwood some money to give to the players?'

'Yes. I remember the secretary giving me the money and me handing it over to Colin to give to the players.'

The above exchange represents an approximation, of course. I was on trial for conspiracy to defraud the Inland Revenue. The jury heard that I was party to giving players some money, the chairman and accountant too. The confusing thing for me was why no one else was on trial. The players were not on trial for receiving it; the directors were not on trial for approving it. And Ossie Ardiles, the manager who replaced me at Swindon, was not on trial for continuing to pay the players money in the same way. I spent a good number of the long hours we waited for the jury to return their verdict wondering why I was on trial for asking for it. I just couldn't see the logic. I couldn't work out how I was any more culpable than them. I was no more or less guilty than the directors or the players.

There were some comic moments that kept me going. Steve Foley was the last of the players to take the stand. He was reluctant to appear at all. My barrister told me that if Steve did not appear, the jury might feel that he had something to hide. In the end I had to ring Chic at Stoke to tell him to instruct Ashley Grimes to bung Foley in the back of a car when he arrived for training the next day and drive him straight to Winchester. Ashley did exactly that. Foley was the big finale. The jury were informed that he was on the way. With bated breath they waited. Eventually, after lunch, in he walked in Bermuda shorts and flip-flops, as if he were on the way to the beach. I glanced at the jury. It was obvious that they thought it was as funny as I did. His testimony was even funnier, delivered in a thick Scouse accent. He made it clear in front of the jury that if the players had not got the money they were asking for they might have gone on strike. He communicated very well that the players were underpaid at Swindon, that the extra payments were fair reward for their efforts and only gave them parity with other players in the same division.

As the foreman stood to deliver the jury's verdict I started to get nervous for the first time. Over the five weeks I had struck up something of a rapport with them. Not verbally, of course, but every day as they came back from lunch they would glance over and make brief eye contact. We laughed together, at Foley and other little things like that. Over time you begin to think you understand how they might be thinking. But now, when it came to giving the verdict, there was no eye contact whatsoever. The rules had changed. This was it.

The atmosphere changed completely and I was gripped by panic. The old heart started to beat a bit quicker. You can't help it. You are moments away from a possible guilty verdict in a criminal case that has lasted for nearly five weeks. You are Lou Macari, a footballer who has played at the highest level for Celtic and Manchester United. There is a lot hanging on this for everybody. You don't know what to think.

Brian Hillier was the first to be judged.

'Guilty or not guilty?'

'Guilty, your honour.'

I was next up.

'Guilty or not guilty?'

'Not guilty, your honour.'

'Mr Macari, you are free to go.'

You'd think I'd have been floating at that moment, elated at being acquitted in court. I didn't feel anything of the sort. I felt terrible walking out of that box and leaving the other two behind. Actually I don't know how to describe how I felt walking through that courtroom door. 'Terrible' only comes close. I was emotional too; I suppose I was in some sort of shock. I subsequently found out that Vince Farrar had also been found guilty. I was gobsmacked. He had hardly been at the club for two minutes. It did not seem right. Of course, he was caught in the responsibility trap. Technically he was the one who prepared the accounts, and the chairman signed them off. I had nothing to do with that side of things, which again begs the question why was I on trial in the first place?

Vince and Brian were to be sentenced the next day. It was a strange half-hour or so sitting in our legal room afterwards with them, me having been acquitted. Outside was the waiting press. If I could play that scene again I would do things differently. I chose to say nothing save for a brief statement read by my solicitor outside the court. I couldn't even tell you what the contents were. I just told him to write whatever he wanted to write. That was the wrong option. I should have put more thought into it. I should have spoken myself, given a personal reaction to the whole episode and aired my feelings about how I really felt and how I had been treated. I should have spoken about the ordeal I had faced, the hype, and of my disappointment at the behaviour of some people in the Swindon boardroom with whom I had worked closely for five successful years. The scale of the media reception told me that they were waiting for a victim, not a free man. That hurt too.

There was no party at my home that night, no euphoria. I returned to Winchester the next day for the sentencing. The judge's summary was harsh in my view. Brian Hillier copped the blame for what had gone on, which I did not agree with. If he was guilty of a crime, then so was a boardroom full of directors. He was sentenced to six months' imprisonment. 'Take him down,' the judge said, which was a bit dramatic too. He was escorted to the cells at Winchester, where he spent something like the next three weeks. He was then transferred to Ford Open Prison. Vince Farrar was given a suspended sentence.

I made a point of going to see Brian in prison. He was in decent shape. The atmosphere was relaxed. He could come and go. He did a bit of cooking for the warden and was active for most of the day. After three months his wife rang to tell me he was going to court in December to appeal against the conviction. I shot down to The Strand in London on the day. Brian had been given all his clothes and the prison had paid him, at the prison rate, for his work. He came up on the train to London. The feeling was that he was going to get a result, though it was by no means clear to me what the outcome would be.

Three judges heard the appeal against the conviction, and turned it down. I thought that was it, he'd be off back to prison. His legal team then asked if the court would hear an appeal against the sentence. Eventually they came back and invited Brian to go home and enjoy Christmas. It was all over. That was him out. Brian was a free man again.

I remember walking down The Strand with him afterwards in a state of bewilderment. I hadn't expected that outcome. There we suddenly were, on our way to Paddington to catch the train back to Swindon alongside hundreds of unsuspecting punters making their way home after work. A bizarre end to a bizarre experience.

22

COMPLETING THE CIRCLE

IT WAS A RELIEF TO GET BACK TO THE DAY JOB. IN MY ABSENCE the boys had added the Isle of Man Tournament to the Autoglass Trophy – a massive lift for me. I knew now that we were on the march. Having reached the play-offs the season before I knew we were capable of mounting another strong challenge in 1992–93, though I never imagined we would clean up with the highest number of points ever recorded by a Stoke team. Like any manager, you hope for the best but you don't really know what lies ahead.

I brought in Bruce Grobbelaar on loan for a month. That's all we could afford to have him for. He was a bit of a gimmicky signing, but he captured the crowd's imagination with those silly wobbles he did with his legs when the opposition were bearing down on his goal. In front of him I managed to get Ian Cranson out on the pitch in forty-five of the forty-six games we played that season. He was crucial for us. Mark Stein took over from Wayne Biggins, who I sold to Barnsley, netting thirty times and never missing a game. From 5 September 1992 to 27 February 1993 we did not lose a League match – a run of twenty-five matches unbeaten. That was the backbone of our campaign and it set us up for the Division Two title (as 'Division Three' was now called in this first season of the Premiership).

When you have a striker scoring like Stein was and others playing the best football of their careers, it doesn't get much better than that for a manager. I could not have asked for more that season. Cranson's contribution in particular was a miracle. He could barely walk between matches. I was pleased for him. He was the club's record signing – £450,000 from Sheffield Wednesday – but until then the supporters had neither seen him at his best nor got value for their money. They did in 1992–93. Cranson and Vince Overson formed arguably the most powerful central defensive partnership in the division. Promotion with ninety-three points was a fitting reward, and it left us within striking distance of the newly formed Premiership, which was already the Holy Grail for all clubs. It is where the money is – the reason why it was formed in the first place. The elite division was actually formed in February 1992 by First Division clubs that wanted to break away from the Football League for financial reasons – in other words a lucrative television deal. The first matches kicked off in August that year.

That promotion with Stoke was my third as a manager, and the second time I had guided a team to a championship with a record points total. Nigel Gleghorn scored the goal that clinched the title, against Peter Shilton's Plymouth at the Victoria Ground. The old stadium was a picture that April day, a sea of red and white, and a reminder of what it must have been like in its pomp when Stanley Matthews was haring down the wings.

I felt I was getting to grips with the management business, really hitting my stride. Others felt the same way. My chairman, Peter Coates, was impressed enough to offer me a new five-year deal. He hoped I might steer the club into the Premiership. Not immediately, of course, but over the period of the contract. That was the plan, and it was certainly my aim, though I did not take it for granted. I knew there was a lot of work to do.

We did not start the 1993–94 season brilliantly: four wins, five defeats and two draws. It was a challenging time. But there was, and there will always be, that first-leg tie in the second round of the League Cup on 22 September 1993. Manchester United, the first Premiership champions, were the opposition. This was the United of Schmeichel, Irwin, Bruce, Pallister, Kanchelskis, Robson, McClair and Hughes. Keane and Giggs didn't play that night, but they were hardly under strength. They had no answer to Steino, who scored a couple of wonder goals for a 2–1 win. We lost the second leg 2–0 to go out of the competition, but we hadn't expected to progress. We'd had our night.

I saw myself as the manager of Stoke City for the foreseeable future. I was happy at the Victoria Ground. I loved the job and the club. But Peter Coates was not the only one paying attention to my achievements. My success at Stoke had alerted interest north of the border. Celtic could not buy a win at the start of that season. Rangers under Walter Smith were dominating the Scottish scene. Celtic had sacked Liam Brady in late October and were looking for a new man. When you have supported Celtic and played for them and they show an interest in you, it is impossible not to show an interest in them, however settled you are at your club. At least that was the case for me, even though most of the people in the game I spoke to about the job said I would be mad to go up there with what was going on.

Celtic were in a mess at the time. There was a consortium trying to take over, demonstrations outside the ground, supporter going up against supporter, boycotts of the club shop. All this was to do with attempts to oust the old regime, chairman Kevin Kelly and his board, from Celtic Park. The Kelly family had been in charge for almost a century. I knew the problems consortia could cause from my time at Swindon. Once the boat starts to rock it is very difficult for those in charge to survive, especially if you are losing on the pitch. Then the fans get really agitated. Worse than that, they stay away. Gates at Celtic had slumped to as low as fifteen thousand. Fergus McCann, the Canadian businessman trying to gain control of the club, played the fans and some of the players very well indeed.

But when the call came I turned a blind eye to the political unrest. Celtic were my club. I wasn't interested in any of the negative stuff. I had my rose-tinted glasses on. I'd stood on the terraces as a kid in the bad old days before Jock Stein took over. I'd played under Jock during the club's glory days. Now I had a chance to complete the circle.

I met with Celtic representatives twice in London and again in Manchester. I wouldn't call them interviews as such, more informal chats to test the water, to sound each other out: for them to determine the strength of my interest, and for me to see how serious they were. When it became clear they were extremely interested, I just couldn't say no. So I left the five-year contract on offer from Stoke unsigned and headed back to Scotland, taking Chic Bates, Ashley Grimes and Peter Henderson with me.

Materially it was the same club I had left. The Jungle was still there, the meat pies were still the best in Scotland, the training ground was the same, and most of the staff working behind the scenes were still the same and were waiting to greet me. What had changed were the club's circumstances, on and off the pitch. The team was poor and the board was fragile.

I took over from Liam Brady on 27 October 1993, three days before the Old Firm derby at Ibrox. I could not have had a harder or, as things turned out, a better start. We won 2–1. I knew from my playing days the value of victory over the auld enemy. With a couple of minutes to go we won a corner kick. The ball came over and Brian O'Neil headed it in. Delirium.

It proved a false dawn. I'd inherited a losing team. That's why I was there. Packie Bonner was in goal. I had Tony Mowbray, John Collins, Paul McStay, an injured Frank McAvennie and Charlie Nicholas. There was some quality, but some of the players were getting old and the dressing room was split, with factions working against each other. Despite the win against Rangers it quickly became clear that I had serious work to do. And no money to do it with. I had been parachuted into a crisis. The board was under siege and the dressing room was all over the place. Within a week or so of me starting one senior player, whom I respected, knocked on my door to complain about some of the others, three or four in particular. 'You have to get them out of here,' he said. 'They are a nightmare. They don't want to work, they don't want to do this or that.' I'm duty bound not to name names. Let's just say there was a group of 'goodies' who were happy to get their heads down and try to pull the club out of the mess, and a group of 'baddies', who were disruptive and did what they could to cause problems in the camp. I had a cancer to cut out, and the only way to do that was to get rid of the element that did not want to play. But that was far from easy. I had no money to bring anybody in for a start.

The attitude of some of the players was shocking, and not just on the pitch. There was constant criticism of the board in the newspapers, and nothing was done about it. Board members would even criticize one another in print. One of them, Tom Grant, stated that his allegiance was with the consortium trying to get in. Three days later we were all sat around the table in the boardroom and I was wondering what was going on. Nothing about the place was healthy. Still, I took the view that if someone did come in, it might improve the situation. I was totally open-minded about that.

Away from first-team and club matters, which were bad enough, another issue was beginning to raise its ugly head at the club. Within a month of my arrival one of the young players asked to see me in my office. 'Here we go,' I thought. 'That didn't take long. Here's a youngster in to complain about not being in the team. Straight away he's going to be into me to give him his chance.' He sat down and told me that he had had problems on a trip to North America with the youth team. One of the fellas in charge had made advances towards him.

As a manager you expect to have to sort out all sorts of problems. But this wasn't one I ever saw coming. I was staggered. To be frank, I didn't know how to respond for the best. Clearly the kid was distressed about what had happened, but I felt I couldn't just approach the accused and ask him to explain himself without proof. My hands were tied, in a way. I felt completely stuck and out of my depth. I spoke to my staff. They were shocked. My gut feeling was that the kid was speaking the truth, but there was no mechanism within the club or within my experience to deal with it. It was a police matter if anything. Any investigation had to start with them. And that's exactly what happened.

A couple of years later it all came out. Celtic Boys' Club founder Jim Torbett was convicted of sexual abuse of three players, including Alan Brazil. Frank Cairney, the manager of the Boys' Club, was charged but not convicted. It emerged that years earlier Jock Stein knew all about Torbett and kicked him out of the club. The wish to maintain the good name of Celtic, if that were ever a good enough reason, was the only thing that kept the issue from coming to light at that point. There was a string of allegations by young lads whose dreams of playing for Celtic were exploited, but it was the testimony of Alan Brazil, David Gordon and James McGrory that brought the matter to court, and Torbett to justice. Before I was approached, I knew nothing about it. I joined Celtic as a youngster in 1965, the year before Torbett set up the Boys' Club. It was completely off my radar then. I had never even heard of him, and subsequently never met him. The details were sickening. I wished I could have done more for the lad, but it was awkward. I had hardly been at the club five minutes. And there were other fires burning.

It seemed only a matter of time before Fergus McCann, who was conducting a clever campaign and who had people inside the club agitating on his behalf, took over. Kevin Kelly was fighting a losing battle. McCann eventually claimed the prize he wanted late on a Friday night in March 1994. It was obvious something was going on from the number of solicitors coming through the door. It was like a legal convention. I and the rest of my staff stayed on while the negotiations played out in various rooms. The chairman and the directors were all there, each with his legal representative, and McCann had his legal team. It was pandemonium. This wasn't the Celtic I knew. People I didn't recognize began appearing in the corridors shouting, 'It's ours!' A shiver ran down my spine. It was all very alarming.

The next day we were playing at St Johnstone. I got a call at Celtic Park on the morning of the match from Kenny Gallagher, a journalist up at St Johnstone and a friend of Brian Dempsey, a director. Dempsey had told Gallagher to inform me that McCann was going to come to see me before the game. About what I did not know. So before kick-off I was ready to meet and greet the new man in charge. McCann walked into the dressing room. He never said a word to me. He walked straight past me, and acknowledged Charlie Nicholas, Packie Bonner and Paul McStay. He had a very unfootball-like exchange with them, then, once he had said what he had to say, he went straight out again. As the manager of Celtic Football Club you would have thought I'd be the first person he would come to see. Instead he just brushed past me. Apart from anything else I thought it was rude. When I was made manager he had been quoted as saying that my appointment was a publicity stunt. Maybe he had already made his mind up about the kind of person or manager he thought I was. I felt immediately undermined, but I wasn't going to lose any sleep over it. 'So be it,' I thought. We won the match by the only goal, scored in the opening minute by Paul Byrne.

McCann had an office maybe fifty yards from mine at Celtic Park. He never came near me for two or three weeks. I wasn't his man. I understood that. But I was still perplexed. I thought his behaviour was probably something of a defensive reflex in case I asked him for money to buy players. But I wasn't so sure he was flush with cash at the time, so I wasn't going to ask for any. I was more interested in seeing what would be forthcoming in the longer term. During the first couple of board meetings we had McCann made no contribution regarding the football team. During the second one he even interrupted me and said, 'Right, have you finished now? We have more important business to discuss' – which were things to do with the stadium, season tickets, etc. He'd be falling asleep when football was on the agenda. He had no interest in it. He was a businessman who wanted to get things up and running as a business.

Not too long after McCann took over we went back to Ibrox with no Celtic supporters in the stadium. It was the first time that had ever happened at an Old Firm game, and it will probably never happen again. I was sent with thirteen players and a security officer. If any trouble had broken out we would have been looking after him. McCann had fallen out with Rangers because they had refused to pay for damage done to seats at Celtic Park. For the return, by way of protest, he chose not to accept any Celtic tickets for fans or directors. There was no one representing Celtic other than those thirteen players and a security officer who set off from the normal retreat of Seamill Hydro.

It was a hell of a day. We picked up Tony Mowbray en route. Tony had been looking after his wife, who was seriously ill with cancer. Even on the way to the ground I wasn't sure if he was going to be in the right frame of mind to play against Rangers. Had he turned round and said to me, 'I'm not up for it, boss,' I would have fully accepted that. He didn't.

'Are you ready for a battle, Tony?'

'No problem, boss. Let's get ripped into them.'

He was our best player by a mile on the night. We were winning 1–0 after a fantastic free-kick by John Collins in the first half, but they equalized with about six minutes to go. That match, for me, as a player and a manager, was my greatest experience at Ibrox. To go there with one end full of your own supporters, you are still up against it. To go there with nobody on the terraces, it was a magnificent effort. Before the game I just couldn't see how we were going to get a result. When we scored you could hear a pin drop, save for one lone voice in the crowd shouting for Celtic. I don't think anyone has seen him since. The baddies had tried to create mischief by making out that there was a problem with morale in the team. That performance at Rangers was my answer to those claims.

There had been a reserve game at Celtic that day. I expected the team to be returning to a hero's welcome. I never even got a 'well done' from Fergus McCann. But that was McCann.

He was an unusual fella full stop. Brian Dempsey tells the story of the day he invited McCann to his house after the takeover to talk shop over dinner. Without warning, McCann lay on the floor and started doing stretching exercises. He obviously did not feel that he had to observe normal codes of behaviour. He thought he was above the conventions that govern the rest of us. He certainly went out of his way to make things awkward for me.

Take the case of Simon Donnelly, for example. I gave Simon his debut as a substitute against Hibs. He was terrific. He then took on Rangers almost on his own up front. A fantastic prospect for us. He was on about £120 a week and had a year of his contract left to run. I had lost Shay Given when I arrived at the club because he had not been tied to a contract, so I didn't want the same thing to happen with Donnelly. I went up to his house, spoke to his mother and father. I was there nearly all day. I came back to Celtic Park about seven o'clock that night, delighted to have his signature on a three-year contract. It was a good deal for Simon, though still some way short of the big earners at the club, who were on three or four grand a week. I had given Simon a deal worth about £600 or £700 a week.

I went upstairs to McCann's office. He was in there with a few people.

'Excuse me for interrupting,' I said. 'I have just been out and got Simon Donnelly's contract sorted. He has signed a three-year deal.'

McCann looked at it, and in front of the other people in the room he ripped it up and threw it in the bin. 'What's it got to do with you?' he asked.

I wanted to do what I think he was hoping I'd do – whack him.

He'd been in business for years. He knew all the moves. If he wanted to get rid of people without paying them off, he knew exactly how to do it. The penny dropped. Everything fell into place. It was obvious that getting rid of me was pretty high up, if not top of, his agenda. I had a sizeable amount of money to come on the remainder of my contract. It was quite clear to me that he wanted me out but didn't want to pay up.

Then the letters started. There were quite a few of them. I came into my office about three weeks into McCann's reign and the first of them was waiting for me. I wrote one back. We became almost like pen pals, he and I, even though our offices were only fifty yards apart. Instead of speaking to me face to face, he'd put everything down on paper. What does that tell you? It told me he wanted a paper trail that might come in handy one day.

The contents were ridiculous. He'd make petty complaints about timekeeping, about how long I spent in Glasgow. He moaned about me spending a day at home to celebrate a birthday. He even had a go about a summer holiday I had planned, even though I'd taken the team on a three-week end-of-season tour to Canada, a trip beneficial to the club. He took issue with me attending a football match on the grounds that I was not the chief scout. How do you respond to that? He thought it was Tommy Craig's job to go looking for players and sign them because he was the chief scout. I told him it was Tommy Craig's job to aid me by looking at players that I had recommended. I'm not going to sign anybody I haven't seen.

There was one final dispute, over my attendance at the 1994 World Cup in America. Long before he arrived at Celtic Park I'd booked tickets to the World Cup matches. I was going to spend my summer months watching the world's best players. That's the way I'd operated all my life. That's the way you get a decent team on the pitch. You watch matches. You watch players. McCann thought otherwise. 'Yes, you can go,' he said, 'but only on my terms. After the first match in New York, you fly back to Glasgow to work at Celtic Park on the Monday and Tuesday. You can then fly out to America for the next game. Then back to Glasgow for two days, then out to the States again.' He had me back and forth over the Atlantic more often than a pilot. I told him he was being ludicrous.

After receiving another letter, I sought the advice of the League Managers Association in England. I got their solicitor to respond in writing to McCann on my behalf. I showed the letter to Pete Henderson and Ashley Grimes. 'What do you think of that?' I asked. 'Is it all right?' I couldn't be bothered to scrutinize the contents myself. I'd pretty much given up caring. They gave me the thumbs up, so I put it in an envelope and left it on McCann's desk.

The following morning, 14 June, I was sacked over the phone while waiting to board a plane at Manchester airport. I rang McCann to give him forwarding addresses and telephone numbers of where I would be in America. He said, 'I expect to see you back here on Wednesday after the first match.' Again, I told him that was ridiculous, that I wouldn't be back. He then adopted a quasi-legal tone over the telephone, as if he had me bang to rights.

'Can I just get this right,' he said. 'What you are telling me is that you are not going to obey my orders, is that right?'

'Yes, that's right. Look, I have to get on this plane.'

'Well, if that's the case, I'm sacking you.'

By the time I got to the US I was officially out of a job. He'd sent the dismissal letter to my digs in Glasgow and copies to my home in Stoke and to a PO box in America at Hilton Head, South Carolina.

I carried on with my World Cup plans. I turned up at the first game to find that I was sitting next to Walter Smith, the manager of Rangers.

'Hi, Lou. Everything OK? Good trip? How are things at Celtic Park these days?'

'I haven't got a problem any more, Walter,' I said. 'I've just been sacked.'

'You are fucking joking,' he said. 'What have you been sacked for?'

'How long have you got, Walter? For coming to the World Cup.'

And that was how my reign as Celtic manager ended – my

first sacking in football. The thing that hurt me the most was that I was never given the opportunity to turn things around. There was a massive job to do, but I couldn't even make a start. Even more frustrating was the fact that the fans never really knew what was happening behind the scenes. They knew about the politics, of course, but not the nasty stuff – the splits in the camp, the nitty gritty that made the job impossible. Immediately after my sacking I took a call from a former Celtic director who advised me to come back to fight my corner, to deal with all the rubbish that would be coming out in the papers from McCann. I should have heeded that advice. I regret not doing so. The papers were indeed full of garbage, all designed to make me look negligent. Meanwhile I was three thousand miles away on another continent watching matches that had suddenly lost all significance.

I'd like to say that was the last time I ever had to deal with Fergus McCann. It wasn't. I had to take him to court in Edinburgh for the money owing on my contract. The case took three years to come before a judge. When it did, the letters we'd exchanged played an important part. They offered the court in abstract some sort of account of our working relationship, but on paper the reality of the situation was completely skewed. What those letters did not do was reflect the atmosphere created by McCann, the subtle moves he made to make my job impossible to execute in the way I knew best. Ask any in the game about the value I place on hard work. Ask my family how much time I have spent at home since taking over at Swindon in 1984. Not a lot, yet the thrust of McCann's case against me was that I was guilty of negligence. Any football court would have laughed McCann out of the place on the opening day. This was different. A legal eagle was sifting through lumps of dry evidence that did little to reflect the reality as I saw it.

It got no better for those who followed me at Celtic during McCann's reign. Accounts in newspapers following the departure of Wim Jansen, for example, would appear to support my case. Much of Jansen's ire was directed at Jock Brown, the filter between the board and Jansen, who enjoyed the title of 'manager' to Jansen's 'head coach'. Jansen resigned two days after taking Celtic to their first championship in ten years. He had been there only a year. He'd replaced Tommy Burns, who was brought in after me only to be sacked as well by McCann. Clearly I wasn't the only victim of the Canadian's methods.

A headline from the *Daily Record* in May 1998 proclaimed: 'Civil War at Celtic Park'. In the article, McCann admitted he would have sacked Jansen if he had not gone of his own accord on the grounds that he was neglecting the club's development. That seems hard to square with a first League Championship in a decade. He made the same accusation against me. McCann offered as an example how Jansen refused to board a private plane to go to watch Harold Brattbakk play. When I was there it was unacceptable in McCann's eyes to go to watch anybody. He wanted me at Celtic Park ten hours a day behind a desk. The job of watching players, he told me, was the responsibility of the chief scout. He can't have it both ways, surely. The discrepancies were in my view strategic, designed to construct a case against a specific employee, should he need to fall back on that some day, which he did with me.

In fact Jansen was hardly through the door before he was eyeing the exit. 'I wanted to quit after two weeks,' he was quoted as saying. Tommy Burns wanted to quit immediately after winning the Scottish Cup for Celtic in 1995. There was a definite pattern there. Working under McCann was difficult. The model was not a footballing one. Let me quote Jansen again. 'I have a good team on paper, but Fergus [McCann] and Jock Brown have no idea what really counts when it comes to football.' Jansen had a charge sheet as long as his hair against his employers, and chose to get out while he was ahead. Of course, McCann saw things differently. The fact that he had gone through three managers inside four years was not a fault of his but of ours. He said of Jansen, 'Sometimes when you appoint a manager you can get it wrong. It is unlikely we would have continued with the arrangement if he had decided to stay. Wim was not incompetent but his style when you don't have co-operation had to change.'

He was right. Someone's style at the club had to change – McCann's. But that was never going to happen. There was no protection from McCann's approach, no matter what position you held. Even some of his closest aides quit the club. Brian Dempsey, who had helped oversee McCann's arrival at Celtic, resigned from the board because he could no longer work with the fella. Director Willie Haughey, one of McCann's loyal lieutenants on the board, went the same way. Dominic Keane left after a boardroom row, citing 'fundamental things I found difficult to accept'.

Eventually I would have my day in court, and I'll come to that later. In my mind the fight was always against McCann, never Celtic. I went to court believing he was my enemy, not the club. How could it be otherwise? Celtic are my team, the club I supported as a boy. I am and always will be a fan at heart. There is nothing in the world that can change that.

23

FAREWELL VICTORIA

I RETURNED FROM THE WORLD CUP WITHOUT A JOB. BUT I didn't stop working. Football is in my blood. I was out and about watching matches, paying attention. And, of course, having moved up to Stoke during my first reign there I was very much in touch with the atmosphere around the Victoria Ground. And at the start of the 1994–95 season you'd have to say it wasn't great. Joe Jordan had never quite managed to win the fans over since replacing me. I have no idea why. A harder-working manager you could not hope for. When you are in that position the last thing you need is a bad start to the season. Joe copped two heavy defeats away from home, at Bolton and Reading, both 4–0. Immediately the fans were restless.

Joe is a close friend of mine, but he wasn't helped by my availability. I'd left only ten months earlier with the club on a high. I was now out of work and living in the town. That must have been tough for Joe to deal with. He survived until

September 1994. After his sacking I got a call from my old chairman at Swindon, Brian Hillier, who was a friend of the Stoke chairman Peter Coates. Would I consider going back? Why not? I could think of no reason why I shouldn't, even though I felt for Joe. He'd been under pressure from the beginning, taking over from a regime that had brought the club success. From my point of view Joe did nothing wrong. He did not waste the club's money. He was a grafter. He didn't deserve the bullet. But football managers are always vulnerable to that, me included. You accept it as part of the job. On this occasion Joe was the loser and I was back in a job.

Well, almost. My attempted return coincided with an escalation of my legal battle with Fergus McCann. Obviously I wanted my contract with Celtic paid up. I believed that McCann had engineered my exit to allow him to get his own man in without paying up. I wasn't having that. I was claiming £400,000 – a huge amount of money. Remember, I was sacked. I did not resign. When I walked away from West Ham I did so without taking a penny out of the club, despite advice from the secretary suggesting that I was making a mistake by not negotiating a pay-off. But that's not the way I work. It was not West Ham's problem, it was mine. I left because I didn't feel I could do the club justice under the circumstances. That was not the position at Celtic.

McCann being McCann, he counter-sued me for failing to win a trophy or to get Celtic into Europe. Ridiculous. That was thrown out by the court within days. But that did not stop my blood boiling. I knew what he was up to. He was trying to deter me from going to court. But my beef was not with Celtic, it was with McCann, and by this time I hated the fella. I was on the warpath. Not only had he made my life hell at Celtic, he was now interfering with my prospects at Stoke. His legal machinery held up my appointment for a good forty-eight hours. If I could have laid my hands on McCann at that point I would have killed him. Thankfully the lawyers sorted everything out and I was soon back in charge at the Victoria Ground.

Nothing had fundamentally changed. Joe had wheeled and dealed to bring a few players in so there were one or two new faces among the playing staff, but behind the scenes it was the same old faces. Joe had brought in Paul Peschisolido in August. He was tricky about the box, had a good work ethic and was capable of getting his share of goals. He was never going to be as prolific as Mark Stein though, who had moved on. It was a question of moulding the team around the requirements of the higher division, which would take time. Every time you step up a division, players need to adjust a notch. The higher you climb, the greater the adjustment. Stoke were just one promotion away from the Premiership, so the standard was creeping up all the time.

Money, as ever, was always a big issue. There was never enough of it. In the lower divisions you can get by with good husbandry. It's not so easy to do when you are up against teams who can go out and sign a player to get themselves out of trouble. Every now and again Mike Potts, the secretary, would indicate that there was a small amount to spend, maybe £70,000 or £80,000. If a player popped up in that price range you could act; anything over and above that, you wouldn't even bother. Joe paid around half a million for Peschisolido out of the proceeds of Stein's £1.5 million sale to Chelsea. Without that he could not have got anywhere near the player.

We picked up sufficiently to flirt with the play-off places

before Christmas, but to sustain that sort of form you need a big squad of a high quality. We couldn't cope with injuries. Martin Carruthers was still a youngster, wholehearted yet inexperienced, nowhere near the clinical finisher you need to succeed. Keith Scott did not work out at Stoke. When he missed from a yard against Portsmouth he took terrible abuse. It wasn't fair – anybody can miss from a yard – but then this game isn't. It was clear Keith's interests would be best served with a move. As luck would have it he eventually played a part in bringing Mike Sheron to Stoke the following season – a brilliant deal for us, and, I hope, for Keith. We ended up eleventh in that first season back. Given the resources I had, that was about all we could expect.

Wembley offered us our only chance of success that season, and that was in the Anglo Italian Cup. We beat Cesena, Udinese and Piacenza, whose players, rumour had it, got lashed in a Stoke nightspot the night before the game. That took some doing. As I recall, there weren't too many mid-week hotspots to choose from in the Potteries. That tournament was quite an adventure. On one trip we got caught out by snow. I can't recall the opposition, but I do remember there was an issue with the pitch. We were told by a club official the night before the game that we would be playing at another ground because they had a big match at the weekend and wanted to protect the surface. That didn't bother us. The only problem was the snow that fell overnight. I went down to the ground on the afternoon of the game with Nello and a couple of the staff. You couldn't see a blade of grass for snow, about a foot of the stuff. While we were there a busload of Stoke fans arrived. They had travelled overnight though the Alps – a major effort on their part. They were knackered. I was looking at the pitch thinking, 'There is no chance of a game here.' I assumed at that point that we would have to go back to the opposition and play on their pitch after all. About half an hour later the officials arrived to formally announce that there would be no game. We went back to the hotel, packed our bags and left the following morning without kicking a ball. At least we were on a plane. The supporters set off for a long journey by road back across the Alps.

The only compensation was the promise of a place in the final against Ascoli at Wembley. To get there we had only to see off Notts County over two legs. But we couldn't even do that. We were on a decent pitch this time, but you would not have known it from the quality on show. A full 210 minutes elapsed across both legs without a hint of a goal. We lost on penalties.

Despite the loss, Notts County still managed to send our fans off on their summer holidays with smiles on their faces, holding neighbours Port Vale to a draw in the last game of the season. We needed to beat Luton at Kenilworth Road to finish above them. At half-time Port Vale were winning 1–0 and we were losing by the same score. Notts County came back to draw and we cracked in three goals in the second half for a 3–2 win – a landmark of sorts in my first season back.

The arrival of Mike Sheron in October as the strike partner to Simon Sturridge, whom I rescued from the reserves, was the catalyst to our run to fourth place in 1995–96. Sheron had been labouring in Norwich reserves. He was bought from Manchester City for big money. Norwich were flying at the time, going head to head with Manchester United for the Premiership and playing in Europe. When they were relegated in 1995, Sheron struggled to break into the team. I went to see him in a reserve game. I could see that he was flat but I also knew he could play. He had an appetite for goals at Maine Road, where he was regarded as a real star of the future. Martin O'Neill was in charge of Norwich at the time. He'd had Keith Scott at Wycombe and knew him inside out. Sheron wasn't doing it for him, so I suggested a swap deal with a cash adjustment. Whatever the amount we paid – and again, memory fails me – Sheron proved a terrific acquisition.

We started the campaign slowly, goals in short supply, but soon, with Sheron and Sturridge on fire up front, life became a lot easier. Scoring goals is the toughest art in football, and it's the difference between mediocrity and challenging for honours. I was also helped that season by two lads I brought in from Celtic, Gary Holt and Justin Whittle, whom I had originally picked up from the army. At Parkhead I was tipped off by Paddy Crerand, who had seen them playing in an armed forces match in Germany. I took them on Celtic's end-of-season tour to Canada then signed them on the books for a fee of £500 apiece – one of the last bits of business I conducted at Celtic Park. They were brilliant characters, and fit as fiddles. Gary was a chef in the army and Justin an accountant. They were two of the best buys I made as a manager. Sheron was another. He broke a club record by scoring in seven successive League games during a run that yielded fifteen goals in twenty-two matches to take us into the play-offs against Leicester.

From where we had started the season, that was a terrific achievement. Six games in, we were second from the bottom of the Division One table and we had just lost to Port Vale. There was also a bit of friction at the club because of a new payment system, which was based on appearances.

Pay-as-you-play was the buzz phrase. Money was always tight, so this was a way of controlling it and making sure it went to those who had earned it. For the players, however, it was an issue. I had no problem with it, but I understood their position. They had mortgages to pay, they wanted guarantees. What if they got injured? What if they fell out of favour? I felt for the lads, but I understood the board's need to run a tight ship. We had acquired a new chief executive by then, Jez Moxey, whose job it was to organize the club's finances and raise revenues. Moxey was responsible for the move to the Britannia Stadium, and ultimately the change of ownership that saw an Icelandic consortium take a controlling interest in the club.

There was a sense in the mid-nineties that change was in the air at Stoke City. I was OK with that as long as it did not affect my ability to do my job. And if there was going to be more money about then great.

Eventually, of course, we overcame our bad start. Sheron sparked the revival. We were also helped by a run in the League Cup, beating Chelsea over two legs. Apart from Vince Overson's majestic tussle with Mark Hughes, the tie was memorable for our late arrival at Stamford Bridge. We got stuck in London traffic and did not arrive at the ground until twenty-five minutes to eight. We barely had time to get our kit on before the ref was blowing for the start of the game. We won 1–0, which makes a nonsense of the modern-day mantra about preparation. It was like a school match. We were practically getting changed on the bus.

On transfer deadline day, Birmingham came in for Peschisolido with a £400,000 bid. Stoke needed the money. Selling teams do not tend to win trophies. Big squads do, and we were moving into the era of the squad system. Gone were the days when the same thirteen players would carry you through the season. Strikers hit dry spells. Sheron would not always be flying. From a footballing perspective we should not have sold Peschisolido. Indeed, I wanted to bring in another striker, Richard Sneekes from Bolton. Instead of coming to us he went to West Brom for £400,000 – the same amount we got for Pesch. That is the position the club was in. Sneekes scored ten goals in thirteen games in the remainder of the season for the Baggies. Meanwhile, Sheron and Sturridge papered over the cracks at Stoke, offering a false sense of security.

Leicester, who we met in the play-offs in May 1996, were managed by Martin O'Neill, and they boasted the likes of Garry Parker and a young Emile Heskey. The first game was at Filbert Street, and we battered them. Four minutes from the end, Graham Potter missed from a couple of yards out with a header. That might have been the decisive moment that took us to the final and a shot at the Premiership. Somehow he managed to put it over the bar. I wasn't too concerned, though. We'd had much the better of the 0–0 draw, and back at the Victoria Ground on the Wednesday night I was confident of progressing in front of twenty-one thousand loyal Stoke fans. We had done the hard work. I had seen nothing to fear. What I had failed to see was the possibility of a negative reaction from us. I could see no reason why, three days later, we would not match the level of performance at Filbert Street. But as can happen on the big occasion, form dips and decisions go against you. It was just not our night. Garry Parker scored from close range to beat us 1–0. It reminded me of the way we lost out to Crystal Palace when I was at

Swindon. A tie that should have been wrapped up in the first leg was stolen from us in the second. It was a bitterly disappointing end to a terrific season for us.

The next season, 1996–97, was to be the club's final year at the Victoria Ground. I didn't know it then, but it was also going to be my last season at Stoke. I was dead against the move to a new stadium. There were two options on the table: one to move, the other to revamp the present ground. I wanted the club to do the latter. But as I was beginning to find, my voice at the club was starting to lose its influence. Moxey was the man to whom the chairman gave an ear. It is not unusual for chief executives to run the show these days. Just look at Peter Kenyon at Chelsea. But as far as I'm concerned the manager should always be the most important figure at any club. The moment people stop listening to the manager, it's over. Without a successful team on the pitch, the rest falls apart.

At Swindon and at Stoke I ran the show as far as football was concerned. I chose which players I wanted to buy. The result was promotions and profits for the club from onward sales of players. That was one element of my relative successes. Another was the hard work and effort of the staff and the players. At Stoke there was a third element that made a difference: the surroundings and the support. It seemed madness to me to take that asset away. This was a venue where teams came down a little tunnel maybe ten or fifteen yards long. The moment the away team stepped out of the dressing room they walked into a wall of noise. As they made their way down the tunnel past the tiny dugouts by the pitch they got abuse. It was hostile. I liked that. The approach to the ground through the narrow streets was also a factor. Teams probably felt intimidated. There was a fella called Harold who led the bawling and shouting. Welcome to Stoke. I was brought up as a football supporter and player travelling to the east end of Glasgow. I understood the value of the atmosphere Celtic's surroundings created. It was worth its weight in gold. It was the same at Stoke, if on a smaller scale. Not every club has that going for them. Stoke did, and I did not want to lose it. I thought it was a daft move to make.

The board disagreed. They had brought in Moxey to move the club along.

I first ran into Moxey in Scotland, where he was a football agent. One of his clients was Celtic's Andy Walker, whom I had brought back to Parkhead from Bolton in one of my last acts as manager of the club. Though he was brought in as chief executive it was clear as time went on that he had a view on the kind of players we should buy and on the lads we already had on the books. I was not overly happy with that. If you are there to build a stadium, fine. But keep your gob shut on football matters. Moxey didn't do that.

The penny soon dropped about why he was so interested in the playing side of things: it was because the trade in players formed part of his scheme to finance the new stadium. He needed money to build it and he saw the sale of Stoke's top players as a legitimate way of generating the cash. I got a little tip-off from an ex-team-mate of mine at Manchester United, Stewart Houston, who was manager of Queens Park Rangers: QPR were interested in Sheron and contact had been made between the two clubs. I knew nothing about it until Stewart let the cat out of the bag. I was not happy. I'd struggled along with Stoke, done the best I could for the club by wheeling and dealing, and was pleased with the results. To undo all that, to break up the team that almost got us into the Premiership the season before, in order to pay for a move to a new ground that the club could not afford seemed to me to be inviting disaster. It is tough enough trying to build a side when cash is tight; when you start selling to fund a new venture, the manager's job is made impossible. After my departure at the end of the season, Sheron duly left for QPR, and Andy Griffin was sold to Newcastle, which brought in around £4 million.

Unsurprisingly, the club went into decline. Yes, they were playing at a new stadium, but on the pitch they were struggling. And a club struggling on the pitch is struggling everywhere. They were relegated the very next season, then spent four years in Division Two before eventually winning promotion.

We started my final year at the Victoria Ground well, winning the first game at Oldham on the opening day. After four games we were top of the League. But as the season progressed I was feeling increasingly undermined, and the goals dried up. Sheron, who started the season like a train, scoring nineteen before Christmas, hit a dry spell. I think the QPR issue was taking its toll. He knew what was going on, that he would be moving on. That changed the whole dynamic of the season for him, and for us. Mike's goal at Charlton on 19 January was the last Stoke scored on an away ground that season. After his move to QPR, we spoke. Mike told me that the sums involved were life-changing for him, that they would set him up for life. That is bound to have an impact on the way you play before the move. To start with, you are not going to want to get injured. And QPR were not the only club chasing him. One of the papers ran a story about a top Premiership club ready to table a £3 million bid. There was speculation that representatives from that club would be at the Victoria Ground to watch him one particular night. Mike had a nightmare. As I said, it looked to me as if he was saving himself, making sure he did not get injured. I would probably have done the same, especially if I knew my club was willing to move me on.

As time went on I felt Moxey was more important to the club than I was. Priorities had changed. The move to the new stadium was dominating everybody's thoughts. At the same time my court case against Celtic reared its head. I was notified that the hearing would take place in the early part of the coming summer. In the spring of 1997 I was back and forth up to Edinburgh to meet with lawyers to help prepare the case. With that going on and the club more bothered about the ground than the team, I felt my time would be better spent taking care of my own business. There was a lot at stake for me. Not only was I fighting for £400,000, I stood to lose around £200,000 in costs if things did not go my way. I can tell you, when £200,000 is all the money you can lay your hands on, that concentrates your mind a fair bit. That's all I had to my name after a career at the top. Stoke were paying me about £70,000 a year. Hardly David Beckham money.

Had things at Stoke been different, I might have felt differently about leaving. As it was, I knew I would have a real slog on my hands for six or seven weeks up in Edinburgh. The club secretary, Mike Potts, who was feeling that he was being edged out himself, advised me not to resign. He thought the court case could be managed without me having to give up my job. It was Moxey's growing influence at the club that made my mind up for me. Not even the prospect of seeing my two boys Michael and Paul coming through the Stoke reserves could change my mind. I actually brought Michael into the first team at the end to help ease the striking problems. That wasn't easy for him or me, but he settled in well and scored a few goals.

I offered my resignation on the eve of the last Potteries derby match at the Victoria Ground, against Port Vale in April 1997. That was a coincidence; it could have been anybody. It would have been nice to leave with a win against the old enemy, but that wasn't to be.

It was disappointing in a way that I was no longer the foremost figure at the club in the eyes of Peter Coates. He knew that I'd managed the club well, that I regarded his money as my own and would never squander his cash. I think I left him with a surplus of around £8 million on player turnover. The chairman was convinced he was taking Stoke forward. I thought they were going backwards. I always had a good relationship with Peter, so it was a shame the way it ended.

That didn't affect my affection for the institution. As I have said, Stoke are a proper club with proper fans. I still live in the town. The writing of this book coincided with the club's push for promotion to the Premiership under Tony Pulis. Stoke have been out of the top flight for too long. No one was happier than me when they claimed that second automatic spot behind West Brom.

24

SOD'S LAW

TO ME, EVERYTHING WAS CRYSTAL CLEAR. FERGUS MCCANN had not wanted me at Celtic Park from day one. In my eyes, he didn't have a case. I wasn't aware of how much of an expert he would be. I was well aware of how much of a novice I was in terms of employment law, and in terms of knowing how a tribunal of this sort proceeds. I was a simple manager who believed he'd been shafted, and it was time to go and get the money owed to me as a result of being taken for a ride. That was the conviction I took into the Edinburgh court. It is the conviction I hold today. If only that had been enough. I was so naive I walked into court believing that my fight was with McCann. In fact it was Macari versus Celtic Football Club. That hurt. Celtic was my club. I had nothing against Celtic. Even if McCann lost, he was not going to suffer. Celtic were bankrolling the case, not him. And if I lost, it was my money down the pan. But that thought did not enter my head.

I was advised that things could go wrong, of course. The

case was heard by Lady Cosgrove, a superstar of the legal scene north of the border and Scotland's first female judge. I am in no way questioning the competence of the judge but I did wonder if any judge would be familiar with the nuances of running a football club; to my mind, a judge was likely to be removed from the ways of football. I think that is fair comment. People familiar with the way the game works would appreciate immediately that turning up every day during the close season to sit behind a desk is not normal; reporting every Monday morning at eight o'clock for a meeting with the catering manager and the groundsman is not normal. It doesn't happen anywhere. If Alex Ferguson had been sitting in judgement he would have been falling about laughing from day one. I mean no disrespect whatsoever to Lady Cosgrove. In fact I liked her a lot. But it is unlikely she would have known how football clubs work. It was a totally different atmosphere from the Swindon case. On this occasion I was the one bringing the matter to court. In terms of press coverage, however, it was on a par with the Swindon trial. The personalities involved and the fact that it was Celtic Football Club in court guaranteed that. Reporters were queuing up to hear the inside story, to listen to people slag off each other; there was a lot of meat on the bone. There was something of a pantomime element to it in that respect.

They heard early on from the former Celtic directors Brian Dempsey, James Farrell and Kevin Kelly, who appeared as witnesses for me. Brian was McCann's side-kick from the outset. When you hear a man as close as he was to the centre of power say that from day one, and I mean day one, the club was never going to keep this fella as manager, you feel that your case is made. That's how I saw it anyway. After Brian spoke I

215

couldn't see the case lasting that long. Brian told the court how he instructed journalist Ken Gallagher to call me after the takeover by McCann to tell me that I was not the chosen one and I would not be staying in my post. That stacked up when McCann arrived at St Johnstone on the Saturday and snubbed me in the dressing room. I also learned that on his first day in his office at Celtic Park, the Monday after the takeover, McCann asked to see a copy of my contract. If you are planning to get rid of someone, it makes sense to identify areas of contractual concern that might prove profitable down the line. As I said, within three weeks of McCann arriving at the club I received the first of many letters drawing my attention to various contractual obligations to which he felt I was not attending properly. The plot was already playing out.

I had no ill will towards McCann. I understand that in football new ownership can mean a change of personnel. If McCann wanted to bring his own man in to manage, I had no issue with that. That's the way it goes. Also I accept that under McCann's regime the stadium and facilities were much improved. He deserves credit for that. I just did not agree with his understanding of what a manager should be, nor did I comprehend his management methods. While I was in charge that obviously became an issue.

McCann made much of my physical absence from Celtic Park. He took exception to my not being at the club on a Monday. I gave the players one day off a week. That day was Monday. Since pussy was a cat, that had happened at Celtic, under Jock Stein and beyond. McCann did not, it seemed to me, understand the rhythm of the football week. He simply saw it as an opportunity to pull me up over a technical issue, to paint a picture of me as an idle manager in neglect of my duties. Not only was that fantasy, it was also insulting. The working day for the manager of a club the size of Celtic, a massive institution comparable to any club in world football, begins the minute your eyes open. It doesn't even end when they close. I used to dream about Celtic issues. It was non-stop. Every waking second is consumed by the demands of the job. But in McCann's view, the only place you could legitimately be doing that job was behind a desk at Celtic Park. If you were being generous you might say that the only defence for the position he took was ignorance. In legal matters, though, McCann was anything but ignorant.

McCann would have people believe that I was at home on a Sunday playing cards with the kids, doing a bit of DIY, wandering around supermarkets with my wife. I wish. There was no time to recover from the match the day before. Before you had poured the milk on your cornflakes you had taken a dozen calls from the daily boys wanting a story for Monday's papers. The phone would not stop all day. The hardest thing for me to take during the whole court experience was to listen to him stand up before the judge and effectively accuse me of being a slacker. I had a reputation among 99 per cent of managers as a workaholic. Then this Canadian fella arrives on the scene, and before you knew it a section of the fans started to invest in the idea that I was a stay-away manager. Absolute crap.

If there was anything that could possibly be done to benefit Celtic and help them win football matches, I did it. There were not enough hours in the day. My prospects for success were indivisible from the club's. I could prosper as a manager only if the club did well on the field. It was absurd to argue that I was negligent in the execution of my duties since that would entail working against my own interests. Nonsense.

Was Alex Ferguson neglecting his duties when he left for South Africa immediately after losing to Manchester City at Old Trafford in the Manchester derby? He would have been by McCann's measure. While Ferguson was in the southern hemisphere, his players were busy at Carrington fashioning the response that would see them thrash Arsenal in the FA Cup. How would McCann's model account for that?

McCann also banged on in the letters about my failure to produce a proper budget for new players and a list of candidates to bring in. He never once mentioned budgets to me when I was manager there. If he had, then why was he against me going to the World Cup? He was against that because there was a chance I'd spot a couple of players, and that would have cost him an amount of money I didn't think he had. Why did he throw Simon Donnelly's new deal in the bin? He didn't want to pay it, that's why. He didn't want to pay anybody anything. When Wim Jansen quit as head coach in 1998, one of his grievances was not being given any indication by McCann as to how much money he had to spend. I knew that feeling, though you would never have known it listening to McCann giving evidence in court.

At the start I felt the case was going well for me. David Pleat agreed to appear as a witness. He was asked about the job of a manager. He simply said it like it is. There is no manual, no guidebook for managers, no one template for doing the job. What he could say with certainty, he told the court, was that in all his experience he had never heard of a manager who sits behind his desk every day, never heard of a manager who does not buy the players. As I have already mentioned, McCann's argument in my case was that the spotting and buying of players was Tommy Craig's responsibility. On paper,

McCann's case had some coherence: it was based on dry contractual detail, on the contents of legal documents no football manager ever read. But in reality it did not in any way get close to representing the real responsibilities and rhythms of a traditional football club. David's evidence made that crystal clear. McCann was making the case against me on obscure contractual grounds.

Halfway through the proceedings my barrister, Colin Boyd QC, told me that he could no longer continue with the case. He had been offered a top job by the new Labour government that had swept to power the month before. He had to take up his post, that of Lord Advocate no less, immediately. That was a bombshell I could have done without, a cruel break. I was now getting a new man, Colin Sutherland QC, who knew nothing about the case. There was a delay in proceedings of a few weeks to allow him to catch up, but I felt that was never going to be enough. I had spent months bringing my brief up to speed with how a football club works. There was never enough time to instruct my new man in the curiosities and subtleties of football life. Not ideal.

Dominic Keane, a witness for McCann, and I, had a chat when the case was over. I confronted him to ask how he could have said what he did in court. He told me that he felt my barrister had not asked questions that were penetrating enough. Had he asked alternative questions or put them in another way, his responses might have been shaped differently, and as such given an impression that supported my view of things.

There was another episode that did not exactly put a smile on my face. The court did not sit on Mondays. One Monday afternoon I was sitting in my hotel room in Edinburgh when I received a call from my legal people informing me that I had to put another £50,000 into their bank account by the close of business that day or they would not be in court on the Tuesday. I was fuming. I had no choice. Paying up front is something I had not considered when I went into this.

It wasn't all bad. Packie Bonner, who also appeared as a witness for McCann, inadvertently ended up speaking for me when he took the stand. Packie's statement was, on paper, a huge disappointment to me. I did not agree with anything in it. But when he gave evidence in the flesh I sat there open-mouthed as he contradicted verbally almost everything that had been written. He said nothing at all derogatory about me. Celtic's barrister tried to shove the words back in his mouth, and Packie would say something like, 'No, no, it wasn't like that.' I'm not sure there was any need for my barrister to question Packie at all.

Peter Grant was comical. His day in court was one of almost total laughter. His evidence certainly added no weight to Celtic's case against me. He mentioned that from time to time I would embarrass him because I was fitter than him. If we did running or physical stuff, Peter told the court that sometimes I would be out in front. Stuff like that. 'Mr Grant, were there times when the manager was absent from the club?' he might be asked. 'Oh yes,' Peter replied, 'but that is the case with any manager.'

Then McCann was called to give evidence. That night was probably the best meal I enjoyed throughout the whole process. Any football person in court that day would have left splitting their sides after listening to his view about how a manager should behave, particularly in relation to timekeeping and the issue of where my family lived at the time. He made a big issue out of my wife and children not moving up to

Scotland. Remember, I took over the club during a period of great uncertainty. Football is a fickle business at the best of times. With a new regime wrestling to take over almost at the time I arrived, only a madman would have uprooted his family until that had worked itself out. We all know what happened when it did. And McCann took over in March, which, as anybody with children of a certain age will tell you, is a critical time of the school year with exams coming up. 'So fucking what?' was the gist of his response when I explained the situation to him. In one of his letters he made the point: you said your wife and kids would be coming up. I replied saying yes, they would be coming up as soon as they could. That was always the intention. I had to get my wife to come to court to give evidence, something I did not want to put her through.

The birthday issue also came up in court. My forty-fifth birthday fell on 7 June 1994 – hardly a critical time in the club football calendar. This was a period when other managers and all the players not involved in the World Cup were lying on a beach somewhere. McCann wanted me behind a desk in Glasgow, despite the fact that I had just returned from an end-of-season tour to Canada. Who exactly was I going to speak to?

As ridiculous as McCann's position was in the round, he threw that much crap in my direction some was bound to stick. And my barrister warned me that what sounded ridiculous to me and to others listening to McCann in court might not to a judge making a ruling on strict legal points. I was not able to judge the strength of McCann's position from a legal point of view. I did not have that expertise. But intuitively, as a football man, I felt I had come out of the proceedings in decent shape. It was obvious to me what had gone on at Celtic under McCann. Was it clear to Lady Cosgrove? I didn't know.

On the last day of the hearing I thought I was home and dry. Seven months later, when she announced her ruling in a document that ran to eighty pages, I got the shock of my life. Lady Cosgrove found me to be amiable if not particularly astute. I didn't agree with the astute part, obviously, but I could live with that. She thought McCann uncompromising and arrogant. She was bang on there. Beyond that I did not grasp much. There were reams of legal arguments explaining how she'd arrived at her decision, not one of which made much sense to me. It was dressed up in legalese, terms like 'pursuant to this', 'pursuant to that'. It was all Greek to me, a bit like attempting to understand the finer theoretical points made by your consultant relating to major surgery you have just had. In other words, you wouldn't bother. All you need to know is whether you are cured or not. How they cured you is beyond your understanding. You take the doctor's word for it. I wasn't that interested in understanding the mysteries of legal theory. All I understood was that I had not won my case. Lady Cosgrove found me to be in breach of contract and rejected my claim for £400,000. She concluded that I had failed to appreciate the change to the regime brought about when McCann became managing director.

My legal team advised me that it was worth launching an appeal. I could not myself establish the strength of my case, but they were telling me I had one, so I went with it. A couple of years later the appeal panel upheld Lady Cosgrove's decision. But by that stage it did not matter to me whether or not the decision went my way. In April 1999, three months earlier, my youngest son Jonathan had taken his own life. Nothing much matters after that.

25

MACARI AND SONS

MY WIFE AND I WERE CHILDHOOD SWEETHEARTS. WE MET AT school. Dale Marie Anderson is American. She came to Scotland with her family when her father, a senior executive with IBM, was posted to the company's Greenock base. It was my last year at school, and it was all very innocent. I was two years older than her and left school shortly afterwards to sign schoolboy forms for Celtic. They were happy days, two young kids having fun. When her dad's posting was up and Dale Marie returned to America, I went to see her whenever I got time off. In between we'd be on the phone, and writing letters.

Flying to America the first time was a huge thing – a lad from Largs getting on a plane and going to New York. It wasn't cheap either. Tickets cost about £100 one way – an awful lot of money to me. My idea of New York was gleaned from watching the movies, things like King Kong climbing up the Empire State Building. To see Manhattan for the first time was mind-blowing. Dale Marie lived out in New City, New

York, a few hours' drive north-east of Manhattan. I took a limousine. Not a car, a limo. I was cock-a-hoop sat in the back of that. It was a real eye-opener. Everything about America was an eye-opener to me. Anybody who owned a house out in New York State owned a fair chunk of land too. I came from Scotland where no one had any land. My back yard was about twelve feet by ten.

The mere fact that I got on a plane showed how serious we were. Dale Marie was my first love, and I was hers. We married young, as people did in those days: I was twenty-one, she was nineteen. The ceremony took place in New City. My mother was ill and did not travel. Dad stayed at home to look after her, so it was just me from my side of the family. My wife's family had no trouble making up the numbers. We had a reception in Scotland later.

We took our honeymoon in Blackpool. It was blowing a gale. Not the best, I know, but at that time we had to cut our cloth. Obviously I had to come back sharpish for the football, too. Jock Stein was not one for extended holidays for newlyweds. I didn't even ask. If I had, the response from Jock would have been, 'Wedding? I'll fucking wedding you!'

We bought a house in Largs. We paid £6,000 for it. Four years later, when I signed for United, we sold it for £14,000. I thought they'd made a mistake, I could not believe there would be £8,000 profit. Of course it all went into the next house in Manchester.

Our first son, Michael, was born in Scotland on 4 February 1973, just after I had signed for United. Paul followed three years later, in Manchester, on 23 August, and Jonathan came along on 15 December 1979, again in Manchester. This was the era before new men. Dads didn't rush off to be at the wife's bedside for the birth of their children. It was unheard of in football. There was a need to play in the team for fear of losing your place and to keep the win bonuses coming in, for what they were. The day after Jonathan was born I was scoring in a 2–1 win at Coventry.

It would be fair to say that the boys' upbringing was largely down to Mum, including their introduction to football. It was as clear as it can be from an early age that all three could probably earn a living from the game. What sort of living, what sort of standard, was in the lap of the gods. Nobody knows. I certainly never pushed them. I might have kicked the ball around a bit in the back garden, but I never offered guidance or advice. As I said, Dale Marie was more involved with them at that age. She was the one running them about to matches. All I can tell you is that they were keen on the game. And they all wanted to be footballers.

Everybody has a story about pushy parents. I was the exact opposite. I think it is foolish to get wrapped up in dreams of superstardom for your kids. I was distressed recently to hear on the way back from a Champions League win for Chelsea over Olympiakos that a lower-league club had just released three eight-year-olds. First of all they shouldn't be there at that age, but if they are, how can anyone dismiss them so quickly? It's absurd. I don't agree with taking kids so early. If one of my boys had come home at a similar age telling me they had been invited to attend a particular club I would have told him to behave himself. Crack on with playing football at school. Too many clubs are taking youngsters just to make sure that no one else gets them. It's shocking. I don't believe a person with a coaching badge can turn my boy into a footballer if he does not have the ability. If he does have the talent, it will emerge through playing with the various age groups in the appropriate setting – school teams, county sides, etc. – as it did for me. A big part of making the grade is having the heart, the commitment and the desire to push on. You can't coach that. And if the hunger is not there, talent alone is unlikely to be enough. It has to come from the child, and part of the process is fighting your way through the ranks.

I watched a few of my boys' games along the way. It was hard for me in some ways. I know how hard it is to break through as a professional. There are no guarantees, even for those who display the most talent at a young age. It is pointless talking about a professional career until kids are at least sixteen. When I was manager at Swindon I didn't see any kids until that age. All this developing youngsters through academies is a relatively recent thing and not something I invest too much faith in. John Trollope looked after the youth set-up at Swindon, but even he would not get them until they were seventeen.

I had just moved to West Ham when Michael started to mature as a player. He was offered YTS contracts by Manchester United, Arsenal and Norwich. West Ham were renowned for their youth system and had produced a long list of players down the years, from Bobby Moore to Joe Cole. Billy Bonds was in charge. Billy is a man you would be happy to trust your son's life with. I had seen Michael play at county level. He had craft, he could finish, and he enjoyed the game. He was about to turn seventeen, so I asked Billy to have a look at him in training. No more than that. If Michael was going to progress he would have to impress Billy, not me. That is the way it should be. Billy took a shine to him and thought he was a bright prospect. Sadly, I moved on after just seven months.

Michael stayed at Upton Park to get on with his own future. Though Billy thought highly of him – he scored fifty-odd goals in two seasons – Michael found it hard to settle. He was a young lad living in digs in the East End of London. For whatever reason, he did not move forward at Upton Park after that two-year spell.

When I went to Stoke, Tony Lacey, the youth team manager, asked me about him. Again, I wasn't going to actively promote Michael. I don't think that is right for the manager of a football club. Tony and Michael would have to sort things out for themselves. We had moved up to Stoke at this point so it was easy for Michael to manage things himself. He came on board with Tony's blessing. I watched him in a few youth games and he looked good, as I expected. He appeared to be enjoying himself again. Quietly, I was pleased with his progress.

At this point Paul also started to work with Tony. Again, there was no pushing from me. Like his brother, Paul was a decent little player. He was strong and capable in the same way. Tony would have picked him up through the usual channels, the local scouting networks. The Stoke chairman, Peter Coates, was a reasonable judge of a player. He saw both my lads and was always saying how well they were doing.

With Michael and Paul making their way at Stoke, Jonathan was picked up by Dick Bradshaw at Nottingham Forest. Dick never came through to me; he dealt directly with Mum. She was the one carting Jonathan around the place, talking to scouts and coaches. I couldn't tell you now where Dick spotted him. The most likely venue was a county game. Dick took a real shine to Jon and convinced his mother that Forest was the place for him. I did not get involved, but I was massively pleased for him. I'd seen him play, of course, and had a gut feeling he was going to be a really good player. It is difficult for me to say which of my sons was the best. They were all strikers in the same mould as me, and they all had ability. The rest was down to fate.

In my last season at Stoke Michael broke into the first team, more at the insistence of my assistant Chic Bates and the chairman than me. Not that I thought he was incapable. On the contrary. It is just an awkward position to be in as a manager having to make decisions about picking your son. The first thing Joe Public talk about is nepotism. I didn't want that. It was music to my ears to hear the chairman and my assistant almost insisting that I played him. He did well, playing regularly after Christmas and scoring a few goals. In one game against Oxford, a live TV match, Big Ron, my manager at United, who was working as a pundit, likened him to me. It was great that others saw him as a talent in his own right. I treated him like everyone else. In fact I was probably harder on him.

When I left Stoke to take on Celtic in court, because of the progress Michael and Paul had made, again in the opinion of Chic and the chairman, I advised them to go in to see about new contracts. They were both progressing well but earning peanuts. Chic told them they still had to prove themselves. I could have knocked his head off. He was the one, along with the chairman, telling me that the boys were coming along. And this was the fella I had taken from club to club with me. I got him a pay-off at Celtic when I didn't even get one myself. I didn't want him to do my boys a favour, or give them any kind of special treatment. I would never have asked anybody to do that. I just wanted him to do the right thing by them. I was livid. They were earning next to nothing under me, and Mike was a first-team regular by the time I left. They deserved proper money. On reflection I blame myself. I should have disregarded the nepotism issue and put them on the decent wages that they fully merited. Unfortunately we all make mistakes. This was one of my biggest. I can only assume that Chic or the chairman were influenced by someone else at the club.

Michael did not play another game for Stoke. Paul broke into the side, making his debut against Stockport. He did OK, according to the reports. On the following Tuesday Stoke were playing at Bury. Paul wasn't even in the squad. Two players who had never played before were brought in. They had probably just stepped off the plane. Much later Paul told me that he thought it was because the club had taken exception to something I had written in a newspaper. It didn't matter that I had made Stoke £8 million-plus in transfers, money that helped build a new stadium. Oh no. I had written something in the newspaper.

Paul was then diagnosed with a fractured back. He had been carrying the condition for a couple of years without knowing what it was. In his case the injury would not heal itself. Surgery was required, which meant fusing the bones together. That kind of treatment restricts movement dramatically. Paul played on, but he knew that the chances of him developing as he might have done were slim. The injury took its toll. Paul had been struck by one of those random events that can afflict anybody, which supports my view that it is pointless parents getting carried away with ideas of greatness for their kids. You never know what is around the corner.

26

THE LONGEST JOURNEY

LOSING MY FATHER OBVIOUSLY MADE ME FEEL VULNERABLE. When you are young you don't realize the effect things like that can have on you. When I think back to the decision I took to leave Celtic as a player, there was a little concern in the back of my mind about whether or not I was doing the right thing. No one ever left Celtic. No one ever joined that club thinking that one day they might leave, other than in retirement. I realize now that the death of my father probably influenced in some way my discussions with Jock Stein. It maybe gave me one or two reasons to do things I might otherwise not have done. I was not totally comfortable, not 100 per cent sure I was correct in standing up to Jock. Now I can see it was absolutely the right thing to do, and I was pleased later to see Kenny Dalglish and David Hay following suit.

Before I went to the World Cup in Argentina in 1978, I lost my mother. I really kicked myself later that I did not do more to help her after Dad died. In that sense, I blame myself for what happened. I left her up in Scotland when I joined Manchester United. I did not judge correctly the impact my father dying would have on her. In fact her life changed dramatically. I could have done something about it.

I was in the Excelsior Hotel in Glasgow again, this time for one of the World Cup get-togethers. I rang my mother. I hadn't been in touch for five or six days – something else I blame myself for now. The phone kept ringing. There was no answer. I rang again the following morning. Again no answer. Later that afternoon I was sitting in the foyer when I saw my uncle, who was a doctor, walk in through the front door. As soon as I saw him I knew something was badly wrong. I hadn't seen him in ages. I thought, 'Fuckin' 'ell, don't tell me.' My mind flashed to something horrific. Within seconds he was telling me that my mother was dead. What made it worse was that she had died in mysterious circumstances.

After my father died my mother had taken up with so-called friends, two people in particular. In a nutshell, she had taken them into her confidence. They would be delving into private matters while at the same time giving her tablets for her nerves. It was all a bit of a mess. I didn't know any of this was going on. Money went missing from her bank account. Mother had signed things over to them she shouldn't have done. Then one night she took too many of the tablets they had been giving her and slumped over on the bed. She fell asleep at a certain angle and never woke up. She was found three or four days later.

It was only years later that it dawned on me what I should have done. I should have brought her down to Manchester with us. It was a kind of double whammy, because I had bought the chip shop I have at Old Trafford for her. I was just starting to smell the problems she was having up there in Largs when she died. Everybody says don't blame yourself, but that is exactly what you do. Why didn't I spot the warning signs? I left it a bit too late. I wasn't quick enough to react. I was quick enough on the pitch to get a career going at Celtic and Manchester United but not sharp enough up top to spot what needed to be done for my own mother.

Years later, of course, I found myself in another horrific situation when I lost my son Jonathan. I can make excuses for myself when I was twenty-odd, playing for Celtic one minute and United the next, but not as a grown man with kids of my own.

When Jon went over to Forest he must have been the happiest kid in Stoke-on-Trent. He was a happy-go-lucky lad, never down or miserable, always had loads of friends. He got on brilliantly at Forest. I shot over to Nottingham on a couple of Saturday mornings to have a look at him and lend a bit of support. I came back once and remarked to his mum that I thought he could go all the way to the top. And I did not say that lightly. He reminded me of a Gazza-type player. He was strong, with good feet. At Forest he was paired with Marlon Harewood up front. It was a little and large partnership. Marlon was the same size and build he is now. He would knock people about. He had pace and power. Jon had a bit more control and perhaps greater awareness. He was also a top finisher. I was really optimistic for him. I didn't get involved in the details at Forest. I wasn't interested in how they did things over there. As far as I was concerned Jon was on a three-year contract, in capable hands, and enjoying his football. The more matches I saw the more I was convinced he was going all the way in the game.

Then, somewhere along the way, something triggered a change in Jon. I will never know what that was. Neither will his mother and his brothers. There were a couple of football incidents that were not ideal, but not enough to turn his world upside down. He stepped out of line during the week once, stayed out late or something of that nature – kids' stuff – and as a punishment was left behind when Forest had an FA Youth Cup tie at Spurs. All the kids stayed in one hostel in Nottingham, about twenty-five of them. When the bus turned up to take them to London twenty-four trooped out and one was left behind. That would have been embarrassing for Jon. I thought that was poor management. He should have been fined, hit in the pocket. Instead they hit him in the head. I didn't think much about it at the time, but just imagine. The FA Youth Cup is a big night for the kids. They play their League matches, but the Cup is a showcase in front of the cameras. And the squad left without him. Not the best. Again, I did not intervene. That was my policy. Other parents might have dealt with it differently. If I was wrong, I have to live with that.

Not long after that he was sent to play with the Under-16s against an England XI at Lilleshall. That was another punishment, a calculated demotion because he was an over-age player. Lilleshall was not that far from us. I went down to watch him and I really couldn't believe what I was seeing. Everything had gone to pot. The timing had gone. His attitude had changed. He wasn't as lively or as focused on the pitch. I went home that night a little bit concerned. Within the space of a couple of months I had seen a lad going from a Gazza to a kid totally off the pace. I recalled a kid at Stoke whom the youth team manager recommended but we did not give a professional contract to. That was down to attitude and overall approach to his job. Maybe he had problems off the field we didn't know about, because he could play.

One Monday morning we got a call at home from the new Forest manager Dave Bassett. He called Jon into his office in front of me and his mother. Dave did everything you would expect a manager to do if he believed he had a player on his books who was really going places. Jon was upset, saying he didn't like it any more, that he wanted to leave. Dave explained the need to buckle down and focus on the job. It was the time of year when clubs release players they feel are not going to make the grade. There was never a question of that with Jon. I wondered if the fact that Jon had seen these discarded kids picking up huge cheques after having contracts paid up might be having some influence on his thinking. These kids were earning good money. If you get cut with eighteen months to run, that adds up to a lot of money, particularly for teenagers. Anyway, Jon agreed to give it another go.

A couple of weeks later, again on a Monday morning, we got another call from Dave. Over we went, back to Nottingham. There were discussions that were similar to what had been said at the previous meeting. We both wanted Jon to stay and did our best to convince him to do so. By the end of the day we had to accept that if he wasn't happy and wanted to leave he could not be made to stay. Forest paid up his contract, and Jon walked out of there with a nice cheque in his pocket.

To me, this system is all wrong. The way football clubs groom young talent when they know the majority will never make it is obscene. Clubs operate a scattergun approach, routinely grabbing anybody who shows any kind of ability in the hope that one of them might make it. If that happens, they stand to make maybe £5 million selling him on down the line. But for every kid who achieves at that level there are nine who don't. The damage clubs inflict on the youngsters they toss aside is irreparable. Telling teenage kids they were not going to be given a contract was the hardest thing I had to do in management. When I was coming through there was no big contract at the age of sixteen like the one kids get today. I was on schoolboy forms. To have allowed the system to progress from the kind of arrangement I enjoyed to the big sums kids get now is shameful. Clubs are bringing kids in at eight and nine and at any time between then and eighteen giving them a contract or the elbow. What does rejection at that stage do to a kid's mind? Equally, what does big money do to those lucky enough to get a deal? Jon was at Forest earning more than my first wage at Manchester United. Kids at bigger clubs get even more. One lad I took on loan from a Premiership club started off on £3,000 a week – £150,000 a year. It's ludicrous. I believe the system should be looked at independently. The football authorities might be horrified at the results.

What happened to Jon at Forest was a mystery to me. When Dick Bradshaw took him on I felt he was destined to be a pro. I never heard Jon say a bad word about the experience until the end. He loved his digs and his work. He'd come home at weekends full of it. My wife and I were two happy parents. Our youngest was getting on well doing something he loved.

Jon left Forest in May 1998 and was back at home in Stoke. Life fell back into its daily routine. I went about my business doing a bit of media work and helping out at Sheffield United under Steve Bruce. I wasn't looking for signs. I assumed everything was for the best and got on with things, as I always had done.

Eleven months later I was heading to Century FM, a radio station serving the North West and based in Manchester, where I worked as a pundit, when I got a call from the police asking me to come back to Stoke-on-Trent. They didn't tell me what it was about, they just told me to come back.

That morning I had had a little warning. I was on the roof of the house trying to clean out the gutter when my lad's girl-friend appeared looking really sheepish. She asked if Jon was in. I said that I thought he was with her last night.

'Did he not come home?' she asked.

My heart sank a little. I felt really annoyed. 'No, he didn't. As I said, I thought he was with you.'

An hour or so later I was travelling up to Manchester and taking a call from the police. I sensed that a disaster was about to unfold.

It's amazing how stupid things can get in those situations. I was apprehensive about phoning Chris Cooper at Century to tell him I couldn't make it. I remember mumbling something to him along the lines of 'Chris, I think I have a massive problem here. I have a bad feeling about this.'

The journey back from Manchester felt like the longest drive in the world. I was trying to convince myself that Jon had been arrested or something silly like that. I was hoping and praying that was the case. On the way back I got a call from a pal of mine, Nigel Sergeant, who was in the police. He said he wanted to see me at a hotel as I came into Stoke. When he said that to me I knew it was bad. I somehow knew that my son was dead.

I can't remember what Nigel said when I arrived. I was just numb. Jon had been discovered hanging from a tree by a cyclist on his way to work that morning. I couldn't take that in.

I then had to do something I never thought I would have to do: identify my son's body. I was not allowed to see my mother when she died, because of the circumstances. My uncle dealt with all of that. This time I had to do it. So I went to the mortuary to identify Jonathan, and it was the hardest thing I have ever done in my life. I can't describe or put into words what it was like.

By the time I got home my wife, Michael and Paul were there. Again, I can't tell you how the next few hours passed. I have no meaningful recollection of them.

The thing is, you never expect that something as desperate as a suicide is going to affect you. Surprisingly, football has had its share of them. I'll never forget taking a call from Joy Morris, the wife of Kevin Morris, my old mate at Swindon. Kevin was a bit of a panicker. A new regime had taken over at Swindon with a new chief executive. Kevin was worried about his position. He'd been called in and told there would be changes at the club, though he wasn't told his position was under threat. He'd call me for reassurance. 'Kev,' I'd say, 'you are a fixture of the club. It would be impossible for someone to come along and get you out of the door.' A couple of weeks later Joy was telling me on the phone that Kevin had fed a hosepipe into his car and killed himself.

Kevin always used to joke that I tried to kill him once when I crashed the car on the way back from a game at Southampton. We'd been watching a player. It was late at night, and we were driving through the country lanes of Wiltshire. I took a sharp bend too quickly and crashed into a ditch. The car was a write-off, and Kevin was right: we were lucky to get out of there in one piece.

It was a heartbreaking call to take from Joy. Calls like that don't come often in your life. I was stunned.

Alan Davies, my old team-mate at Manchester United, did exactly the same thing in 1992. Alan was a quiet lad, a neat and tidy footballer. You would never think he would be capable of taking his own life. He was found dead in his car at the age of thirty. Three or four days before that he had played for Swansea at Stoke. He'd seemed his normal self, the happy fella I knew at United. Justin Fashanu was another high-profile case.

Again, you never think your family will be touched by it. But we were. Our son was gone. You never get over it.

The next few days were just a nightmare, though in truth the nightmare never leaves you. Reporters were camped outside the house. It was the first time I had ever refused an interview. I didn't have any answers to give. I don't have any now. That does not stop me spending hours going over in my mind what I could have done, what I should have done, to prevent Jon from taking his life. I just didn't see it coming. Losing a child in any circumstances is tough; this was even worse. We'll never know what he might have gone on to achieve with his life.

Whenever I go to the cemetery to visit Jon's grave I see next to his headstone one for someone who died at the age of eighty-six. On the other side the person was in his seventies. Jonathan was nineteen years old. A young life snuffed out.

I'm not a frequent visitor to the cemetery. It is just too painful for me. My mind starts racing away, playing tricks with me. The whole thing becomes too big to contemplate, because it can never be resolved to anybody's satisfaction. There are too many questions that remain unanswered, no way of ever finding peace.

People say time is a great healer. It isn't in my case. Others say that there is nothing I could have done to prevent what happened. No one will ever convince me of that. My mind tells me every day that I could have done something. Some have suggested grief counselling. It would not be worth my while, because I cannot accept that what happened to Jon was unavoidable.

A lot was written at the time and many things were speculated on. The coroner recorded an open verdict which indicated that he wasn't even convinced it was intentional. The only truth is that we don't have any definitive answers. We never will. Jon is not here to answer those questions. There is no point in further speculation.

The inquest was very difficult for all of us. It was another big media affair, lots of TV cameras and reporters. It was a distressing time. The court looked in detail at the last few hours of Jon's life and established that they were spent with his girlfriend. I was given an opportunity to put questions to her, but I didn't want to dig too deep and turn it into a big public affair. Jon was gone. I couldn't bring him back by asking his girlfriend a series of probing questions.

More than five hundred people attended Jonathan's funeral, including his team-mates at Forest. It passed in a blur. I was numb with grief, overwhelmed by emotion. Consequently I remember very little about the day. I don't know what I said or who I spoke to. As a family we made it through the day, no more than that.

After the funeral I thought the best place for my wife and family would be with her parents in America for a few weeks. I thought that might help. But when that plane set off along the runway at Manchester airport I felt terrible. I felt like I was leaving Jon behind. I was thinking to myself, 'What am I doing on this plane? I shouldn't be on it.' I can't honestly say I feel any better now.

It is five years now since I was last interviewed for a job. I haven't given up on the idea of returning to management. I'm open-minded about the future. But if I don't manage again I won't feel that I have missed out. My life changed in 1999.

Does walking up the steps at Wembley matter any more? Does getting into the play-off finals matter any more? Would winning a championship be as good as it was in the past? The answer is probably no. I can imagine going home delighted, then waking up the following morning no longer on a high. The kind of tragedy that struck my family leaves an indelible mark. You can't escape it. Anybody in the same position will tell you that. Your life is turned upside down and inside out. Nothing is ever the same again.

Every day is a battle I know I can never win. Some days I feel I could go under any minute. I feel that I let my son down, that I failed as a parent to discharge the most important duty: to protect your kids. I stay afloat by reminding myself that I still have a wife, two sons and now grandchildren to support.

These days I find myself reading the births, deaths and marriages columns in the newspaper. It makes me realize I am not alone in dealing with loss. There is a crumb of comfort in that. I picked out this message which sums up the way I feel. Somehow it's easier to write things down than to speak.

> They say there is a reason
> They say that time will heal
> But neither time nor reason
> Will change the way we feel

Those words are spot on.

Jon's death has become the defining event of my life. You like to remember all the great things you have done. That's what life is about. But what can I celebrate now? Having played for Celtic? Having played for Manchester United? Having represented my country? Having won promotion at

Swindon and Stoke? None of that means as much to me now.

The one thing you have to do as a footballer is make decisions on the pitch. As a manager you have to make decisions not only on your behalf but on behalf of others. I believe that I got most of the decisions I made in my career right. My judgement has been good. Yet in the one area that really mattered, looking after my son, I did not make the right calls. I did not get it right when it mattered. That is a hell of a thing to have on your conscience.

The search goes on for a solution that will make things better, not just for me but for every member of the family, something that Jon would want, a magic formula to take the pain away. It is like being in a maze. You hope there is a way out somewhere, but you can't find it. Even if you could, you probably wouldn't take it because it would feel like you were deserting him. I loved my son. We all did. Jon knows that.

27

HERE WE GO AGAIN

STEVE BRUCE TOOK OVER AS SHEFFIELD UNITED MANAGER IN
the summer of 1998 – his first managerial post. The court case
was over and I was deeply out of pocket. Steve called me and
invited me to join him at Bramall Lane to help out about the
place and do some scouting. I like Steve. I needed to work and
I was grateful just to be around a football club again. I had
been out of the game for twelve months. I was happy to be a
dogsbody.

I spent a fair amount of time abroad. I can't say I unearthed
any great talent, but then I'm hard to please. For me, scouting
is more about not signing players than it is about snapping
them up. If you listened to the recommendations of agents
you'd think you were going to watch Pelé and Maradona playing every week in Poland and Slovakia. I was going to rule
them out. That wasn't hard given the budget Sheffield were
working with.

Then, getting on for a year after linking up with Steve,

Jonathan was suddenly no longer with us and everything became irrelevant overnight.

A month after Jonathan's tragic death, in the summer of 1999, Steve left Bramall Lane to take over at Huddersfield. When the time was right he gave me a call to see if I felt ready to get back into the swing of things. I was more than grateful to hear from Steve again. It gave me a chance to clear my head and immerse myself in something I had always been used to. I didn't care what the job description was, I was just happy to be thinking about something else. In a sense, losing the court case probably helped in a perverse sort of way. Had I retired as a footballer with significant wealth I would probably have rotted away at home. Certainly all I wanted to do after losing my son was curl up and die. But I didn't have that luxury. Necessity forced me out the door. And for the hours I was at work it was a great help.

Barry Rubery, the owner of Huddersfield, had great ambitions for his club. I remember Steve telling me just before Jonathan's death that he had been approached by Rubery. He was promising £10 million to build a team. That was a fair amount of money. But like a lot of business people coming into football, Rubery probably got the shock of his life when he saw how clubs operated, how difficult it is to make an impression. He took Steve on to shape this brave new world at the McAlpine Stadium, to take the club on to the next stage. But inevitably at small clubs when money becomes tight, the manager and chairman or owner end up locked on a collision course. What starts out as an amiable relationship often deteriorates when the money supply dries up and results start to suffer. This is what happened between Steve and Barry.

Steve wasn't helped by the sale of top scorer Marcus Stewart to Ipswich in February 2000. The fee was £2.5 million – too much for a club like Huddersfield to turn down. Scoring goals became a problem. We were top of the First Division table going into Christmas but encountered a rocky holiday period, taking just one point from nine and dropping down to fifth. On the day Stewart scored on his Ipswich debut we went down at home to the only goal of the game against Portsmouth, a team fifteen places below us in the division. And guess where our next match was? At Ipswich. Marcus scored. We lost. The slide continued. We managed to lose our last two games of the season to slip out of the play-off places to eighth – a disaster for Steve. Things had looked so promising in the first half of the season. Steve was never able to recover the momentum after that.

The 2000–01 season started well with two straight wins. We then lost Clyde Wijnhard in a car accident. He crashed his Jeep on the A1 and was lucky to escape with a broken arm. It was a bad omen. The club chairman, Ian Ayre, resigned shortly afterwards, adding to a growing sense of instability. By the time we arrived at Grimsby for our thirteenth game of the season, we were at the wrong end of the table. We went in at half-time 1–0 down. The directors' box at Grimsby is on the opposite side of the pitch to the dugouts. From nowhere, Barry Rubery appeared in the tunnel, grabbed Steve, pulled him around to face him and demanded to know what the bloody hell was going on. 'How can we be losing 1–0 to Grimsby?' The question illustrated how little Barry knew about the game. History will tell you that Grimsby is a tricky place for anybody to go to on any day. And, let's be honest, we were talking Huddersfield Town here, not Manchester United or Arsenal. Someone in the directors' box had probably remarked that it was not good to be losing at a place like this. A ding-dong followed in the tunnel, with Steve giving as good as he got. Then he had to go into the dressing room and try to lift the players. Steve was seething. It was ridiculous. We lost the game and were now in serious trouble. A meeting followed and, inevitably I suppose, two days later Steve was out.

Barry turned to me and John Deehan to take over. It was the last thing on my mind. After what I had been through with the court case against Celtic and the death of my son I didn't know if I was ready to hold the management reins again. At the same time I did not have the luxury of choice. I was not in a position to turn down work. I had to have a job to pay the mortgage and try to recoup my losses. Reluctantly, John and I agreed to take temporary charge and see what developed.

The very next day we were back at Bramall Lane. Funny how fate plays tricks with you. We lost 3–0 and were lucky to escape so lightly.

A week later I was approached by Trevor Cherry, who was working alongside Barry Rubery, and asked if I would consider taking on the job permanently. Initially I said no. He then explained the obvious: if I didn't take it somebody else would step in, and they would almost certainly have me out the door. I felt backed into a corner really. I was still vulnerable. I made the decision to take the job, bringing in Joe Jordan as my assistant. Just twelve days after Steve was axed I was back in the game. And in a familiar position.

Huddersfield were at the wrong end of the division and there was no money to spend. Not only that, I was told I had to release as many high-earners as possible. Players like Ken Monkou were on big wages. All this came with a plea not to get relegated. An escape was unlikely, but we gave it a go. A run of five wins and a draw just before Christmas lifted us off the bottom. 'Here we go,' I thought. In March I brought Andy Booth back from Sheffield Wednesday. He scored on his debut in a win over Portsmouth. Hope springs eternal. We got to the last game of the season needing to beat Birmingham to ensure we stayed up (fate again). Portsmouth and Crystal Palace, who started the day below us in the relegation zone, were both away. Palace won at Stockport in bizarre circumstances. The crowd at the McAlpine went wild with a minute to go when the fans listening to radios thought Stockport had been given a penalty at Edgely Park. The referee did not give it. With the Stockport players still chasing the referee, Palace went up the other end and scored. I saw it later on TV. It was a stonewall penalty kick. That's life. If one of them lost we would stay up, no two ways about it. One team did lose – us. Incredibly, both our rivals won away from home. I experienced relegation for the first time as a manager.

We started our Division Two campaign in 2001–02 with three wins out of four. Then in October I picked up Leon Knight on a loan deal from Chelsea. Leon had got involved in a bit of a skirmish down at Brighton, him and Carlton Cole. It was in all the papers. That's where I came across the story. I'd seen him play. I thought he was a real talent. I thought I'd take advantage of his situation and get him out of there, away from the London scene. I rang Chelsea and they agreed. 'Great,' I thought. 'This is too good to be true.' He was just eighteen.

You never really know what a player is like until you have seen him in your own environment, and the first training session he had with us was a bit of an eye-opener. He arrived in a blacked-out BMW. We ran one lap just to warm up. He finished about thirty yards behind everybody. The alarm bells started to ring. 'There must be something seriously wrong with this kid,' I thought. So I pulled him to one side and asked what was the problem with the running.

'Do you have an injury? Can you not run?' I asked.

'Yeah,' he said. 'I haven't got a problem with running.'

'Well, why are you not running then?'

'It's a waste of fucking time, running. I'm all about what I do on the pitch.'

'Oh right, great. I think you can't run.'

'Let's do another lap then.'

I lined everybody up. 'Right, lads, one more lap around the pitch.' And who won? Leon Knight, by fifteen yards. I now knew he could run. I also knew that I had to get into his head. I had to find a way to connect with him.

We moved on to do some shooting, and a bit of five-a-side. I couldn't believe what I was seeing. He looked special every time he struck the ball. Good connection, nice and crisp and hard. In the air he was brilliant. My size, too. I was thinking that this kid could do everything. By the end of the season he'd scored sixteen goals in thirty-one games to help us make the play-offs. Except he didn't make them.

On 1 April we were at Oldham Athletic for a meaningless game. Four minutes into the match Leon elbowed their centre-half in the face and was sent off. This was no April fool. In those days suspensions for red cards did not kick in for a couple of weeks, which meant I'd lost my star striker for the play-offs. I had Andy Booth back from injury, but it wasn't enough. Not for the first time in the play-offs my team failed to make dominance at home pay. Andy had two goals disallowed and hit the woodwork in a 0–0 draw against

Brentford. At their place he scored just two minutes into the second leg but we still lost, 2–1. Very frustrating.

Leon was one of the most difficult lads I've had to manage but I got on well with him. I had to be his dad, not his manager. If he got the hump he'd just tell you to fuck off. There were a few incidents during the season. Nothing I couldn't handle, though. He did well for us, but he could have done even better for himself. After we had both left the club I came across him playing for Sheffield Wednesday reserves against Manchester United reserves. I was doing a bit of work for MUTV. He was standing up front throwing his hands in the air, shouting at people, shouting at the referee. He didn't get a kick that night. He didn't make it at Wednesday and ended up moving on. He is one of the best players I have seen playing football in the lower divisions of English football. Here was a man who had everything except the one thing that could have made him great: the right attitude. He didn't recognize that. He didn't want to. I just wish I could have sat him down and got it through to him that his career could go one of two ways: right to the top, or right to the bottom. The lad should be playing in the Premiership. If he had come through in my time as a player, he might have made it to the top flight. He'd certainly have got through the door at Celtic, though he'd have been straight out of it again unless he changed that attitude.

In January 2002 I had been affected by yet another takeover. This time a four-man consortium bought a controlling interest in Huddersfield Town and I ended up with a new chairman, David Taylor. One member of the new board wanted greater involvement with the team, to come to the training ground, to travel with the team to games, to come into the dressing room before matches to listen to my team-talk.

It was all very bizarre. The answer was no, of course.

At the end of that 2001–02 season the board congratulated me and Joe for doing so well after being relegated the previous year. Joe's contract was up. Ann Hough, the secretary, popped up to the training ground on two or three occasions before the end of the season to iron out the details. Joe declined, saying that he would tie everything up at the end of the season.

Given the circumstances at Huddersfield, I thought that season in Division Two, getting into the play-offs, was one of my best achievements as a manager. To celebrate, my wife and I went on holiday to America. We spent a week in Hilton Head with my wife's parents then headed west to Las Vegas. We stayed at Caesar's Palace on the Strip. 'Right,' I thought, 'for the next few days I'm going to switch off my phone.' It had been a long time since I'd been able to relax in any meaningful way.

A couple of days later curiosity got the better of me and I turned the phone back on. I had at least fifty missed calls. I immediately feared the worst. After what happened with Jonathan I thought it must be another family problem of some kind. I did not really want to start listening to the messages. The first was left by Jim White, the Sky TV presenter. 'Give us a ring the moment you pick up this message,' he said. I rang him. He asked me straight up if I would go on air and give the programme a view on my sacking.

'What are you talking about?' I asked.

'You've been sacked by Huddersfield,' Jim said.

I was stunned. I thought he was taking the piss. I had to ask him two or three times if he was being straight with me. Most managers know when the sack is coming. It had only happened to me once, at Celtic, and I'd been well aware it was coming then. I did not see this coming at all. There were no signs. We'd left with pats on the back all round and Joe talking about a new contract as my assistant.

I was dumbstruck for a while, then I agreed to speak to Jim on air. On I went, admitting that I'd heard of my sacking by chance through Sky. Of course I trawled through my messages afterwards to find that there was one from chairman, David Taylor. I rang Joe. He hadn't heard anything either.

'Joe, we've been axed.'

'You are fucking joking, aren't you?'

On this occasion, no.

My mind went back to the director who wanted to see how it was done from the inside. I wondered if he had not had something to do with this. But I never discovered the reason because I never asked. Neither did Joe. We were angry. We were not in the business of trying to convince the board of our credentials. We had both played at the highest level and enjoyed successful careers as players and managers. We weren't about to start justifying ourselves to this lot.

A new manager, Mick Wadsworth, was appointed but the club agreed to continue paying me until my contract was up. Joe took them to a tribunal over the new contract he had been promised. I spoke on his behalf and he won the case. Joe was awarded £35,000. A few months later the club went into administration. Joe didn't get his money, I stopped receiving mine, and Huddersfield were relegated. David subsequently admitted that it was a mistake to get rid of Joe and me.

That experience left me wondering if I were not simply unlucky as a manager. I ran into Fergus McCann at Celtic, the Inland Revenue after I took over at West Ham, then I went to Huddersfield to turn around on a shoestring a club that had been relegated the previous season. The standard reasons for sacking a manager did not seem to apply to me. I didn't fail on the pitch. I didn't cost clubs any money. In fact the opposite is true in both cases. At Swindon and at Stoke I left them in surplus to the tune of millions. I worked my socks off, gave as much to these clubs as it was possible for a manager to give. And what did I get? Multiple kicks in the bollocks.

A little over a year after I got the sack at Huddersfield, in October 2003, the Tranmere job came up. They had lost heavily at Luton in a match televised live on Sky. The job was advertised shortly after that. I fancied it because I felt I could take the club on and that Tranmere had potential. They had a solid cup tradition as underdogs. I felt it would not take much to get them back to that position of taking the odd cup scalp and enjoying solid League campaigns.

I gave John Aldridge a ring to ask him about the job. Ironically, Aldo had been sacked as Tranmere manager in 2001 after losing to Huddersfield when I was at the McAlpine. He warned me that the boss, Lorraine Rogers, was very hands on. She liked to be involved in the recruitment of players and things like that. That concerned me a bit.

I was interviewed by a panel of four including Lorraine, the chairwoman, and Peter Johnson, who was a former chairman at Everton. I spelled out what I was about, the kind of manager I was, that I expected total commitment from the players, that I would train them hard, and that I would not tolerate drinking. As a manager I believe I have a duty to the players. They are my responsibility. As part of that responsibility I must make sure that I give each one of them every opportunity to be a professional footballer for as long as possible. You can't do that if you allow drink at your football club. What they do away from the premises I can't control, but at the club, on the bus, in the players' lounge, wherever, no drink. That is not an easy habit to establish. Players are used to going into the players' lounge after games to get tanked up. But if I allowed that I would be contributing to their downfall. I take no pleasure in looking at, for example, the state of Paul Gascoigne and others like him who have fallen foul of drink.

I spoke from the heart. I was not selling them a line about the drink, it's always been my position. I think it struck a chord. There was no tactical talk, no talk about budgets and suchlike. I simply explained that I would be looking to bring on young players and to get the older ones into better condition. It was a template that had worked for me before. I had a track record in that area.

They asked if I would retain John McMahon, the caretaker manager. I had no problem with that, and told them so. We shook hands and that was that.

As I left the room, I noticed outside Steve Cotterill waiting to go in. I didn't think that was the best move, lining up interviewees as if they were in a doctor's surgery. Steve was not alone. He had a couple of fellas with him and a couple of suitcases. I thought, 'Bloody hell, I've just driven up from Stoke without so much as a scrap of paper with me.' I didn't have any notes prepared. I saw Steve and his suitcases and was gripped immediately by the thought that the panel must have viewed me as terribly unprofessional.

A couple of days passed, then the phone rang. It was Tranmere, inviting me back to see them again. It was a Thursday afternoon. Peter Johnson broke the ice by thanking me for returning. I explained that I was worried I might have sold myself short at the first meeting.

'What do you mean by that?' he asked.

I mentioned Steve and his team of advisers and the suit-cases. 'If you don't mind me asking,' I added, 'what was in them?'

It was projectors. He'd used them to show the panel how he would conduct training sessions and suchlike.

'I don't have that kind of equipment,' I said. 'This is my equipment – me.'

'Don't worry about that,' Peter Johnson said. 'We want you to be the manager of Tranmere Rovers.'

At that point we had not discussed terms, which is typical of me. I was principally concerned with the potential of the club. Only when I'd established that did I mention money. I didn't raise any of the issues Aldo had highlighted. I didn't want to put Lorraine on the back foot and force her to answer to me about how she ran her operation. I was just happy to take the job. A three-year contract at the market rate was on the table. They asked me if I wanted to bring anybody in. I said I would like Joe Jordan to join me. Lorraine said she would have to interview him. I wasn't overly happy with that, but it wasn't a deal-breaker. The only condition I imposed was to have a copy of the contract so that I could forward it to the League Managers Association for the lawyers to have a look at. She was happy with that. Before I drove home as the new manager of Tranmere Rovers, Lorraine added that she would like me on the bus the next day for the away game at Plymouth. No problem.

I arrived home to find the contract sitting on the tray in the fax machine. It was full of the standard jargon. One thing stood out, a clause that said I could be dismissed with twenty-eight days' notice without cause. Alarm bells rang. Despite sitting through two lengthy court cases my legal knowledge was not all that, as I've said, but it sounded to me as if they could get rid of me without a reason.

I rang Lorraine first thing on Friday. They were due to leave Tranmere at eleven a.m., head south and pick me up at Stoke. I explained that I wouldn't be on the bus. I had seen the contract and wanted a few points cleared up by the LMA before I proceeded. John McMahon had taken them for training all week, prepared them for the Plymouth match. I had not even met the players. I explained that the team's prospects would not be affected by my not being there. Lorraine wasn't too happy with that. I insisted that I could not set foot on that bus as the possible next manager while there were issues to clear up on my contract. Sure enough, the LMA's John Barnwell called me later that day to tell me that the contract was not acceptable, that I would be leaving myself wide open to dismissal at the drop of a hat. He also pointed out a further seven clauses he wasn't happy with.

Again, I was straight on the phone to Lorraine to confirm that my being with the team that weekend at Plymouth was a non-starter and that the major issue for me was the notice period; the other stuff was minor in comparison. She was very insistent, which to me was an indication, as Aldo had warned, of how she could be. This wasn't about money, which is the usual stumbling block. There were no hardball negotiations in that regard. Lorraine asked me to think about it, but there was nothing for me to think about. I wasn't going to go to the match without signing a contract. The old me might have got on that bus, but not the post-Celtic Lou Macari. I learned the value of attending to contractual details in a courtroom sat opposite Fergus McCann.

The next day I spent an anxious afternoon waiting for the result at Plymouth. It was another hammering. I was thinking, 'Bloody hell, what's going to happen now?' What happened was this: they were even more desperate for a manager, and double quick. Later, Brian Little, whom I know very well, told me that the club rang him on Sunday morning and asked if he could come up to Tranmere for a chat that day. They'd told him earlier in the week that he wouldn't be getting an interview. It all turned out well for Brian, he got the job, and good luck to him, I thought. The following day, Monday, I watched the story unfold on Sky Sports News. Tranmere expressed relief at finally getting their man. He was always first choice, they said. I was sitting at home laughing. 'Typical,' I thought. That's how football proceeds. The story that is presented to the world is somewhat different to the way events actually happened.

Lorraine never came back to me. I didn't expect her to. I'd told her that the contract was with the LMA and it could be days or weeks before they got in touch. I'd more or less invited her to make other arrangements. 'Don't wait for me,' I'd said. 'If you feel you need someone then go and get them because I won't be signing until I understand fully how the contract is going to work.' I had been caught out by small print at Celtic. Had I had my contract looked at thoroughly before I went there, maybe I could have closed all the doors for McCann, making it difficult for him to get me out the way he did. I didn't, and I paid for that with my job and a bill for £200,000 in costs. You could say I had learned my lesson.

I was disappointed not to take the Tranmere job. In another life, without the Celtic fiasco and without the death of my son, I would have been Tranmere manager, no question. I took the

Huddersfield post because I would have been out of a job if I hadn't. Trevor Cherry made that perfectly clear to me. I was quite content not to be in the hot seat that soon after losing Jon. A whole year passed after my sacking at the McAlpine before I considered another management post. Since the Tranmere interview I have had quite a few offers thrown at me from abroad and at home. If someone caught me at the right time, as the Tranmere job did, I might take the plunge again, but the job would have to be right for me to consider jumping back in. Everything would have to be right. I went to Swindon at the right time. I went to West Ham at the right time, though I wasn't there long enough to achieve what I wanted to. I went to Stoke at the right time. I went to Birmingham at the right time. The only place I went at the wrong time was Celtic. I just couldn't resist it.

Thus far I have been vindicated in saying no to the clubs that have offered me a job. None of them have done anything to prove me wrong. I still keep a special eye on Tranmere, though, waiting for them to make the step I've always thought they were capable of.

28

REALITY TV

AFTER MISSING OUT ON THE PRENTON PARK HOT SEAT I DID A bit of scouting for Brian Kerr while he was in charge of the Republic of Ireland. I knew him from my Stoke days, when he was a manager in the League of Ireland; he would come over at the end of the season looking to take players. Brian did well with the Republic's youth team and got the nod after Mick McCarthy's reign. He asked me to report on the opposition during the qualifiers for the 2006 World Cup. There was no money in it for me, just expenses. I enjoyed it. The reward, had the Republic of Ireland qualified, would have been to go to the World Cup Finals as part of the management set-up. Switzerland put paid to that at Lansdowne Road. We needed to beat the Swiss to get into the play-offs, but the match fizzled out in a 0–0 draw. So it was back to the television and radio studios for me.

I'd made my first appearance in a TV studio in 1986 as a football pundit on the BBC alongside Jimmy Hill. Over the coming years I was called upon from time to time to appear on a variety of football programmes, including *Gillette Soccer Special* on Sky, and to do some radio work with TalkSport. I was delighted to be asked and happy to oblige, if my schedule allowed. Post-Huddersfield, that schedule has been wide open. And I consider myself fortunate these days to be spending most of my time at Old Trafford working for MUTV.

The hardest shift I have ever had to put in was for TalkSport in Barcelona at the 1999 Champions League final. It was barely a month after we lost Jonathan. I had agreed to do it months before if United made it to the final, and when they did I felt I could not let TalkSport down. For a time afterwards they replayed the commentary of me going mad, shouting and screaming after Ole Gunnar Solskjaer poked the winning goal over the line in the closing seconds of the match. It was only a brief release. I was dead inside.

I took Jonathan's brothers, my two older boys, to the game. I knew exactly where they were behind the goal. I also knew that one of my sons was missing. It was an emotional evening for me. Not because United won the Champions League for the first time since 1968 in such dramatic fashion, but because of everything else surrounding it. When the final whistle went and the place went mad, I immediately thought about my two lads, which in turn triggered the painful thought that their brother was absent.

It was a surreal evening, one of the great nights for Manchester United. Everybody was jumping up and down, hugging each other. There was a function afterwards at the team hotel near the marina complex, but I didn't want to go anywhere near it. I went back to my hotel alone.

My sons flew back to Manchester. The only person I bumped into was Statto, aka Angus Loughran, who was chuffed with himself having acquired a pile of signatures on his programme.

To this day I view my work with MUTV as a release, an opportunity to clear my head and concentrate on an issue far removed from the circumstances at home. I take my work seriously. I understand that an opinion is required. Even though it is Manchester United, the club I played for, I like to think I call it as it is, say what I feel. I'm not going to say they were great on a day when they weren't. I have not really had any run-ins with the United staff, but I'm not silly enough to believe that at some point I have not got up the noses of one or two of the players.

The only time for me to be concerned is if the manager loses it with me. If he's aggrieved then things might get awkward. I've had no direct run-ins with Fergie, but I have on the odd occasion had to make contact through an intermediary to smooth things over. I've woken up some mornings and read things in the papers that I haven't said, or that I have said but the words have been twisted for greater impact. 'Macari blasts Fergie' – that kind of stuff. I'm not going to blast someone I regard as the best manager United have ever had. A punter might come on after a game and have a go. I might take a view that some of what he says is justifiable. The next day I'm reading that I agree with a punter who has had a moan at Alex. That usually results in me sending him a recording of the show to demonstrate that I also contradicted the same punter on just as many points, claiming he was talking a load of crap. This must have worked because thus far I've not had the hairdryer treatment. Maybe he defers to the days when we were both players in Scotland, though we never had a relationship back then. He was slightly older and a former Rangers player. I was at Celtic. Our paths never really crossed. But whenever he sees me around Old Trafford he always lets on.

As a former player, some think it natural that you would have a relationship of some sort with the current squad. It's not really like that. The modern player is not connected to old-timers in the same way they were in previous generations. Things have changed. There's a similar dislocation nowadays between players and fans, and players and journalists. Money and celebrity have put up a wall between the modern player and football's support cast. I often wonder how players these days would respond to being asked to visit supporters clubs up and down the country. We were obliged to go to as many as twenty functions a year, and that involved jumping in the motor and driving off the length and breadth of the country, from Carlisle to Plymouth. I used to volunteer. I suspect not many hands go up for that duty these days.

So much has changed since I first ran out in front of the Stretford End, or the West Stand as it is now known. The stadium has changed beyond belief. In my day the Megastore was known as the Souvenir Shop. If there were ten people in there no one else could get in. The capacity was around 61,500 in 1973, and that included the terracing. Now it's fifteen thousand bigger, and of course everybody has a seat. The massive state-of-the-art training complex at Carrington has replaced The Cliff. There was nothing wrong with The Cliff; the new set-up is just on a different planet.

In my role as a pundit, and as a scout for Brian Kerr and the

Republic, I've been around the world and back again watching matches over the last five years or so. Hand on heart, I can't say I've seen any players that make my pulse race. In fact I would argue that global standards are dropping. The days of fearing Brazil are over. The days of trembling at the sight of France are gone. Thierry Henry was too easy to blot out of games. He did brilliantly for Arsenal, but not towards the end. For France he was never as influential. Arsène Wenger eventually took the view that his time was up at Arsenal. He wouldn't have done that if he'd been worth his salt. Italy managed to win the last World Cup without a decent striker. Francesco Totti was poor. Alessandro Del Piero was just as bad. I'm still embarrassed about Luca Toni. I built him up to a pal of mine. 'Watch him,' I said, 'he's a real goalscorer.' He scored twice in the whole tournament, in the quarter-final against Ukraine. That was it. Awful.

The game will keep going, of course. It is now a massive media entity, the ultimate reality TV show, filling up a huge amount of space on TV and radio schedules, and in newspapers. We build it up, analyse it to death, take it apart, examine every nuance of the game and a player's performance. Footballers are the twenty-first-century soap stars, packaged in celebrity lifestyles. I'm part of that process now, so I can't knock it. It is not necessarily a bad thing. The only point I'm making is this: the ramping up of football from a working man's pasttime to a middle-class accessory has not been accompanied by a great rise in standards. The only thing we don't seem to talk about, in my opinion, is great players in the same numbers. There are plenty of high-earning, headline-grabbing performers for sure, but in the context of today's product I would argue that very few compare with the greats of old. And that's not me being an old curmudgeon. It is the evidence presented to eyes that have been glued to the game for half a century.

The money circulating at the top end of football has changed everything. It is not the game I knew, though it remains the staple of my life. Football I can trust. It gives my life a welcome structure, especially after it was torn apart in 1999. And I love going to Old Trafford.

In the context of modern-day football, the 2007–08 United squad deserves to sit on their lofty perch at the summit of the European game. They still play with panache and are managed by one of the greats in the history of club football, a figure comparable in Britain with Stein, Busby, Shankly, Paisley and Clough. Cristiano Ronaldo is up there with the world's best. Wayne Rooney is not far behind. The same can be said of Ryan Giggs, Paul Scholes and Gary Neville. Rio Ferdinand and Nemanja Vidic are as solid a pairing as you could wish to see. Of course, other teams have great players, too, but arguably not as many as we have seen in the past.

Manchester United have done well by me, as a player and an ex-player. The club, in my view, looks after the old-timers well. I'm always made to feel welcome, part of the extended United family. Some people are still there behind the scenes from my time; others have passed away. Until recently, Norman Davies, the kit man, was one of Alex's trusted aides. He was there in my day. I used to drive him mad on the bus. Every two minutes between London and Manchester I'd be shouting, 'Norman, cup of tea!' By the time we got back to Old Trafford, I'd have consumed a gallon of Tetley's finest. He worked for Alex a long time before falling seriously ill. Norman died in the summer of 2008. Things like that mark the passing of time. In the imagination of the fans, though, time stands still. Denis, Bobby and George are still scoring goals in the memories of millions. For the supporters, you are always one of their own and will always be a massive part of the club. I played at Old Trafford for eleven years. It is a place I feel I have never really left.

I get the same warm glow at Celtic Park, despite my brief time there as a manager. I was up there for the Barcelona game in February 2008. The roar was deafening when the players walked out of that tunnel. I've stood in that tunnel. I know that feeling, one of indescribable excitement. As they walked out I was thinking quietly to myself, 'What lucky players they are. I wish I were still in that tunnel.' Celtic was and will always be special to me. I was still a boy when I left. I became a man at Old Trafford. Manchester United represents a different phase of my life, and one I'm obviously much closer to. And, of course, there is the Lou Macari name plastered over the chip shop I bought for my mother, which I still own. It has become a local landmark. I look at that and think, 'At least I did something right.' It helps keep the memory of little old me alive.

Wherever I go in the world someone remembers me. Not because I was a footballer, not because my name is Lou Macari. I get noticed because I played for Manchester United. Of that association I'm immensely proud. I signed in 1973. If you'd told me then that I would still have an association with the club thirty-five years later, albeit as a pundit on MUTV, I'd have said you were bonkers. I still get a tingle down my spine when I set off down Sir Matt Busby Way. Sometimes I get there four hours before kick-off. The place is already buzzing. That's Manchester United.

Of course, it's only a game. It's given me a great life. But there are more important things, and inevitably I can't help wondering how much better my life would have been had I been able to share it for longer with my mum, dad and Jon.

CAREER RECORD

Playing Record

CELTIC 1970–73

League debut: 29 August 1970 v Morton (Home)

	Appearances	Goals
League	58	27
Scottish Cup	8	8
Scottish League Cup	24	14
European Cup	12	8
Total	102	57

MANCHESTER UNITED 1973–84

League debut: 20 January 1973 v West Ham (Home)

	Appearances	Goals
League	329	78
FA Cup	34	8
League Cup	27	10
European Cup Winners' Cup	4	0
UEFA Cup	6	1
Other competitions	1	0
Total	401	97

SWINDON TOWN 1984–86

League debut: 25 August 1984 v Wrexham (Home)

	Appearances	Goals
League	36	3
FA Cup	1	0
League Cup	4	0
Other competitions	2	1
Total	43	4

Honours won:

Scottish League Championship	1970/72
Scottish Cup	1971/72
Second Division Championship	1974/75
FA Cup	1977

SCOTLAND

Debut: 24 May 1972 v Wales (Home)

Caps: 24   **Goals:** 5

Tournaments played:

World Cup 1978

British Home Championship 1972, 73, 75, 77

Managerial record

SWINDON TOWN 1984–89
Division 4 Champions 1986
(league record for number of points in a season)
Division 3 Promotion 1987
Division 2 play-offs 1989

WEST HAM UNITED FC 1989–90
Division 2

BIRMINGHAM CITY FC 1991
Division 3, Leyland Daf Trophy winners 1991

STOKE CITY FC 1991–93
Division 3 play-offs 1992
Division 2 Champions 1993
Autoglass Trophy winners 1992

CELTIC FC 1993–94
Scottish Premier League

STOKE CITY FC 1994–97
Division 1 play-off semi-finalists 1996

HUDDERSFIELD TOWN FC 2000–02
Division 1, relegated 2001

PICTURE ACKNOWLEDGEMENTS

INDEX

269